MARTIN LUTHER KING, JR.
AND
THE FOUNDATIONS
OF
NONVIOLENCE

James P. Hanigan

UNIVERSITY
PRESS OF
AMERICA

LANHAM • NEW YORK • LONDON

Copyright © 1984 by

University Press of America,™ Inc.

4720 Boston Way
Lanham, MD 20706

3 Henrietta Street
London WC2E 8LU England

Library of Congress Cataloging in Publication Data

Hanigan, James P.
    Martin Luther King, Jr. and the foundations of
nonviolence.

    Includes index.
    1. King, Martin Luther. 2. Nonviolence. 3. Afro-
Americans—Civil rights. I. Title.
E185.97.K5H27   1984   323.4'092'4   84-15162
ISBN 0-8191-4215-8 (alk. paper)
ISBN 0-8191-4216-6 (pbk. : alk. paper)

All University Press of America books are produced on acid-free
paper which exceeds the minimum standards set by the National
Historical Publications and Records Commission.

TABLE OF CONTENTS

Introduction   p. 1

Chapter I   -   The Images of a Man   p. 31

Chapter II   -   The Faith of a Man   p. 69

Chapter III   -   The Vocation of a Man   p. 115

Chapter IV   -   The Mind of a Man   p. 141

Chapter V   -   The Principles of a Man   p. 181

Chapter VI   -   The Matter of Means   p. 207

Chapter VII   -   The Matter of Law   p. 235

Chapter VIII   -   The Matter of Suffering   p. 263

Chapter IX   -   The Dream of a Man   p. 293

INTRODUCTION

The word "nonviolence" -- to the extent that it conveys any substantive meaning at all -- is intimately linked in the minds of most people today to the names of Mohandas Gandhi and Martin Luther King, Jr. For those more familiar with the history of nonviolence, names like Henry David Thoreau, Leo Tolstoi, Dorothy Day, Albert Luthuli, Cesar Chavez, Danilo Dolci(1) and other saints or dreamers of our age may also come to mind. These figures are by no means universally admired, although they are given credit by and large for sincerity of motive and nobility of intention. The grounds upon which they are accorded honor, however, are frequently as varied and ambiguous as are the grounds on which their critics fault them. After reading both a flattering and uncomplimentary assessment of a practioneer of nonviolence, the reader is not at all sure that the two assessments are talking about the same person or describing the same practice.(2) Aside from the psychological characteristics and material interests that account for this discrepancy in evaluation by different authors, there are other, more objective reasons for this confusion.

Nonviolence is simply not a very intelligible or useful word. It points to no specific reality, no clearly indentifiable practice, no precisely defined set of concepts. To some people nonviolence suggests a cowardly and parasitic way of life, a refusal to take responsibility for one's own life and well-being and a willingness to let others bear the burden of one's own security and defense. To others it is an idealistic dream that is ultimately impractical and foolish at best, deliberately deceitful and enslaving at worse, an ideological promise of something that can never be. Still other human beings regard nonviolence as a way of life that embodies the highest form of heroism and the most intense degree of moral courage. Nonviolence has been used to mean or refer to all of the following practices: civil disobedience, primary and secondary boycotts, strikes, sit-downs and sit-ins of all kinds, protest marches and rallies, simple political acts like voting, the practice of conscientious objection to war, the refusal to honor specific obligations of citizenship such as paying taxes or giving information to the police, burning draft cards, the

1

renunciation of all political and social participation and responsibility, including the right to vote. While the word itself projects the idea that nonviolence means <u>not</u> doing something, the proponents of nonviolence seem to have understood it in a more active, positive way: as a way of life, a method for effecting social change, a political strategy to influence public opinion, a moral imperative, a commandment of God, a philosophy of life, democracy in action. Certainly the above survey represents an awesome number of meanings for one single word to convey.

Perhaps the most direct answer that can be given to the question, just what is nonviolence, is simply that it is what Gandhi and King did with their lives, it is the way that people like Chavez and Day went about trying to improve human life. But for an outsider, one who was not a confidant or coworker of these men or this woman, such an answer remains highly ambiguous. It is certainly no clearer than to say, for example, that Christianity is what Jesus of Nazareth was about, although there is a sense in which both those answers are quite true and absolutely fundamental.

If, however, one does approach the subject of nonviolence through the lives of its advocates, he or she will soon begin to suspect that nonviolence is inherently a normative concept rather than a purely descriptive or pragmatic one. It is a concept which embodies an ideal or a norm of what constitutes properly human behavior, a concept which has been formed only after making some specific value judgments, and a concept which makes implicit truth claims. Such an approach to nonviolence requires some defense. For from a sociological perspective it is quite possible to distinguish two forms of nonviolent understanding and strategy. Following the analysis of Houtart and Rousseau, the two forms may be usefully described as conscientious nonviolence and pragmatic nonviolence. The first understanding of nonviolence "is based on the fundamental harmony of social relations and is opposed to every form of coercion or violence." The latter understanding "flows from an evaluation of conflict...as a healthy element of reality, and of nonviolence as the least costly way of resolving it."(3)

2

The second or pragmatic view of nonviolence is by far the more common one. It is the view taken for instance, in Gene Sharp's major work on nonviolence,(4) as well as in the more popular presentation of Richard Gregg.(5) As Sharp considers the possibilities of nonviolence, he presents the issue in this way.

> ...Alternatives to violence in meeting tyranny, aggression, injustice and oppression are needed. At the same time it appeared evident that both moral injunctions against violence and exhortations in favor of love and nonviolence have made little or no contribution to ending war and major political violence. It seemed to me that only the adoption of a substitute type of sanction and struggle as a <u>functional alternative</u> to violence in acute conflicts - where important issues are, or are believed to be at stake - could possibly lead to a major reduction of political violence in a manner compatible with freedom, justice and human dignity.(6)

While it is undoubtedly possible, for the purpose of analysis, to separate the conscientious approach to nonviolence from the pragmatic approach, it is not at all certain that this separation always exists in reality, or that, where it does exist, one is talking about two forms of the same reality. Sharp himself is undeniably concerned with morality and human values when he speaks about a compatibility with freedom, justice and human dignity. Surely such a concern is conscientious as well as pragmatic. The assessment of conflict as a healthy element of reality involves no less a value judgment and a truth claim. The fact that in the specific cases of Gandhi and King nonviolence developed from a general, formal ethical imperative to a concept with growing political content(7) indicates that there may be an unavoidable relationship between the normative and practical content of nonviolence. On the face of it, it seems likely that the normative meaning given to nonviolence and the practical content given to it will be reciprocally determinative of what one means by nonviolence in reality.

One reason for hesitation in the face of this analytical distinction is that both King and Gandhi explicitly eschewed the purely pragmatic approach to nonviolence. They did so on the precise ground that tactical nonviolence alone is not nonviolence at all, but merely an alternate form of violence.(8) If, as this book will argue, nonviolence is necessarily rooted in an ethical vision of reality, it seems doubtful that it can be intelligibly discussed if divorced from its ethical foundations. If the case for nonviolence is to be made on purely practical or functional grounds, and not also as a matter of right and truth, it is hard to see how it will escape the charge of being one more form of bourgeois cowardice rather than of moral courage. For it will be put forth as "the least costly way" of resolving conflicts for people unwilling to pay the cost themselves for what they claim to value,(9) and we will hear again the condemnation of middle-class moral mediocrity.

A second reason for hesitation in the face of the distinction is that there is a not-so-implicit utilitarian ethic in the pragmatic approach to nonviolence. Both King and Gandhi explicitly repudiated the utilitarian, situational ethic without turning their backs on so-called practical considerations.(10) It was the utilitarian ethic with its claim that the end justifies the means(11) they considered to be the chief ideological justification for violence, and rightly so. For there is no question but that violence in certain circumstances may have functional significance, or that it can be rational in terms of a means-to-an end scheme of thought.(12) But to discover the functional significance of violence, to perceive the rational relationship between the means of violence and the end sought by those means is not at all the same thing as justifying violence. Any ethical theory that defends nonviolence on practical grounds will inevitably also find violence appropriate on certain occasions. It will have a hard time supporting nonviolence on any kind of firm and consistent basis. It will also have trouble showing how nonviolence does, in principle and in fact, differ from violence in both its moral and practical aspects. Given those difficulties, any such ethical theory has a very dubious right to call itself nonviolence.

There is also a third reason for hesitation before the distinction between conscientious and pragmatic nonviolence. Both Gandhi and King looked

4

upon nonviolence as a way of overcoming the separation between the moral life and the political life of
humankind. Whatever they understood nonviolence to
be, they thought they found in it, not distinction,
but unity. For them the wholeness or integrity of
human life depended upon the unity of ethics and
politics, the oneness of principle and practicality,
the integration of personal and social well-being.
For King, quite simply, "religion is life."(13)
Religion, or the sphere of the ethical,(14) is life,
the sphere of the practical. The human person's
moral health and political health go hand in hand.
It was not for him a matter of choosing one or the
other. This same emphasis on unity and wholeness in
Gandhi's life has been noted by Thomas Merton in a
brilliant short essay on the Hindu sage.

> It cannot be too often repeated that with
> him non-violence was not a simply marginal
> and quasi-fanatical indulgence of personal
> religious feeling. It belonged to the <u>very
> nature of political life</u>, and a society
> whose politics are habitually violent,
> inarticulate, and unreasonable is a subpol-
> itical and therefore subhuman society.(15)

The problems that emerge in understanding
nonviolence only as a functional alternative to
violence, only as one means or technique among
others, have been well explained by John Macquarrie
in his perceptive essay on <u>The Concept of Peace</u>.(16)
Peace, Macquarrie argues, and I would include nonviolence here, is both a set of techniques and also a
concept. What Macquarrie writes about peace is <u>pari
passu</u>, true about nonviolence.

> Peace cannot dispense with objective
> knowledge - indeed it demands a vast store
> of such knowledge, such as could be sup-
> plied by a whole host of experts in many
> different fields. But it cannot dispense
> either with an intellectual understanding
> of what peace essentially is. It is a pity
> that although there is a universal longing
> for peace and sometimes enthusiastic
> demonstrations for peace, it is not always
> appreciated that these are doomed to
> futility unless they are matched by an
> intellectual grasp of the problem.(17)

Without a similar intellectual grasp of nonviolence, then, as more than a set of techniques, as something more than a functional alternative to violence in the resolution of conflict, two things at least will result. The first result, certainly less harmful, will be a failure to understand what people like King and Gandhi were trying to tell us about our human existence. The second result will be an inability to judge the effectiveness of the techniques associated with nonviolence, for how are we to judge the means if we do not clearly understand the end being pursued. Without the unity of wisdom and science, of vision and technique, of the moral and the practical, what is the meaning of language such as "a functional alternative"?(18) Nonviolence clearly must embrace a vision, an understanding of the potentiality of human being, both individual and social, if there is to be any intelligible direction to the social change it seeks to effect. What this understanding of the potentiality of human being was in the life and language of Martin Luther King, Jr. will be one of the major concerns of this book.

Nonetheless, it is true that nonviolence is not a clear and agreed-upon concept. One reason for this is that we also lack any common agreement for what we mean by its verbal opposite, violence. In his now classic work on violence written more than eighty years ago, the French Marxist, Georges Sorel, noted that the problems of violence still remain very obscure.(19) Upon taking up the same topic for our own times, Hannah Arendt pointed out that the same unfortunate state of affairs continues for the discipline of political science.

> It is...a rather sad reflection on the present state of political science that our terminology does not distinguish among such key terms as "power," "strength," "force," "authority," and, finally, "violence" - all of which refer to distinct phenomena...To use them as synonyms not only indicates a certain deafness to linguistic meanings, which would be serious enough, but it has also resulted in a kind of blindness to the realities they correspond to.(20)

If Arendt was correct, as I think she was, we do not know what the reality is which we designate violence and, consequently, we do not know how to recognize either its presence or absence.

It is not only political scientists who are aware of this difficulty; philosophers have recognized the same problem. Robert Paul Wolff, for example, has claimed that "the concept of violence is inherently confused, as is the correlative concept of nonviolence; these and related concepts depend for their meaning in political discussions on the fundamental notion of legitimate authority which is also inherently incoherent."(21) Wolff's confusion is shared by other philosophers, even by those who do not agree that it is the concepts themselves that are to blame. Numerous efforts have been made to bring some linguistic and conceptual clarity to the term violence and related concepts. One possibility is to distinguish between descriptive and normative definitions of violence(22), a distinction which only roughly corresponds to the pragmatic, and conscientious forms of nonviolence. Another approach, similar to Arendt's, is to make careful distinctions among the concepts of force, coercion and violence.(23) In attempting these distinctions ethicians and social philosophers find themselves pondering once again a whole range of related questions: whether and under what conditions violence is ever morally justified;(24) whether the traditional pacifist position on the use of violence is inherently inconsistent;(25) whether politics, power and violence are intrinsically related or essentially contradictory.(26) Finally, under the impact of these initial reflections and in unwitting confirmation of Wolff's claim, they have been forced to reconsider the basic meaning of such fundamental terms as freedom, justice, obligation and public order.(27)

One thing that clearly emerges from these varied attempts at clarity is that both the hidden and overt forms of oppression present in our social life call into serious question some traditional democratic assumptions and values. This challenge to traditional values comes from several quarters. The proponents of nonviolence point to the oppression and violence in social life that is the result of a competitive and militaristic society. In this challenge they are joined by strange bedfellows. A similar challenge is present in the Marxist and socialist critiques of bourgeois individualism,(28)

7

as well as in the anarchist critique of totalitarian democracy and bureaucratic socialism.(29) These critiques are often marked by paradox, if not by outright contradiction. Some brief examples are illustrative. Gandhi claimed to be a socialist of some kind while sharing at the same time the Jeffersonian assumption that that government governs best which governs least. Added to those hard to combine notions was his overall vision of democracy as "an ordered anarchy," whatever possible meaning that could have.(30) In the late 1960's and early 1970's the phrase law and order became for many people in the United States little more than a reactionary, racist slogan, a covert expression meaning the repression of all dissenters and minority discontent. Yet Martin Luther King, Jr. began his public career with a simple plea, not for freedom now, but for law and order. He could see no more pressing need or precious blessing for the black citizens of the United States than the restoration of law and order in the South.(31) Today from every corner of the globe liberation movements complain of powerlessness and raise the cry for power in a variety of ways. Many groups frequently resort to violent acts in the hope of seizing the elusive thing called power. At the same time, taking a cue from Lord Acton that power corrupts, other groups are convinced that it is power itself which is intrinsically violent and immoral.(32) As one tries to make sense of this discordant conversation, it becomes strikingly evident that, even while using identical words, the speakers are often talking about quite different realities.

Historians of American life, taking their lead from H. Rap Brown, the anomalous, one-time leader of the Student Nonviolent Coordinating Committee (SNCC), have discovered that violence is as American as cherry pie. It has become almost commonplace now to emphasize the traditionally violent character of American life. Depending on an author's temperament and politics, we are either warned or reassured that the present outbreaks of violence are nothing new in the American life-style.(33) The historical concern with violence is more direct and specific than that of the philosophers. It focuses more on particular acts and defines violence accordingly. Richard Hofstadter's definition is representative. "Acts of violence are those which kill or injure persons or do significant damage to property. Acts of force are

8

those which prevent the normal free action or movement of other persons, or which inhibit them through
the threat of violence."(34)

Working definitions of violence which have been
proposed by various government-appointed study
commissions, while of some use for their own purposes, reveal this same concentration on specific
acts. As one might expect, the commissions tend to
focus on those particular acts of violence which
occasioned them being called into existence. The
result is a carelessness in conceptual clarity and
definitions that are at once too broad and too
narrow. Such definitions of violence, as for example
that of the Eisenhower commission - "behavior designed to inflict physical injury to people or damage
to property"(35) - if rigorously applied, would count
as acts of violence the activities of every forester,
bull-dozer operator and surgeon in the world. Such
definitions would also discount as violence any kind
of institutional or psychological violence.

Behavioral scientists have also addressed
themselves to the question of violence. Like the
philosophers, many of them have found it necessary to
make careful and elaborate distinctions. Rollo May
has undertaken "a search for the sources of violence,"(36) a search which eventually led him to
locate the source of violence in weakness. In the
course of his study he found it necessary to distinguish five specific kinds of power in human life, as
well as to distinguish carefully between self-assertion and self-affirmation, and between aggression and
violence.(37) Even then, violence was not found to
be an unambiguous phenomenon of human life. Another
student of human psychology, Frantz Fanon, was more
blunt about the sources of violence and emphatic
about the positive healing values of violence when
used by oppressed people.(38) Yet critics of Fanon
have pointed out that the words "radical and uncompromising action" could easily be substituted for the
word violence in his writing without any loss of
functional meaning. Hence Fanon can be read to
support nonviolence even when he writes violence.(39)
The same oddity is true about Sorel. Many of the
behaviors he mentioned as violent responses to
oppression and injustice would be generally accepted
today as legitimate nonviolent forms of protest.(40)
William Grier and Price Cobbs have explored in
particular the causes of violence among black Ameri-

9

cans. They, too, mention the interplay between social conditions and the psychological resources of individuals, but they remain indifferent to social forms of violence such as war and crime. Nor do they evaluate the positive or negative function of violence. Because they blame a great deal of black violence on white racism, they leave us ignorant in regard to the nature and origin of that racism and they fail to help us understand why racism, the violence they consider primary, but which is an attitude, should be considered a form of violence at all.(41)

Ethnologists and social anthropologists have contributed their insights and theories on the nature and origins of violence in the human condition. Authors like Konrad Lorenz, Desmond Morris, L. Ashley Montague and Robert Arbry base their ideas on the study of animal behavior and the habits of our pre-historic ancestors.(42) Here again, however, conceptual clarity is not all it might be. In general terms the basic argument regards all aggression as violence and sees aggression as the human inheritance of the evolutionary process, as developmentally innate in human beings. Lacking instinctual controls over their violent or aggressive proclivities, human beings must learn to develop social systems and mechanisms to control or to suppress their more disruptive tendencies. This position is not very far from a Hobbesian view of humanity, nor from a Hobbesian solution.(43) Unfortunately all such a position does is move the question of violence away from the individual to the social sphere, without affording any insight into the nature, causes, or ways of limiting social violence, or any evaluation of the positive and negative uses of aggression in human affairs.

In a major work of the first importance Erich Fromm has analyzed and summarized the data from a host of disciplines to construct An Anatomy of Human Destructiveness.(44) He, too, has found it necessary to make careful distinctions, in his case between benign and malignant aggression, and then within the framework of that distinction, to sub-distinguish further between pseudo-aggression and defensive aggression, and between sadism and necrophilia. The basis of all these distinctions is the function that aggression plays in the development of the human personality within a given social context, as well as

10

the intended purpose of the aggression. Among the many merits of Fromm's book is the clear relationship he establishes between aggression and character structure. In plain words he recognizes that it is a human person who perpetrates violence and human persons who suffer it. Hence he acknowledges both the moral and practical importance of the issue and points clearly to the dialectical interplay among the instinctual, psychological and social dimensions of the human person.

In his own way, then, Fromm deals with both technique and vision. For technique he suggests that

> an increasing number of people have become aware of the fact that it is not the presence of one or two conditions that have an impact, but a whole system of factors. This means that the general conditions conducive to the fullest growth of man - and, of course, each stage of individual development has its own specific conditions - can only be found in a social system in which various favorable social conditions are combined to secure the right soil.(45)

At the same time that he notes the importance of social conditions for human development, and consequently the key role to be played by objective knowledge and technique, Fromm is equally insistent on the need for vision and wisdom. "Man's reason and will are powerful factors in the process of his development, individually and socially. It is not history that makes man - man creates himself in the process of history."(46)

Once again it appears from the behavioral sciences that the issues surrounding the problem of violence are many and complex, and that we do not have a clear vocabulary yet in which to discuss them. It is clear that violence cannot be simply equated with aggression or power or self-assertion, or even with any form of social restraint. It is also clear that while violence is essentially destructive, it is not always psychologically or socially harmful. No simple identification between violence and evil is sound.

By way of contrast to the philosophical and behavioral disciplines, most theological reflection

11

on violence has tried, not to distinguish, specify and limit the meaning of violence, but to extend the meaning of violence to more forms of human behavior. It is not always a lack of attention to precise analysis that is responsible for this inflation of meaning. It is due more to the directly ethical concern of the theological discipline and its emphasis on vision to the neglect at times of technique and practicality. Nonetheless, such inflation of meaning is not without its problems.

Most traditional theological thinking about violence has centered on the questions of war and tyrannicide, and, in the contemporary discussions, on the issues of revolution and political terrorism. Much of the two discussions has reflected the continuing argument between just war theorists and pacifists. Most of this literature(47) is of little or no help in understanding the nature and causes of violence, possible alternatives to violence, and the positive and negative uses of violence. It does illuminate certain aspects of the human capacity for self-deception and self-justification as well as the real dangers in adopting an a priori or dogmatic position about the moral permissibility or wrongness of violence.(48) In addition, some of the arguments of classical Christian pacifism against violence have an affinity with the contemporary nonviolent position. But the effectiveness claims - the pragmatic emphasis - of contemporary nonviolent theorists are quite foreign to the classical pacifist perspective. The just war-pacifist discussion, therefore, reflects once again the division between the moral and the political, the conscientious and the pragmatic.

It is true that many theological discussions of the problem of violence are less precise than would be desired by students in other disciplines. A profound and careful thinker like Karl Rahner can discuss power as a metaphysical and theological reality, yet see no need to distinguish in any way between power and violence.(49) One must draw the conclusion from his essay that power is violence. Jacques Ellul, who prides himself on his realism, in his otherwise splendid book on violence seems to know what violence is, but leaves his readers with the message that violence is violence is violence.(50) Colin Morris, writing out of his pastoral experience as a missionary in Zambia, makes the depth of his pastoral compassion clear but adds little clarity to the confusion with his impassioned rhetoric and lofty denunciations of evil. His approach suggests the weakness of moral passion divorced from practical understanding.

> To starve people is violence, to rob them of their dignity and self-respect is violence; to deny them their political rights or discriminate against them is violence. Elaborate structures of violence make a terrorist what he is, and he faces them as the weaker adversary.(51)

Perhaps the most outrageous example of this inflation of the meaning of violence is offered by the liberation theologian Juan Luis Segundo. In a deliberate effort to move the question of violence off the center-stage in the discussion of liberation in Latin American, Segundo argues that we do violence to one another simply by being present to one another and sharing a common world. To impinge upon the existence of another, to do anything that makes the other take notice of me is already a form of violence. Hence violence is unavoidable, nonviolence a chimera, and the use of violence in liberation movements is an altogether peripheral question.(52)

Not all theologians are insensitive to the rhetorical expansion of the meaning of violence. George Edwards has seen the difficulty such statements as Morris' can cause or such attitudes as Segundo's can foster. In a telling way he has warned against the careless use of the word violence.

> Education is violence; technology is violence; matrimony is violence; work is violence. The list can be multiplied and the predicate nominative (violence) can sit in the subject position. But it is also clear that words that acquire too many meanings eventually have no meaning at all.(53)

It may be, as some theologians are suggesting, that anything may be used to perpetrate violence, and that violence is a pervasive, ever-present reality. But if anything might be used to inflict violence, it does not follow that to use anything is to do violence. The refusal to make careful distinctions in the interest of an absolute position for or against

13

violence does not help us know how we are to tell the difference either morally or practically.

Charles West has identified one of the more important psychological factors that makes it difficult to determine what constitutes violence. He points out that the self-interest and emotion which frequently accompany the charge of violence are to blame.(54) In commonplace terms it all depends upon whose ox is being gored whether a specific act is perceived as violence or as a proper exercise of power. That insight again emphasizes the importance of an intellectual grasp of violence and nonviolence if we are to avoid falling victim to subjective whim and arbitrary judgment. One does not have to be an essentialist to recognize the necessity of first establishing a frame of reference or a point of view before deciding what is and what is not violence and passing judgment on its moral legitimacy.

The establishment of such a frame of reference is a major merit of Robert McAfee Brown's book, Religion and Violence.(55) It is Brown's explicit purpose to expand the meaning of violence far beyond ordinary usage. While he is alert to some of the dangers in this procedure, Brown argues that violence is a more widespread reality than we usually acknowledge. He proposes a definition of violence as "the violation of personhood," and distinguishes four manifestations of such violation which encompass the psychological and sociological dimensions of human life and the visible and hidden aspects of each dimension.(56)

To expand the meaning of violence in this way is quite simply to equate violence with any form of oppression or injustice. One advantage of such a procedure is that it places Brown in accord with the meaning of violence operative in many liberation and revolutionary movements today.(57) It points concretely to an important aspect of the problem of violence by revealing that violence is not simply or even primarily a matter of particular acts, but is also a condition of human relationships to a greater extent than is commonly realized. This expanded understanding of what counts as violence is helpful, finally, in identifying the dynamics of violence and oppression, or in recognizing the "spiral of violence" as Dom Helder Camera has called it.(58) For

14

it specifies the area where any serious attack upon the causes of violence must begin.

On the other hand, this expansion of meaning has its problems. Violence, understood as the violation of personhood, has at the outset a morally negative meaning. Oppression, injustice are simply morally evil. To be consistent, if violence is injustice, then nonviolence is a moral requirement of human life for everyone in every situation. It is always morally wrong, by definition, to perpetrate injustice, to oppress, to violate personhood. Hence nonviolence becomes an overly elaborate way of saying human beings should act morally. Even more questionable about the simple identification of violence and injustice is the resulting impossibility of making any meaningful distinctions between criminal violence and due self-protection or due defense of others, or between revolutionary, progressive violence and reactionary, regressive violence, between a violence aimed at overthrowing oppression and violence aimed at oppressing others. Indeed, that such distinctions cannot be made was precisely the point Jacques Ellul was making in his intriguing claim that Hitler won the second world war because all his enemies imitate him in their unbridled use of violence.(59) Ellul's claim seems to be supported by the understanding of violence which Brown proposes. Yet surely there is something premature, if not false, about such a definition. While the circumstances of an act and the intentions of the actor do not exclusively determine the moral quality of any act or relationship, they are a necessary consideration. Brown himself is reluctant on circumstantial grounds to draw the obvious conclusion from his own argument that violence as a means to political and social liberation is immoral.(60) One is led consequently to question the adequacy of his understanding of violence.

This widespread interest in the problems and possibilities of violence, particularly on the part of religious thinkers, is not only a sign that violence has become one of the more pressing social concerns of the modern age. It is also, I would suggest, an indication that we are face to face with one of the essential questions of human life. How we live together and treat one another as a society is taking on the same kind of basic importance as the questions of meaning and trust and sexuality. It is

becoming an issue that must be understood and resolved in some way if we are to make a success of the
human enterprise. While the forbidding and increasing presence of nuclear weapons reminds us that our
physical survival as a species is at stake, it is
also the case that the moral stature of humankind,
the very meaning of our human-ness, is on the line.
The freedom and dignity of the human person have
become problematic. There are those who have rejected such language as no longer meaningful, if it
ever was.(61) More than a few political and intellectual leaders argue and act on the conviction that
human problems of relationship are not essentially
moral at all, but technical, requiring proper manage-
ment and techniques for their solution. Control,
which some authors see as the very essence of violence, becomes the new category for reflection and
planning because it is said to be the only true
one.(62)

    The difficulty in determining just what violence
is and what kinds of acts and types of relationships
count as violence did not escape either King or
Gandhi. For one example, Gandhi came to realize that
the threat imposed by deliberate hunger strikes could
easily be used as a blatant form of psychological
manipulation and so become a form of violence. He
was highly sensitive to the pseudo-innocence that
masked itself as nonviolence and played upon its own
weakness and cowardice to control others.(63) Yet
the fact that violence was not always a clearly
defined reality was not a particularly crucial
problem for the advocates of nonviolence. For they
approached the problem of violence in quite a different manner. Nonviolence was not understood primarily
as a means to an end or as a technique that was a
functional alternative to violence. Initially
conceived as providing a clue to the truth of reality
and as an attitude structuring a whole way of life,
nonviolence developed as a method for opposing
injustice and effecting social change only in the
working out of that way of life. Hence the implications of nonviolence could not be determined a priori
nor could its demands be listed in a series of do's
and don'ts. What nonviolence demanded could only be
perceived in the actual practice and living of it.
Gandhi's description of his own life as "my experiments with Truth" is an accurate illustration of this
point.(64)

A meaningful interpretation of nonviolence and the problems of violence, therefore, could do well to take seriously the lives and beliefs of those people who most fully and directly strove to practice nonviolence. That does not mean, of course, that everything people like Gandhi or King believed or did is to be accepted uncritically. They themselves were learners as well as teachers, and they made and admitted mistakes in judgment and abuses in practice. But the starting-point for an interpretation must be the actual thought and practice of such individuals and that will be the approach adopted in this work.

To my knowledge no adequate philosophical or theological interpretation of nonviolence has been written to date.(65) There are a number of excellent studies of Gandhi's ideas and practice which take the form of biographies, theories of conflict resolution, political philosophies, or partial understandings of his thought on a particular issue.(66) A recent study of high quality(67) deals comprehensively with his moral and political thought and is of great interest for a study of nonviolence. But Gandhi comes out of a Hindu religious tradition which, with its doctrines of kharma, reincarnation, and nirvana,(68) makes immediate sense out of "a-himsa" or nonviolence, though Gandhi radically transformed and extended the significance of the term. There is no similar tradition of nonviolence in the Christian religious tradition out of which King came, although the pacifist tradition certainly has influence upon the nonviolent perspective.(69) To understand nonviolence on western and Christian grounds, as King perceived it, represents something of a problem.

Not a great deal has been written in a scholarly way about Martin Luther King, Jr. Aside from a few biographies of unequal worth,(70) most of which will be referred to in the notes, the only attempts at a systematic presentation of his ideas and practice with which I am acquainted are the slim volume by Hanes Walton, Jr.,(71) dealing with King's political philosophy and a work by Kenneth L. Smith and Ira G. Zepp, Jr., which the authors describe as "an intellectual biography."(72) In addition there are two quite recent books,(73) one focusing on King's ethics, the other on his intellectual formation. The study undertaken here does not pretend to be a total systematic presentation of nonviolence according to King. The materials needed for such a study are non-existent. Rather it is a critical, reflective study in which I have attempted to understand exactly what King meant by insisting that nonviolence was an absolute moral imperative of human life, the basis on which he rested such a claim, and some of the implications and problems flowing form the claim. For that reason I regard this study as a critical effort to delineate the foundations on which nonviolence is thought to rest or to examine the formal philosophical and theological grounds of nonviolence. An alternate way to understand the issues pursued in this book would be to raise two questions. What did King hold to be true about reality and human life in this world that led him to embrace nonviolence? What can be said critically about the coherence, meaningfulness and truth of King's position?

As has been amply demonstrated elsewhere,(74) and as will quickly appear in this study, the basis of King's commitment to nonviolence is to be found in his religious faith. The basis is theological, although the theological tradition from which he came put no important stress on the difference between theology and philosophy as to either method or content. For his theological tradition nonviolence was certainly not a dogmatic position nor can it be derived in any systematic fashion from the major tenets of that tradition. The commitment to nonviolence is not a matter of logical argument. That is bound to make the philosopher unhappy, the theologian of another tradition uneasy, and the social scientist bemused if not outright amused. It may effect the general reader in all three ways. Still, many questions about nonviolence and many objections to it disappear or take on new forms once it is understood that the grounding of the argument goes back to the question of God, and that the central point at issue is the free moral commitment of the self in response to reality. Certain faith convictions must be made clear if King's views are to make any sense. Certain choices about the meaning of human life must be possible if his views are to have any truth.

One such obvious consideration has to do with the basic fact of death. Both King and Gandhi were assassinated, fell victims to acts of violence. Does such a tragic and untimely end mark the failure of nonviolence and prove its ultimate lack of effectiveness and wisdom? To some the answer is an unqualified yes so that, despite the nobility of their lives, King and Gandhi must be counted as failures and their method of nonviolence judged to be fundamentally flawed. For those who see some value in the ideals and inspiration that their lives contribute to the human adventure, there is more optimism about the personal success of King and Gandhi as human beings, though much less about the worth of the nonviolent method. For Christian believers, however, who profess to find the key to the mystery of life in a man who was crucified ignominiously as a political criminal, the answer is much less certain.(75) But whatever one's answer, it is impossible to come to grips with the issues of violence and nonviolence, unless one also comes to grips, both personally and philosophically, with the stark and mysterious fact of human mortality.

To a considerable degree King's "philosophy of nonviolence" was a matter of testing experientially certain faith convictions and theological understandings in the harsh world of reality. Accordingly a substantial part of this study is devoted to an examination and critical evaluation of those convictions and understandings. It might be regarded as an exercise in ecumenical theology. As a Roman Catholic theologian, I stand a good distance removed from the liberal Protestantism that was King's theological inheritance and with which I have little affinity and only slightly more sympathy. Yet I have tried to share both his concern and approach to questions as far as possible and to offer the most intelligible interpretations I could manage. The study makes no claims to be a systematic theology. It is not a biography, still less is it hagiography. While the personal events of King's life are not without importance for his understanding of nonviolence, my focus is not on the psychological and sociological factors that explain King the man. My concern is rather with the meaning and the truth-claims of nonviolence. I have not sought to explain why King came to believe and value as he did. Instead I have tried to account for what he believed and valued about reality and human existence and to reflect critically on those beliefs and values.

Despite the central theological focus of the study, King's "philosophy of nonviolence" is not without significance for the social and psychological possibilities of human beings. One of the implications of seeing nonviolence as a way of life is that it has something to say about every aspect of human existence. It contains a theory of social change as well as a theory of personal conversion and a method for the personal appropriation of objective truth. It has ideas about how to deal with emotions and instinctual drives. It has views about the ordering of the economy, about personal and communal wealth, about the practice of democracy. Philosophically it is a challenge to behaviorists, social utilitarians and defenders of reàl politique. It is not possible here to explore all these aspects of nonviolence, but some indications, questions and possibilities will be mentioned along the way.

Finally, it is not my aim to arrive at a precise definition of either violence or nonviolence. Such precise definitions seem to me to be impossible since the two words represent open or growing concepts(76), similar to concepts like freedom, justice, love and sin. As I see it, the importance of non-violence is that it points us to certain human possibilities, holds out a vision of human life, and charts a way to the realization of those possibilities and vision. Above all else it makes lucidly clear the central question of the nature and extent of human respon-sibility for our own common growth in humanness. Starting with the words and work of Martin Luther King, Jr., I have tried to analyze and interpret them to present the meaning and worth of non-violence and to make clear its religious and rational foundations.

A considerable portion of this study relies upon the material collected in the Martin Luther King, Jr., File at the Mugar Library of Boston University. The author is grateful to the King estate, Boston University and the library staff for access to and cooperation in the use of those materials. I am also indebted to Professors Henry B. Clark of the Univer-sity of Southern California and Frederick Herzog of Duke University who initially guided me through some of the vagaries of King's thought: to the editors of The Journal of Religious Thought, Debate and Under-standing, and Horizons, to use materials here which appeared in print in those journals in slightly other form. My indebtedness to my fellow scholars is evidenced and acknowledged in the end notes. I owe a special thanks to my colleagues in the theology department at Duquesne University who provide an environment that gives one hope for the coming of the beloved community and to Mrs. Constance Taylor and

Mr. Edward Scheid for help in the preparation of the manuscript. Above all others, however, I express lasting gratitude to my father, now dead, who made it easy for me to understand what King's father meant to him, to my mother, the very model of a strong and tender non-violent love, and to my wife, Elizabeth Coulbourn Hanigan, who more than fulfills her biblical role of beloved helpmate and mediator of God's love. It is to these three I dedicate this book.

NOTES: INTRODUCTION

1. The literature on non-violence advocates is voluminous and uneven. Some useful works by and about the figures mentioned in the text: Jacques E. Levy, Cesar Chavez: Autobiography of La Causa (New York: Norton, 1975); Mark Day, Forty Acres: Cesar Chavez and the Farm Workers (New York: Praeger, 1971); Peter Matthiessen, Sal si puedes: Cesar Chavez and the New American Revolution (New York: Random House, 1969); Beverly Fodell, Cesar Chavez and the United Farm Workers: A Selective Bibliography (Detroit: Wayne State University, 1974); William Robert Miller, A Harsh and Dreadful Love: Dorothy Day and the Catholic Worker Movement (New York: Liveright, 1973); Dorothy Day, the Long Loneliness: The Autobiography of Dorothy Day (Garden City, NY: Doubleday, 1952); Loaves and Fishes (New York: Harper and Row, 1963); Danilo Dolci, The Man Who Plays Alone, trans. Antonia Cowan (New York: Random House, 1968); A New World in the Making, trans. R. Munroe (New York: Monthly Review Press, 1965); Outlaws, trans. R. Munroe (New York: Orion Press, 1961); Report From Palermo, trans. P.D. Cummins (New York: Orion Press, 1959); Waste: An Eye-Witness Report on Some Aspects of Waste in Western Sicily, trans. R. Munroe (New York: Monthly Review Press, 1964); James McNeish, Fire Under the Ashes: The Life of Danilo Dolci (Boston: Beacon Press, 1965); Jerre Gerlando Mangione, A Passion for Sicilians: The World Around Danilo Dolci (New York: W. Morrow, 1968); Albert Luthuli, Let My People Go: An Autobiography (New York: McGraw-Hill, 1962); Henry David Thoreau, Reform Papers, ed. Wendell Glick (Princeton, NY: Princeton University Press, 1973); Leo Tolstoy, Tolstoy's Writings on Civil Disobedience and Non-Violence (New York: Bergman Publishers, 1967); The Kingdom of God and Peace Essays, trans. and introduction Azlmer Maude (London: Oxford University Press, 1960). A general overview of nonviolence is Peter Meyer (ed.), The Nonviolent Tradition (New York: Union Press, 1964). The most comprehensive bibliography can be found in Gene Sharp, The Politics of Nonviolent Action: Part III: The Dynamics of Nonviolent Action (Boston: Porter Sargent, 1973), pp. 819-840.

2. For one such interesting contrast see William Robert Miller, <u>Martin Luther King, Jr.: His Life, Martyrdom and Meaning for the World</u> (New York: Weybright and Talley, 1968); and John A. Williams, <u>The King God Didn't Save</u> (New York: Howard-McCann, Inc., 1970).

3. Francois Houtart and Andre Rousseau, <u>The Church and Revolution</u>, trans. Violet Neville (Maryknoll, NY: Orbis, 1971), p. 17.

4. Gene Sharp, <u>The Politics of Nonviolent Action</u>, 3 vols. (Boston: Porter Sargent, 1973).

5. Richard Gregg, <u>The Power of Nonviolence</u> (New York: Schocken Books, 1966).

6. Sharp, <u>Part I: Power and Struggle</u>, pp. v-vi; italics added.

7. Houtart and Rousseau, p. 19.

8. Martin Luther King, Jr., <u>Stride Toward Freedom: The Montgomery Story</u> (New York: Harper & Row, 1964), p. 83; Mohandas K. Gandhi, <u>Gandhi on Non-Violence</u>, ed. Thomas Merton (New York: New Directions, 1964-65), pp. 36-41.

9. <u>Gandhi on Non-Violence</u>, p. 41; "There is nothing more demoralizing than fake non-violence of the weak and impotent." Georges Sorel, <u>Reflections on Violence</u>, trans. T.E. Hulme (New York: Peter Smith, 1947), pp. 71-73 and <u>The Illusions of Progress</u>, trans. John and Charlotte Stanley, Foreword by Robert A. Nisbet, intro. John Stanley (Berkeley and Los Angeles: University of California Press, 1969) makes the strongest case against the moral mediocrity of the middle-class. As John Stanley expressed it in the introduction, "Sorel's purpose in <u>The Illusions of Progress</u>, and in much of his other writings is to show that moral superiority has long ago been separated from political progressivism... and has attached itself to the socialism of independent producers," p. xxxi; "This is the basic theme of the <u>Reflections on Violence</u>.", p. xxxi, n. 48.

10. King, <u>Stride Toward Freedom</u>, p. 74; <u>Gandhi on Non-Violence</u>, pp. 24-33.

11. The popular defense of this position is Joseph Fletcher, _Situation Ethics_ (Philadelphia: The Westminster Press, 1966), pp. 120-133; for how widespread such a view is see G.E.M. Anscombe, "Modern Moral Philosophy" _The Definition of Morality_, eds. G. Wallace and A.D.M. Wade (London: Methuen and Co. Ltd., 1970), pp. 222-223.

12. Hannah Arendt, _On Violence_ (New York: Harcourt, Brace and World, Inc., 1969), pp. 63-66.

13. _Martin Luther King, Jr., Collection_: File # XIV (29); Mugar Library, Boston University, Boston, Massachusetts. Referred to hereafter as _B.U. Coll._

14. Religion, of course, is not to be equated simply with the ethical, but that was the interpretation of religion King inherited and accepted from liberal Protestantism, as will be indicated in Chapter 4.

15. Thomas Merton, "Introduction," _Gandhi on Non-Violence_ (New York: New Directions, 1964-65), p. 8.

16. John Macquarrie, _The Concept of Peace_ (New York, Evanston, San Francisco, London: Harper and Row, Publishers, 1973).

17. _Ibid._, p. 10.

18. For an effective criticism of the value-neutral quality of social functional analysis see Alvin W. Gouldner, _The Coming Crisis of Western Sociology_ (New York, London: Basic Books, 1970).

19. Sorel, _Reflections on Violence_, pp. 47-48.

20. Arendt, p. 43.

21. Robert Paul Wolff, "On Violence," _The Journal of Philosophy_, LXVI, 19 (Oct. 2, 1969), p. 602.

22. Francis C. Wade, "On Violence: A Comment," _The Journal of Philosophy_, LXVIII, 12 (June 17, 1971), pp. 369-378.

23. Ronald B. Miller, "Violence, Force and Coercion," Violence, ed. Jerome A. Shaffer New York: Daniel McKay Company, Inc., 1971), pp. 9-44.

24. William R. Marty, "Nonviolence, Violence and Reason," The Journal of Politics, 33, 1 (February, 1971); Robert Audi, "On the Meaning and Justification of Violence," Violence, ed. Shaffer, pp. 45-99.

25. Jan Narveson, "Is Pacifism Consistent?" Ethics, 78, 2 (January, 1968), pp. 148-150; William R. Marty, "Nonviolence, Violence and Reason," The Journal of Politics, 33, 1 (February, 1971).

26. D.M. White, "Power and Liberty," Political Studies, XIX, 1 (March, 1971); Anthony de Crespigny, "Power and Its Forms," Political Studies XVI, 2 (June, 1968); Steven Lukes, Power: A Radical View (New York: Macmillan, 1974); Michael Foucault, Power and Knowledge (New York: Pantheon Books, 1980).

27. John Rawls, A Theory of Justice (Cambridge, Massachusetts: Harvard University Press, 1971), pp. 363-391; Ernest van den Haag, Political Violence and Civil Disobedience (New York: Harper & Row Publishers, 1972).

28. Herbert Marcuse, One-Dimensional Man (Boston: Beacon Press, 1964), pp. 3-16.

29. A useful work here is Stanley Moore, Marx on the Choice Between Socialism and Communism (Cambridge, Mass. and London: Harvard University Press, 1980), esp. pp. 3, 12-14.

30. Gandhi on Non-Violence, pp. 54-55; "The ideally non-violent state will be an ordered anarchy."

31. B.U. Coll., I (11A); in testimony before the National Democratic Platform and Resolution Committee, August 11, 1956.

32. Michael Selzer, "Politics and Human Perfectibility: A Jewish Perspective," Cross Currents (Winter 1971), pp. 98-112; John Howard Yoder, The Politics of Jesus (Grand Rapids, Michigan: William B. Eerdmans Publishing Co., 1972), pp. 135-162.

33. Richard Hofstadter, _American Violence_ (New York: Alfred A. Knopf, 1970); Karl K. Taylor and Fred W. Sondy, Jr. (eds.), _Violence: An Element in American Life_ (Boston: Holbrook Press, 1972).

34. Hofstadter, p. 11.

35. Cited in George Edwards, _Jesus and the Politics of Violence_ (New York, Evanston, San Francisco, London: Harper & Row, Publishers, 1972), p. 3.

36. Rollo May, _Power and Innocence: A Search for the Sources of Violence_ (New York: W.W. Norton & Company, Inc., 1972).

37. _Ibid._, pp. 137-163.

38. Frantz Fanon, _The Wretched of the Earth_ (New York: Grove Press, Inc., 1968), esp. pp. 35-106; _Black Skin White Masks_ (New York: Grove Press, Inc., 1967).

39. Barbara Deming, "On Revolution and Equilibrium," _Revolution: Violent and Nonviolent_. Cited in Arendt, p. 71, n. 96.

40. Sorel, _Reflections on Violence_, p. 136.

41. William H. Grier and Prince M. Cobbs, _Black Rage_ (New York: Basic Books, 1968) and _The Jesus Bag_ (New York, Toronto, London: Bantam Books, 1972); the latter work has a particularly fine bibliography, pp. 171-291.

42. See the selections in Ashley Montague (ed.) _Man and Aggression_ (London: Oxford University Press, 1973) and _Learning Non-Aggression_ (New York: Oxford University Press, 1978); also Desmond Morris, _The Naked Ape: A Zoologist's Study of the Human Animal_ (New York: McGraw-Hill, 1967).

43. Thomas Hobbes, _The Leviathan_, ed. by Michael Oakeshott (New York: Collier Books, 1962), p. 100; "...and during the time men live without a common power to keep them all in awe, they are in that condition which is called war; and such a war, as is of every man, against every man."

44. Erich Fromm, _An Anatomy of Human Destructiveness_ (New York, Chicago, San Francisco: Holt, Rinehart and Winston, 1973).

45. _Ibid._, p. 260.

46. _Ibid._, p. 265; see also n. 32.

47. Ralph B. Potter, _War and Moral Discourse_ (Richmond, VA: John Knox Press, 1969), pp. 87-123, has a splendid bibliographical essay to this effect.

48. _Ibid._, pp. 58-61.

49. Karl Rahner, "The Theology of Power," _Theological Investigations_, IV (Baltimore: Helicon Press, 1966), pop. 391-409.

50. Jacques Ellul, _Violence: Reflections From a Christian Perspective_ (New York: Seabury Press, 1969), pp. 97-100 and his clarification in _Christianity and Crisis_ (October 19, 1970), p. 221. "...the idea that there are two kinds of violence is utterly mistaken. From whatever side the problem is approached, it invariably turns out that all violence is of a piece..."

51. Colin Morris, _Unyoung, Uncolored, Unpoor_ (Nashville: Abingdon Press, 1970), p. 97.

52. Juan Luis Segundo, _The Liberation of Theology_ (Maryknoll, NY: Orbis Books, 1976), pp. 154-182.

53. Edwards, p. 7.

54. Charles West, _Ethics, Violence and Revolution_ (New York: Council on Religion and International Affairs, 1969), pp. 14-15.

55. Robert McAfee Brown, _Religion and Violence_ (Philadelphia: The Westminster Press, 1973).

56. _Ibid._, pp. 7-8.

57. For some examples, Gustavo Gutierrez, _A Theology of Liberation_ (Maryknoll, NY: Orbis Books, 1973), p. 48, 89; James H. Cone, _A Black Theology of Liberation_ (Philadelphia and New York:

J.B. Lippincott Company, 1970), pp. 185-190; Judith Plaskow, Sex, Sin and Grace: Women's Experience and the Theologies of Reinhold Niebuhr and Paul Tillich (Lanham, MD: University Press of America, 1980), pp. 62-70. Cone and Plaskow speak of sin and oppression, but clearly understand both as experiences of violence in the sense Brown proposes.

58. Helder Camera, Spiral of Violence (Denville, NJ: Dimension Books, 1971).

59. Ellul, p. 29.

60. Brown, pp. 85-88.

61. The classic work here is B.F. Skinner, Beyond Freedom and Dignity (New York: Alfred A. Knopf, 1971).

62. Skinner, p. 181.

63. Gandhi on Non-Violence, pp. 69-70.

64. Mohandas K. Gandhi, An Autobiography: The Story of My Experiments With Truth (Boston: Beacon Press, 1957).

65. The closest attempt is William Robert Miller, Non-Violence: A Christian Interpretation (New York: Association Press, 1964).

66. Some representative works are Geoffrey Ashe, Gandhi (New York: Stein and Day, 1969); Joan V. Bondurant, Conquest of Violence: The Gandhian Philosophy of Conflict, rev. ed. (Berkeley and Los Angeles: The University of California Press, 1965); Dhirendra Mohan Datta, The Philosophy of Mahatma Gandhi (Madison: The University of Wisconsin Press, 1953); Erik H. Erikson, Gandhi's Truth: On the Origins of Militant Nonviolence (New York: W.W. Norton & Company, Inc., 1969). William L. Shirer, Gandhi: A Memoir (New York: Simon and Shuster, 1980) which misses the religious and metaphysical basis of Gandhi's nonviolence; Gene Sharp, Gandhi as a Political Strategist (Boston: Porter Sargent, 1980).

67. Ranaghan N. Iyer, <u>The Moral and Political Thought of Mahatma Gandhi</u> (New York: Oxford University Press, 1973).

68. <u>Ibid.</u>, pp, 18-21, 67-73 for the eclectic quality of Gandhi's religious thought.

69. The clearest account of the relationship and the difference still remains Reinhold Niebuhr, <u>Moral Man and Immoral Society</u> (New York: Charles Scribner's Sons, 1960), pp. 257-277. Also of help is John Howard Yoder, <u>Nevertheless: The Varieties of Religious Pacifism</u> (Scottdale, PA: Herald Press, 1971).

70. By far the best biography of King, both in its comprehensive and scholarly quality, as well as in its ability to capture the human flavor of the man and the period, is Stephen B. Oates, <u>Let the Trumpet Sound: The Life of Martin Luther King, Jr.</u> (New York: Harper & Row Publishers, 1982). Its chief weakness is an uncritical acceptance of King's intellectual understanding.

71. Hanes Walton, Jr., <u>The Political Philosophy of Martin Luther King, Jr.</u> (Westport, Connecticut: Greenwood Publishing Corporation, 1971).

72. Kenneth L. Smith and Ira G. Zepp, <u>Search for the Beloved Community: The Thinking of Martin Luther King, Jr.</u> (Valley Forge, PA: Judson Press, 1974), p. 14; the methodology of this book seems to me to be badly flawed. To expound Rauschenbusch and Niebuhr and then to attribute their ideas to King on the grounds that he studied them is illegitimate. See chapter 2 for comments on the method of interpreting King.

73. Ervin Smith, <u>The Ethics of Martin Luther King, Jr.</u> (New York and Toronto: The Edwin Mellen Press, 1981); John Ansbro, <u>Martin Luther King, Jr., The Making of a Mind</u> (Maryknoll, NY: Orbis Books, 1982).

74. Smith and Zepp, p. 12; Daniel Day Williams, <u>The Spirit and Forms of Love</u> (New York: Harper & Row, Publishers, 1968), p. 270; Louis E. Lomax, <u>To Kill a Black Man</u> (Los Angeles: Holloway House Publishing Co., 1968), p. 93; John H. Cartwright "The Social Eschatology of Martin

Luther King, Jr.," in Essays in Honor of Martin Luther King, Jr. (ed.) John H. Cartwright (Evanston: Leiffer Bureau of Social and Religious Research, 1971), pp. 1-13.

75.   Ellul, p. 144.

76.   Stanley Hauerwas, "Situation Ethics, Moral Notions, and Moral Theology," Vision and Virtue (Notre Dame, Indiana: Fides/Claretian, 1974), pp. 20-22; Herbert McCabe, What is Ethics All About? (Washington, Cleveland: Corpus Books, 1969), pp. 17-25.

CHAPTER I

THE IMAGES OF A MAN

In the life of every nation and people certain men and women emerge from the obscurity of day-to-day existence and assume the status of public heroes.(1) It is not easy to point precisely to what it is that marks some human beings rather than others as heroes beyond the admiration and prestige accorded to them by their contemporaries or by later generations. While we speak occasionally of unsung heroes, this is usually done in the hope of elevating such figures to the requisite level of public admiration and prestige at which they will qualify as heroes. Such attempts rarely succeed. For not all human beings whose qualities or achievement we admire qualify as public heroes, as heroes of their people. Those men and women who achieve the status of public hero seem to have a larger-than-life quality about them or better, perhaps, to be especially favored by the gods. They are indisputably central figures in the drama of which they are a part, while that drama is itself one which is central to the life of their people or nation.

But the hero's niche among his or her people is rarely secure or unquestioned. More than one person has earned the esteem of his or her contemporaries only to be scorned or rejected by later generations as a rogue or a villain. Two of the major heroes of western civilization, Jesus of Nazareth and Socrates of Athens, were accorded a criminal's death by the people of their own time and place, only to be elevated beyond all imagining to the heights of admiration and prestige by people of other times and places. In similar fashion, men and women regarded as heroes by their own contemporaries are seen by later generations as only marginal figures or yet worse, as misguided or malevolent fools.

One thing that makes the hero's course a precarious one is that the very nature of the hero's role in history requires the more ordinary among us to make choices. It is not simply a matter for us of liking or disliking, of admiring or ignoring the hero. Rather, we are forced to choose for or against the hero, for or against the vision, or dream, or message, or course of action the hero proposes to us.

One hallmark of the hero's authenticity as a hero is precisely that he or she forces us to choose; we cannot remain indifferent to this presence among us, even if we would. For not to be with the hero is automatically to be against him or her.(2)

Because of this demand for choice that a hero makes upon people, he or she confronts us with the problem of values or of moral truth.(3) Faced with a choice, we must decide what is good and what is evil, what is right and what is wrong. The truth of our existence(4) is called into question, not, however, in a way that is theoretical and abstract, but very practically and concretely.(5) Heroes are not academicians or theorists or even scientists, though there is much that can be heroic about such vocations. Heroes are not discoverers or explainers of truth; they are doers and makers of truth, a truth that for the most part comes to be embodied and preserved for posterity in their own persons and in the images of them that their followers fashion and propagate. Hence heroes become "mythological" figures,(6) images of both inspiration and explanation for the truth which they have embodied and made real.

Martin Luther King, Jr. was, and is still considered today to be, a hero of his people.(7) Whether posterity will so esteem him is a question that is best left to posterity to answer. But our own memory of him and our own understanding of the truth he embodied will in significant measure contribute to their estimation. For we have, indeed, already begun the process of "mythologizing" him. His picture appears reverently placed on the walls of home and public buildings; his name is invoked on solemn occasions and used to consecrate schools and other public places; his words are remembered and quoted, his day of birth and day of death commemorated.

But all of this hallowing is by no means in the same cause or universally accepted. Like all heroes, King is an ambiguous one, as much villain to some as hero to others. To many of his contemporaries he was a troublemaker,(8) a communist dupe,(9) a publicity seeker,(10) a man of dubious personal morality.(11) To others he was a saint,(12) a genius,(13) and savior.(14) Such a range of feeling and opinion about the man suggests something of the difficult path heroes - and villains - have to tread through history, as well as the difficulty we humans have in understanding and making the choice heroes demand of us.

King is most readily associated with his insistence upon nonviolent resistance as the method of social change and as the most moral and effective path to human freedom. Yet what exactly King meant by nonviolent resistance, or by militant nonviolence as it will be called throughout this study,(15) how effective he actually was in using it to achieve the goals he sought, and how we are to assess today the significance of his teaching and action for ourselves; all these remain questions of bitter dispute and high passion. It is unlikely that any common answers to all of these questions will soon appear. Yet it does seem possible to acquire a clearer understanding of what King meant by militant nonviolence and why he insisted upon it so continuously and unequivocally.(16) If that much is possible, it will focus much light upon the significance of his truth for us today as well as upon the meaning of King himself and his time among us.

It was mentioned above that the person who has the hero's role confronts other people with the question of moral truth and with the demand to choose between competing values and alternate courses of action. The hero does not, of course, create the problem or situation which requires choice. That is created simply by the way people live together. The hero merely exposes and interprets the problem, makes the need for choice both evident and urgent, and points to an alternate course of action to the status quo. The hero may or may not be original in his or her perception and interpretation of the situation; he or she may or may not offer a novel solution to it. What is always characteristic of the hero, however, is the inescapable urgency for a choice in regard to the problem which is the hero's central concern.

The problem which was to claim King's energies and life was an old one and it had long received a more complete and scholarly exposition and interpretation than he himself was ever to give it. When Gunnar Myrdal's landmark study of the Negro in the United States appeared in print for the first time in 1942, it bore the highly fitting title, An American

Dilemma.(17) In its succinct way that title completely captured the problem, the thesis, the frame
of reference and the state of the question of
Myrdal's study. For what he analyzed and discussed
for over 1400 pages was precisely a dilemma -- not
yet a finished tragedy as some feared, nor a settled
issue as some hoped, nor a condition beyond possibility of remedy, but a choice between two
irreconcilable courses of action, two incompatible
futures. The dilemma to which the title referred,
the problem with which Myrdal was fundamentally
concerned, he understood to be an essentially moral
question, a growing clash of beliefs and values. He
offered as a basic definition of the dilemma the
following description.

> The 'American Dilemma'...is the ever-raging
> conflict between, on the one hand, the
> valuations preserved on the general plane
> which we shall call the 'American Creed,'
> where the American thinks, talks, and acts
> under the influence of high national and
> Christian precepts, and, on the other hand,
> the valuations on specific planes of
> individual and group living, where personal
> and local interests; economic, social, and
> sexual jealousies; considerations of
> community prestige and conformity; group
> prejudice against particular persons or
> types of people; and all sorts of miscella-
> neous wants, impulses, and habits dominate
> his outlook.(18)

The concrete arena in which this ever-raging
conflict of opposed values took place Myrdal judged
to be the mind and heart of the individual American;
indeed, even more specifically, the mind and heart of
the white American.(19) With a remarkable and direct
perceptiveness he announced to one and all, long
before the angry voices of the 1960's blared out the
same truth,(20) and despite the subtitle of his
book,(21) that the negro problem was in fact the
white American's problem, and that racial prejudice
was a fundamental and integral part of a whole
complex of problems in American life.(22) The words,
"institutional racism" do not appear as such in
Myrdal's study,(23) but he marshalled more than
abundant evidence of how deeply and pervasively
racial prejudice had infected every aspect of American life to support the more contemporary slogan.

34

For Myrdal the American Dilemma was a classic and painful moral conflict. Certain key principles, derived from the founding documents of the American polity and from the American brand of Christianity, formed a common political and social creed which had sunk deep roots in the American people.(24) These principles, which were intended to order the social relationships of American life, and which were thought to make the United States a beacon of freedom and truth or an object lesson for the world, were taught, honored and embraced in every class and segment of society, including the black population of the United States. In many ways the common creed was more honored and obeyed in the black community than in any other single, identifiable group in the population. In many cases it could be fairly said that the black American was the most Americanized of all the nation's inhabitants.(25)

The principles which were intended and thought to rule the social life of Americans were, in fact, more honored in the breach than the observance in one main area of the nation's life - its treatment of its black citizens. So important was this exception, so basic to every aspect of daily personal and social intercourse, that it established at the very core of American life a fundamental contradiction, a contradiction between what every American knew ought to be and what he knew to be the reality. Nor was it a contradiction that touched only a part of life or one that could be contained within the bounds of occasional times or certain places.

To be sure, white Americans employed all the techniques of rationalization, equivocation, willful ignorance, good intentions and self-justification to explain away or to hide from the painful contradiction that festered at the roots of their lives and continually spread its poison to every aspect of those lives. But the pain was real, the contradiction fundamental, escape or oblivion impossible. For Myrdal, then, there were two major questions to be asked about this situation: how long could America go on living with a bad conscience? what forces, if any, would and could move that conscience to repentance and change?(26)

Myrdal did not regard the problem of black people in American life as the only social problem facing the American people, nor even as the most pressing among several problems. Its significance was rather that it was an integral facet of every problem and, therefore, crucial to the future of America.(27) He considered America's treatment of its black citizens to be its greatest failure, "but also America's incomparably great opportunity for the future. If America should follow its own deepest convictions,...the century-old dream of American patriots, that America should give to the entire world its own freedoms and its own faith, would come true."(28) Given the state and nature of the problem, Myrdal thought it would be changes of the American mind, changes in people, changes in their beliefs and valuations, that would be most important for the realization of the dream.(29) Although he was optimistic about economic and social trends in his prognostications,(30) Myrdal insisted upon the essentially moral character of the social problem. Quoting American's own philosopher, John Dewey, he made clear his reason for such insistence.

> Anything that obscures the fundamentally moral nature of the social problem is harmful, no matter whether it proceeds from the side of physical or of psychological theory. Any doctrine that eliminates or even obscures the function of choice of values and enlistment of desires and emotions in behalf of those chosen weakens personal responsibility for judgment and action. It thus helps create the attitudes that welcome and support the totalitarian state.(31)

Such was the overall framework in which Myrdal studied the life situation of black Americans. It was this general conception of the American dilemma which he endeavored to support and clarify in his investigation of the various aspects of their life in the United States. There is no direct evidence that Martin Luther King, Jr. ever read Myrdal's monumental study or was in any way directly influenced by his conception of the American dilemma. On the face of things it would seem likely that a young man at Morehouse College in 1945 majoring in sociology would have had some acquaintance with the work, but that remains only a likelihood.(32) What is certain is that King's initial perceptions of life in the United States and the different problems it posed for black and white Americans was in every important aspect

36

but one(33) identical with Gunnar Myrdal's conception of the American dilemma.

There is no question but that King understood the nature of the black man's existence in the United States to be at the most profound level a moral problem which would determine the essential character of the American spirit as good or evil. The struggle that was to absorb all his energies during the adult years of his life was to him in the most direct and literal fashion a struggle for the soul of a nation.(34) He did not think that the situation of the black American was one among many problems which the country faced, one among a number of ills the society needed to remedy. It was the problem, the ill. And it was the problem precisely because it posed the most fundamental contradiction to American political and Christian principles; posed to the American people the question of good and evil, right and wrong, in the most basic and decisive way. Just as Abraham Lincoln's moral stature is reflected in his awareness that the nation could not live half-slave and half-free, so too King's moral sensitivity is reflected in his radical insistence that the continued practice of discrimination and segregation spelled the death of the American dream and the promise and hope it held out to all men.(35) Myrdal's major question of how long America could live with a bad conscience and what forces could or would bring to that conscience repentance and amendment of behavior, Martin Luther King was to make urgent, concrete, and inescapable.

What was unique about King, however, was not that he shared Myrdal's interpretation of the problem. Many scholars and activists have done so and still do. Nor was he unique in addressing his energies to the problem nor in the solution he offered to it. For, as will appear, King did little more that ask America to be true to itself and its own public principles. He was not even unique in proposing nonviolent activity as a method to address the problem. Many of his brothers in color were long ahead of him in this. What was unique about him and makes him worthy of attention is the moral absoluteness with which he insisted upon militant nonviolence as the one way to solve the problem, and the inescapable demand he was able to impose upon his countrymen to choose for or against it.

King's personal role, both in the formulation and dissemination of the one means of solution, as well as his own understanding of it and his effectiveness in imposing the demand to choose for or against it, are all matters of dispute. The more thoughtful, if no less impassioned, observers of the man and his work have employed a widely varied assortment of images to capture the meaning of the man and his activities. King himself was a very private person and his soul is obscure and hidden from public scrutiny; it is likely to remain so for some time.(36) But a review of some of the more common and more profound images used to interpret him will be helpful here, not only to indicate the wide diversity of opinion about him -- his hero-villain ambiguity -- but also to suggest something of the complexity and richness of the man and his message. For although we are mainly concerned in this study with the theoretical foundations of militant nonviolence, it is necessary, in order to find them, to study King's deeds and person as well as his writings and speeches. Some of the images point to his function in a social movement, some to the origin of his message and inspiration, some to his legacy to his fellow men. Some of the images are complementary, others are incompatible with one another. All of them will tell us something about King's impact on his world.

Shortly after King's assassination Herbert Richardson, writing in Commonweal, suggested that King was a theologian of singular contemporary relevance who merited our heads as well as our hearts,(37) a somewhat surprising assessment of a man who wrote not one word of formal theology after finishing his unpublished doctoral dissertation.(38) But Richardson claimed that King "was the most important theologian of our time...because of his creative proposals for dealing with the structure of evil generated by modern relativism, viz., ideological conflict."(39) It was Richardson's contention that King's importance lay in the fact that he created a new theology, new types of piety, and new styles of Christian living, a formidable achievement if true. Richardson's specification of King's achievements, however, is less hopeful than his claims. He understood from King that faith is a power of reconciliation or the commitment of a man to oppose the separation of man from man. "It is a commitment to struggle against attacks on the common good, against racism and segregation, and against the fragmentation of man's intellectual and spiritual life."(40) In King's theology, according to Richardson, faith affirms reconciliation as opposed to relativism which denies its very possibility. King's was a faith which worked and hoped not only against the factors which deny reconciliation, but for the factors which affirm it. Ultimately it affirmed the power of divine unity working in all things. This means a vision of faith which perceives an invisible unity behind all appearances of difference and separation. Such a description of faith tells us little more than that King believed in some sort of absolute principle of unity behind the multiplicity and variety of finite reality, hardly enough to support a claim for a new and relevant theology.

The opposite pole of faith is the structure of evil which Richardson claimed is ideological conflict. Hence King's struggle -- or the effort to affirm his faith -- was against the forces or structure of evil itself, not against persons or groups. Richardson thought that this suggests the need for asymmetry between the form in which evil manifests itself and the form of our opposition, which seems to be no more than an elaborate way of repeating the Pauline injunction to overcome evil with good.(41) Richardson concluded from this that King's argument for non-violence was not an eschatological appeal to the Lordship of Christ nor based on confessional grounds, both of which he was convinced will fail every time, but on the sole practical grounds that non-violence is based on a right understanding of reality. Whether this conclusion is sound or not, it indicates at least that Richardson thought that King based himself on philosophical grounds rather than on theological ones.(42)

The goal of the struggle of faith was the beloved community, an often used expression of King's which Richardson interpreted to mean that friendship or personal communion is the ultimate value of human life. This also helped him locate King's emphasis on suffering and self-sacrifice as less than ultimate human values or acts, but rather as acts which grow out of and are for the sake of personal communion and friendship, as acts which do not establish but only manifest friendship.(43) As a theological interpretation of the cross of Christ, or an interpretation of the suffering of black people at, e.g., Birmingham or Selma, to say nothing of Watts or Harlem, this seems seriously inadequate. As an explanation of King's words and deeds, as will appear below, it is simply wrong.

The only other commentator on King who has suggested the image of an innovative theologian as a way of understanding him is the man who was King's right arm in all his endeavors, Ralph Abernathy. In an open letter to the dead man shortly after the assassination(44) Abernathy mentioned how the two of them once talked theology and later made it. There is no record or report of what those conversations contained and Abernathy makes no mention of what theology it was that they made. Whatever he thought it may have been, there is no way of deciding whether or not it is the one represented by Richardson.

An image of King that runs directly counter to Richardson's picture of King, the theologian, is one put forward by Joseph Washington, Jr. While an admirer of King as a man and a Christian, Washington was also severely critical of King even before his death.(45) In his view King was hardly touched by his academic exposure in the North and was not an intellectual in any ordinary usage of that word, a judgment, incidentally in which I by and large concur.(46) He was rather an exemplary instance of the Baptist preacher for whom the method of speaking lends whatever importance and substance there may be to the content of what is said. "The key," suggested Washington, "to being a successful Baptist preacher is being able to speak at once as a philosopher and as a man of religion without distinguishing between the two."(47) He found a perfect example of such syncretization in King's first speech as the newly elected president of the Montgomery Improvement Association (MIA), on the eve of the bus boycott. King's advocacy of passive resistance on that occasion was basically the thought of the philosopher, not of the theologian, and the absence of any real theological content and understanding was blatant. King, argued Washington, was basically an eclectic syncretist, mixing in one bowl parts of Socrates, Thoreau, Hegel and Jesus. As a Baptist he was undisciplined by any theology or by a community of faith. And it was Washington's contention that King came to advocate love and the importance of Jesus through philosophy rather than through a vision of Christian faith.(48)

40

The superficial veneer that faith and theology were for King's own self-understanding was further revealed by the direction he took after Montgomery and by the character of his influence and inspiration. For, claimed Washington, when King left Montgomery he faced a choice. "The choice was between presenting an image of a militant civil rights leader with a deep private religious faith, or one of a spiritual leader with a concern for civil rights."(49) The choice King made was the former, with the result that religious influence grew increasingly unimportant in the movement, even if the external trappings of hymn singing and prayer in the streets remained. King's emphasis shifted from love to justice and rights too long denied. He himself remained an inspiration to thousands of young blacks, not, however, as a man of God, but as a man of nonviolence and a champion of freedom and justice for black people. Nonviolence itself came to be seen as a powerful technique for instigating social change, and, as such, had no necessary connection with Christian love or faith. In sum, King became for a time the symbol of the most militant of civil rights activists, but was trapped by the rhetoric of his Baptist preaching and the un-related ideas of nonviolence, with the result that the movement passed him by and he and his message became a force that impeded rather than advanced the movement.(50)

In a later book,(51) written before but published after King's death, Washington resumed his criticism of King's failure to proclaim a theological understanding of Christian faith. Indeed, he asserted that not only was King not a theologian, not a proclaimer of the Christian gospel, but he was also clearly not a prophet in the tradition of the Old Testament, nor was his movement a work of God. "Faith in man, not in God, is too clear too often - for the movement to be the movement or mission of God. The dominant voices of our time rejoice in Martin Luther King, Jr., a sure sign that he is not an Old Testament prophet."(52)

Washington's far-reaching deflation of the image of King as a man of faith, a proclaimer of the gospel, an interpreter of the Christian message, was based largely on his own particular interpretation of the scriptural testimony.(53) Whatever is to be said about Washington's own position, and we will have to say a good bit about it later, it was not widely shared by any commentators who are not involved in some form of black theology, nor is it shared by all who are so involved.(54) Most observers of King saw some religious significance in his words and work. A great variety of images taken from both the Old and New Testaments, as well as from secular history, have been used to capture something of this significance: prophet, preacher, apostle; the black Moses, the American Gandhi, a modern-day St. Paul, a modern Job, a Socrates, even a Jesus, which was reflected in the not always flattering appellation of King by many of those close to him as "De Lawd."(55)

C. Eric Lincoln saw deep religious significance in King. For Lincoln, King was in his own person the manifestation of what Myrdal's book had made known to those who had troubled to read it and understand it. King was, in Lincoln's words, "the symbol - the unbearable symbol - of what is wrong with ourselves and our culture. Because he articulated...clearly and expressed...perfectly the central message of Christian doctrine,"(56) he became the contradiction of the contradiction that lay at the root of American life, the negation of the negation, that would either force transformation or have to be eliminated. The choice that would be made, Lincoln thought, was altogether predictable.

Lincoln shared with the historian, Louis Lomax,(57) an image of King as a modern-day St. Paul whose parish knew no boundaries and expanded until it embraced the whole world, an image that seeks to take in the extension of King's concerns to include the war in Vietnam, the plight of all the poor in the United States, and the pervasive problems of economic imperialism and colonialism. But for Lincoln, King was even more than a St. Paul. He judged King's special genius to have been an ability "to translate religious fervor into social action, thereby creating political leadership under the rubic of his religious ministry at an extraordinary level of involvement and commitment."(58)

The image of King as a political leader is not altogether peculiar to Lincoln. That King was a leader of one kind or another is unquestioned and unquestionable. The more common assessment of his leadership, however, was that it was mainly symbolic in a movement that was far wider and more independent of him than public appearances indicated. King's visibility, the ease with which he could get a hearing and actually be heard, the fact that he was well known and could raise large sums of money, contributed to keeping him, while he lived, in the forefront of national consciousness. More important, however, was his visibility to the black community as a symbol of their hopes and aspirations. William Miller, a biographer of King, interprets his significance in this way.

> Whatever his other roles, King's symbolic role was supreme, his charismatic stature was universally recognized...King as the individual apostle of nonviolence and the voice of the movement - His moral authority and personal image transcended matters of organization and stategy [sic].(59)

Whether this symbolic leadership was due to King's personal gifts, or, as many have thought, was a creation of the communications media, it was and is a widely held image of the man. David Lewis, in his sympathetic but critical biography of King, reported that both "Ella Baker and Charles Sherrod" - two of King's close associates in the Southern Christian Leadership Conference (SCLC) - "believed that Martin was a phantom of the news media, a symbol without more substance than that of hundreds of other Southern Baptist preachers."(60) Lewis did not altogether share this opinion, but he admitted the largely symbolic role of King's leadership. His full assessment of King is reminiscent of Lincoln's image of King as a political leader, but not as positive. For Lewis, King was only on the verge of moving from symbolic to political leadership when he was shot to death. Chicago is seen as the turning point. King left Chicago, writes Lewis, "with a much clearer understanding of the forces he was up against. More important, he began to identify lucidly the forces that the impoverished black American was up against. The period of rhetoric...was closing and a brief season of political realism had begun."(61) Lewis saw King as in transition from preacher to politician, from moral exhortation to the realistic practice of politics. King, he wrote, "was killed at the climacteric [sic] point at which he might have helped to create a coalition of racial, populist, intellectual and national groups."(62) The evidence, insisted Lewis, pointed to the idea that King was

looking for a national political base in which
support would no longer be based on the vagaries of
pure humanitarianism but on specific mutual benefit."(63)

The idea that King was in transit from preacher
to politician in the last years of his life was one
shared by a number of writers interested in the rise
of the Black Power slogan and approach. Not all were
as positive or as definite as Lewis, but the general
image is the same. John A. Williams dedicated his
book on King to "the memory of the man Martin Luther
King could have become, had he lived."(64) He found
that King's denunciation of the war in Vietnam in his
now famous sermon at Riverside Church in New York in
1967 "revealed a man in the process of breaking his
own shackles."(65) In his view it was neither civil
rights nor the poor that was the key issue in King's
development. Rather Vietnam became the catalyst for
the formation of a new populist party, and in the
last years of his life, suggested Williams, King was
moving rapidly toward the political integration of
blacks and whites designed to bring an end to the
war.(66) But his assessment of King was less positive than that of Lewis. For he thought that King
did not have any power and lacked awareness of the
power whites had and used to manipulate him. King
was, he wrote, "more a symbol than a power in the
civil rights movement but there was always the chance
growing with each campaign that King could end up
with a genuine power to join to his prestige."(67)

The evaluation that Williams made of King's life
and work was based largely on Williams' own admitted
antipathy to religion and moral preachment.(68) For
him King was a vacillator and indecisive,(69) a
dreamer who dealt in the never-never land of intangi-
ble goals and moral ideals.(70) The Democratic party
national convention of 1964 and the struggle there to
seat the Mississippi Freedom Democratic Party in
place of the regular delegation represented for
Williams both King's great opportunity and his
failure. That struggle he regarded as "King's
biggest opportunity to break out of the mold of moral
suasion into something of infinitely more value -
power politics."(71) In accepting the compromise of
the established white power, King lost his greatest
chance to deal with the tangible.(72)

What King contributed to his people in a positive way, according to Williams, was the initial
impetus to many groups and individuals who continue
today to attack the structure of authority. He
judged King to be responsible in large measure for
the various polarizations - economic, racial, moral
and political - that currently affect the United
States. King's failure to achieve moral gains made
others see that the gains could only be political."(73)

The notion that King's contribution to his
people centered in his failure to achieve his moral
goals with the resulting insight that only political
goals make sense was a common one among the proponents of Black Power. This is not surprising, for
Black Power had its origin in such a reading of
King's activities. The idea itself is not so much an
interpretation of King's work as it is a justification of Black Power as the means of social change.
In the book that bears the title Black Power, the
authors Stokely Carmichael and Charles V. Hamilton,
said next to nothing about King or his contribution
to the movement. They allowed that he, along with
others, helped to build the frustration which provides energy for the movement,(74) and that his
failures led to the change from moral to political
means and ends, the change from invoking good will to
seeking self-interest.(75) Two alternate ways of
expressing the same idea were common and both re-
volved around the method of militant nonviolence.
One form of the idea involved the rejection of
nonviolence as a way of life to see it merely as one,
sometimes useful, political technique for effecting
change, but by no means the only method.(76) The
second form in which the same general idea was
advanced involved a more radical rejection of nonviolence. What King's life and work proved was that
nonviolence is useless and self-defeating. In this
form King's death was also the death of nonviolence,
and his failure was also the final dispelling of
illusions about white good will.(77)

Whatever is to be said about the validity of
this idea in its various formulations, it should be
noted that none of the forms tell us very specifically what militant nonviolence means. The idea seems
to assume a radical divorce between the political and
the moral dimensions of human existence, as well as a
total identity between power and violence, when, in

fact, these would seem to be the very points at issue. Finally, to be an accurate assessment and criticism of King, it requires the assumption that his goals were in some way identical with the goals of his critics. The assumption may prove to be true, but it remains an unfounded one in his critics.

The more secular interpretation of King's work and its historical significance was best caught, perhaps, in an image used by Hanes Walton, Jr., in his book, The Political Philosophy of Martin Luther King Jr.(78) Walton portrayed King as a social critic after the model of Socrates in fifth century Athens - "a sort of gadfly, given to the State by God to stir it to life, to hold it - or move it closer - to its own ideals."(79) Needless to say, neither the fifth century Athenians nor the twentieth century Americans welcomed the gadfly's presence and sting with the unsurprising result of extermination.

While the image of King as a twentieth century American Socrates is highly suggestive of the function King actually played in the United States, it is limited mainly to his role vis-a-vis white Americans. It also implies a favorable estimate of King's message and function. A negative assessment of King's function which runs along the same general line of interpretation was offered by Lionel Lokos.(80) He did agree that King was a gadfly, a social critic, a prod toward change. Yet he passed quite a different judgment about the worth of King's work. "I am," he wrote, "perfectly willing to grant his brilliance, his basic sincerity, his charismatic effect upon hundreds of thousands of Americans - and still regretfully conclude that primarily Martin Luther King left his country a legacy of lawlessness."(81) This negative evaluation of King's legacy to his countrymen reflects rather accurately the Athenian fear of Socrates, for its main concern is not with the form or intent of King and his work, but with its content. Socrates was thought to be introducing into the Athenian society something new and alien to it. Such, too, was Lokos' judgment about King.

> His concept of civil disobedience...
> stripped to its essentials...was the
> concept that every man could be his own
> judge and jury and legislator - that no law
> was binding upon any American unless he

46

could 'conscientiously' obey it. It was a
concept that a minority has the right to
flout the law...to force its will upon the
majority. It was the doctrine that Martin
Luther King could harness the forces of
lawlessness to compel the passage of
law.(82)

The images that have been projected to explain
Martin Luther King have a distinct temporal association. Men observing him in the earlier stages of
his career were more apt to see him as one more black
minister concerned about civil rights, albeit a more
important one. He was considered, for example, as
the Billy Graham of the civil rights movement,(83) as
the keeper of the nation's conscience on civil
rights;(84) primarily he was seen as a preacher, a
man of faith concerned about morality. Carl Rowan
thought that King reached the pinnacle of his influence because of "an ability to wear the mantle of the
church in such a way as to suggest a special close-
ness to God."(85) James Baldwin found King to be a
man "solidly anchored in spiritual realities" and
engaged in a spiritual battle with evil and with
himself.(86) One of King's earliest biographers
judged him to be "one of the great spiritual leaders
of mankind."(87) It was only with the passage of
time and the development of King's career that he
seemed to be something else than "a man of God." It
was his temporal development that led later commentators to the previously mentioned judgments that King
changed or was in the process of changing from
preacher to politician.

There were some early intimations of this image
of the politician. Indeed, it was the first and
standard criticism thrown at King in the early days
of the Montgomery bus boycott that ministers should
stick to their pulpits and not get mixed up in
politics.(88) But even more detached evaluations saw
King, as early as the middle sixties, as the leader
of a reform movement which would effect economic and
social change throughout the country. August Meier
offered an image of King as a "Conservative militant,"(89) a mixture of righteousness and respectability, in which lay the secret of his great success.
It was by maintaining this delicate balance between a
purely moral appeal and militant displays of power
that King gained for his movement respectability, an
essential condition for the success of any reform

movement in the United States.(90) David Halberstam,(91) while covering King's anti-war activities,
saw in him not only a mystic and a prophet who
believed his own myth, but a fairly pragmatic moral-
ist who did "not intend to lose his position with the
young, militant, educated Negroes."(92)

With the increasing perspective afforded by
time, observers tended to see a change in King from
preacher to politician at an earlier and earlier
point in his life. One of his more recent biographers, Jim Bishop, dated King's transition from
religion to politics at the earliest point of any
writer. "As he was about to leave India, King thrust
aside his narrow shielding cloak of the cleric for
the broad and vulnerable one of the politician."(93)
But for Bishop the real key to understanding King
lies neither in his faith nor in his movement,
neither in religion nor in politics, but rather in
his personal ambition. Of King he asserted:

> His ego was such that he dealt solely with
> presidents and premiers, avoiding second
> and third-echelon politicians. His heart's
> desire was to play Gandhi or Christ, or a
> combination of both, but the modesty and
> self-denial required by those roles were
> foreign to him, so he tried to play states-
> man himself.(94)

One of the most popular images of King was that
of the black man's Gandhi, or the American
Gandhi,(95) an image greatly favored by American
groups like the Fellowship of Reconciliation and the
Society of Friends, who themselves had been deeply
influenced by Gandhi, as well as by Indian admirers
of King. The image, was, perhaps, a natural and
inevitable one in as much as comparisons of the two
men came so readily to hand. It was certainly
fostered by the quickness with which Gandhian language was injected into King's movement,(96) as well
as by King's own readiness to acknowledge the inspiration and influence he drew from Gandhi.(97) His
trip to India in early 1959 - "To other countries I
may go as a tourist, but to India I come as a pil-
grim"(98) - and the fact that he kept a picture of
Gandhi over his desk did nothing to discourage the
comparison. Finally, Gandhi's now famous hope-
prediction that someday the American Negro might show
the world the true power and meaning of nonviolence

hit too close to home for it not to be elevated to the level of fulfilled prophecy.(99)

Most Indian commentators on King took his own account of Gandhi's influence on him, in Stride Toward Freedom,(100) for granted. Mithrapuram K. Alexander, for example, saw the "philosophy of Jesus Christ and the techniques of Mahatma Gandhi" as the two central influences on King's own thinking,(101) and claimed that King "started to formulate Gandhism long before he was even exposed to the theory of nonviolence."(102) It was his contention that King was influenced by Gandhi's techniques of nonviolent resistance from the outset of the Montgomery boycott. The fact that there is no actual evidence to support such a claim does not prevent the idea from being frequently repeated.(103)

The grounds for a comparison of the two men, however, are more readily available than any evidence of a direct and deep influence of Gandhi upon King. The situation of Afro-Americans in the United States lent itself to a reasonably close comparison with the situation of the Harijans (the untouchables) in India, and thus provided an easy picture of Gandhi and King as champions of the oppressed peoples in their countries. Further parallels between the two men were equally plain. Mulford Q. Sibley,(104) in a short appreciation of King, mentioned several. Both men were preachers of a method of social change that excluded violence; both held that nonviolence was a way of life, not merely a technique; both admitted to serious errors at times; both were assassinated and praised extravagantly in death; riots followed the death of each of them and neither man's ideas were followed. Other similarities could be mentioned, all of a like nature. They all have to do with the external setting of the two men's lives and the events which surrounded them. The similarities say nothing about the inner vision, the content of the message, the meaning of either man. Whether the image of King as the American Gandhi has more than an external validity to it is simply a study that has not yet been made.

The most penetrating and suggestive images of King were four figures taken from the Old Testament. Used alone, or sometimes in combination, the images attempted to make clear, not only something of King's

functional significance to his time and place in
history, but also something of the man himself, his
roots, his motivation, his goals. The most general
of the four is that of prophet, understanding prophet
here in the scriptural sense of both the Old and New
Testaments, as one who speaks on behalf of God and
interprets His present Will to men.(105) Robert Hoyt
shared this image of King and explained it this way:
"a man who sees very plainly the moral condition of
the human community and describes it in harsh,
burning words."(106) The task of such a man who is
thus given to see, said Hoyt, "is not only to hold up
lofty ideals of goodness but to pinpoint evil -
particularly the insidious evils of injustice and
hypocrisy - and to fix responsibility."(107) In this
view of King there are two things about him which set
him apart as a prophet rather than merely a social
critic. The first is his own nobility of character -
he was himself a good man. Both King and his wife
have testified to his consciousness of the burden his
role put upon him in this regard.(108) This side of
the prophetic role takes in both its symbolic character and the claim it makes upon the prophet himself
for holiness or obedience to his God. Secondly,
there is the nature of his message. King did not
attack people, but structures and systems that
institutionalized evil. He spoke against those
powers that enslaved his people and poisoned the very
life of man.(109) King was not, properly speaking, a
theologian at all, nor an original religious thinker.
His writings and speeches on religion were aimed at
persuasion and action rather than at analysis and
understanding. His theology was in no sense a
discovery, but a synthesis, not creative but traditional. "He was not a sage who proclaimed a new
truth, but a prophet who renewed an old one."(110)

     The remaining three images of King were more
specific and concrete in that they pointed to three
personalities in the Old Testament: Joseph, Moses,
and Job. The Joseph image is best understood from a
text of Genesis that has been inscribed on the marble
tablet at the Lorraine Hotel in South Memphis where
King was killed. "They said to one another, 'Behold,
here cometh the dreamer. Let us slay him and we
shall see what becomes of his dreams.'" (111)
Primarily the Joseph image suggests what King meant
to many of those closest to him in the SCLC, for they
are the ones who selected the text. (112) Yet it
also captured the essence of King's life and purpose

50

as that was enunciated in his most famous speech, "I have a dream," delivered at the close of the now famous and historic March on Washington in 1963.(113) But the image also suggests the whirl of human passions, resentments, jealousies, and guilt feelings which threatened repeatedly to destroy both the dream and the dreamer. The image also suggests the special giftedness and chosenness of King - for Joseph's dreams were given him by God to prepare for the salvation of his people.

The Moses image for King was undoubtedly the most popular one. It has very deep roots in Southern Negro spirituality and religion, and was readily evoked in both sermons and songs. Ralph Abernathy took the image as far as describing himself as the Caleb to King's Moses.(114) While the image was quite a common one, it was also quite vague. It was understood that King was God's chosen instrument to challenge Pharaoh on behalf of his people, to lead them out of captivity and toward the Promised Land. His fate, as Moses' fate is reported, was never to reach there himself, but to view it from the mountaintop and reassure the people that it would be theirs. But what the concrete referents were in contemporary life for the biblical symbols varies greatly.

Albert Cleage, Jr. called King a Moses to his people,(115) and this despite the great disparity between his own outlook and King's views. Wrote Cleage, "I never agreed with most of the things he said, but I have loved everything he did because the things he did had no relationship to the things he said."(116) For Cleage, King was a doer, a creator of situations which needed to be interpreted through the mind and words of Malcolm X. A fanciful use of the Moses image might, therefore, see Malcolm X as Aaron to King's Moses. The exodus King led was, in Cleage's view, a psychological one - "the victory was not in what white people did; the victory was in how we were changing and in what was happening in our minds. This was Dr. King's victory all through this crucial period in the Black Revolution."(117) Yet despite the Moses image, despite the victory of psychological liberation which he attributed to King, Cleage insisted that King "was not a national black leader, because he had no way of giving a program on a national scale to black people."(118) This last, somewhat disjointed and incomprehensible sentence, suggests something of the looseness of the Moses image as applied to King.

For another ardent exponent of Black Theology the Moses image was also apt for King. James Cone saw in King's early career a return to the spirit and style of pre-Civil War black preachers whose emphasis in their ministry and sermons was on freedom and equality in the present political structures.(119) Like Moses, King did not get to reach the Promised Land--actual freedom and equality in America for the black man--but he "retained the unshakeable certainty that God's righteousness will triumph."(120) Cone considered the religious aspects of the image to be of great importance. Of King he wrote:

> King saw clearly the meaning of the gospel with its social implications and sought to instill its spirit in the hearts and minds of black and white in this land. He was a man endowed with the charisma of God, he was a prophet in our own time...Like the prophets of old, he had a dream, a dream grounded not in the hope of white America but in God.(121)

The exodus that King led was the move from acceptance of a system to confrontation with it. Because of King's work the beginning stages of real confrontation between black and white Americans has arrived. Like many exponents of Black Power, Cone argued that the concept of Black Power was a result of King's work, and that King, whether he agreed with the conception or not, preached black liberation in Jesus Christ.(122)

The attribution of the Moses image to King tells us more about the yearnings and aspirations of black people in America than it does about King himself. His own use of the image in regard to himself, especially on the night before his death during his last speech in Memphis,(123) indicates how much his own life and work were inspired by those aspirations. James Baldwin pointed out this identity of King with his people in the early 1960's. In a telling and sensitive way, Baldwin captured the inner meaning of the Moses image as applied to King, though he did not use the image himself.

> It is true that it was his congregation who
> had begun the struggle of which he was now
> the symbol and the leader; it is true that
> it had taken all of their insistence to
> overcome in him a grave reluctance to stand
> where he now stood. But it is also
> true...that once he had accepted the place
> they had prepared for him, their struggle
> became absolutely indistinguishable from
> his own, and took over and controlled his
> life. He suffered with them and thus he
> helped them to suffer.(124)

If King is to be considered a Moses, it is mainly
because of such a deep identity of his own person
with the situation and hopes of his people, who found
the image of Israel's captivity in Egypt and their
exodus to the Promised Land to be the best means of
interpreting their own history and their own hopes.

A final biblical image which sought to portray
more of the character and meaning of King's own
person was the image of Job. It was an image suggested by Maurice Friedman in a short appreciation of
King written shortly after his assassination,(125)
but the image itself and its meaning are derived from
a book Friedman wrote much earlier concerned with
images of modern man.(126) The key to understanding
Job, according to Friedman, is to grasp that Job both
trusts and contends with God, and knows that the two
are not incompatible.

> At the heart of Job's contending lies the
> question of trust in existence....It is not
> his belief in God that is undermined but
> his trust in existence: if he affirms his
> relationship with God throughout yet
> refuses to give up his demand for justice,
> it is because his trust in existence is at
> stake.(127)

This suggested to Friedman the need for openness in
finding values in genuine dialogue, even where that
dialogue is with the absurd - an openness teaching us
to meet others and to hold our ground when we met
them. This holding on to one's ground will bring a
man, as it did Job, into confrontation. He will
become a rebel. But "he is not a rebel on principle.
He is a rebel only where he is called to be one by
the situation which confronts him. He meets what

comes with clear-sighted trust, affirming where he
can affirm, and withstanding where he must withstand.(128)

It is this understanding of Job, not the patient
Job of legend, which Friedman suggested would illuminate the meaning of King, both in his person and his
work. His militancy and his insistence on nonviolence; his refusal to settle for less than 'freedom
now' and his willingness to negotiate and compromise;
his refusal to condemn persons while condemning
institutions and structures; his opposition to some
laws while defending the rule of law, all are seen as
efforts to affirm and withstand. More importantly,
King's effort to transform or win over those he
confronted is a model of the strongest kind of
rebellion, one that is able to hold its own ground
and confirm the worth of the other at the same time.
"Only this double action prevents that transformation
of rebellion into a new tyranny,"(129) an outcome
which King deeply feared and warned against. Because
King spoke and acted concretely from his real historical situation, he spoke his unique self, at the same
time speaking what was valid for all human beings.
He discovered in both the national and international
situations not only what personally affected him, but
his complete duty as man.(130) So Friedman finally
concludes that not only is Job a fitting image of
King, but that King in his own unique person is
himself "an image of what - in this time of great
confrontation and little dialogue - it means to be
human."(131)

The images of King which we have presented here
raise as many questions as they answer. Undoubtedly
they tell us more about how King impressed his
contemporaries than about what he himself actually
taught and did. Certainly King could not have been
or meant all the things that men have read into his
deeds and words. It is hard to see how he could have
been both an innovative theologian and no theologian
at all, or a prophet and also a tool of the white
power establishment. Yet a number of the images are
complimentary. There is no prima facie reason why
King could not have been a preacher of the gospel, a
symbolic leader of a black freedom movement, and a
politician all at the same time. Nor do the Old
Testament images stand in conflict with one another,
as long as they are not pushed too far.

54

One thing that few of the images shed any light upon is the content and meaning of militant nonviolence, nor do they illumine the grounds on which it is based. If King was a prophet who renewed an old truth, what was that truth? If he was a Joseph with a God-given dream, what were the meaning and consequences of that dream? If he was a Moses, what commandments did he bring to his people? If he was a Job trusting and yet contending with God, in what did he trust and for what did he contend? The fact that the images fail to inform us about the content and deeper meaning of his message may be an indication that the power of King's personality and example was far more impressive and important than anything he had to tell us.(132) On the other hand, it may also indicate that the choice he forced upon his fellow citizens was an unwelcome one, and the fact that he is accorded honor in death is but a sign of an uneasy conscience and relief at his passing.

While it is certainly clear from the many images that the mythologizing process in regard to King is well under way, and is, on balance, highly favorable to this point, the more interesting fact about the images is the difference between the political and religious evaluations. Most observers who employ a political image for King, or give a religious image political content, are either critical (Williams, Lokos, Bishop) or only tentatively affirmative (Lewis, Cleage, Walton, Meier). Those who favor a religious image are uniformly favorable (Hoyt, Friedman, Richardson, Miller, Bennett), with the exception of Washington whose whole effort is to deny the validity of such images as applied to King. The black-white correlation is also of interest, since the dominant tendency of white commentators is toward a religious image and an emphasis on King's religious significance, while most black writers look toward the political impact and meaning of King's life. The white critics of King attack his political methods and aims, while the black critics fault him for the confusion and inhibiting effect that religious ideas and rhetoric had upon the political movement.

Despite the favorable balance of assessments, it would appear that the images of the man to date are by and large ignoring what was most distinctive about King and what was essentially both his hope and his legacy. In an article on King's legacy, his wife suggested that essentially it was the church in action,(133) a combination of the religious and the political, of faith and social relevancy. The two were seen to be completely interdependent, for it was King's conviction that the moral and political had to be combined for any kind of justice to be the result.(134) The way of relating the two, of seeing faith and politics together, or of unifying theory and praxis correctly, was precisely militant nonviolence. This was King's charter of action from the earliest days in Montgomery, and it remained his conviction that one without the other rendered both empty and impotent. Militant nonviolence was neither a faith nor a technique. It was not a slogan for King nor an accidental accretion upon an entirely different enterprise. He may, of course, have been wrong in his claims for militant nonviolence, but in his own mind at least, there was an intimate and necessary relationship between what he believed and what he did.

In the pages that follow, therefore, it will be important to explore what King did believe and why he so believed. How did he understand his own calling in the light of this faith? How did such an understanding lead him to the insight that nonviolence was the one way of living to effect social change, and what exactly did he mean by this? The first part of this study will explore these questions. The second part of the study will be concerned with a critical assessment of the more practical implications of his convictions to see whether militant nonviolence represents a coherent and relevant vision of life in the world.

NOTES: CHAPTER I

1. The conception of hero operative here takes its
    starting point from Webster's Seventh New
    Collegiate Dictionary (Springfield, Massachu-
    setts: G. & C. Merriam Company, 1967), pp. 389-
    390. See also Sidney Hook, The Hero in History
    (New York: The Humanities Press, 1943),
    pp. 156-157.

2. See, for example, Luke 11:23. It is not the
    saying of these words that marks the hero, but
    the power of the hero's presence to make them
    true about himself or herself.

3. In expressing the choice as a problem of moral
    truth, I only mean to indicate that it is not a
    matter of degree, of something better or wiser
    or more effective, but a matter of kind, an
    either-or situation.

4. Eric Voegelin, From Enlightenment to Revolution
    (Durham, NC: Duke University Press, 1975),
    pp. 298-303, is the inspiration for this formu-
    lation.

5. The distinction here is important. The choice
    is not about a theory, or a principle, but about
    a real, time-bound, localized situation.
    Therefore the only test of one's choice is one's
    deeds.

6. I am using "mythological" here in the sense in
    which it has been frequently used in modern
    theology. It certainly does not mean false or
    imaginary. For a clear explanation of the usage
    see Mircea Eliade, Myths, Dreams and Mysteries,
    trans. by Philip Mairet (New York and Evanston:
    Harper & Row, Publishers, Harper Torchbooks,
    1967), pp. 14-17; "It can only be grasped, as a
    myth, in so far as it reveals something as
    having been fully manifested, and this manifes-
    tation is at the same time creative and exem-
    plary...," p. 14.

7. Though some regard King as a villain, his name
    at least is accorded public honor. I mean to
    claim no more than this. Precisely who his
    people are remains to be seen. He has been
    claimed by many, blacks, all sorts of

minorities, by Africans, Indians, and even by some white Americans. Possible his people are all humankind.

8. For one example, Lionel Lokos, House Divided: The Life and Legacy of Martin Luther King (New Rochelle, NY: Arlington House, 1968).

9. He was certainly not an official member of the Communist Party. For the alleged associations of King with party members see Ibid., the appendix; Jim Bishop, The Days of Martin Luther King, Jr. (New York: G.P. Putnam's Sons, 1971), pp. 318-319, 489-490, 454.

10. See Bishop, pp. 163-164, 264-265; 264-265; John A. Williams, The King God Didn't Save (New York: Coward-McCann, Inc, 1970), pp. 166-167, 189.

11. Information on King's supposed sexual activities is of the most elusive kind; it is rumor and innuendo. Both Bishop, pp. 83, 356-361, and Williams, pp. 129-130, 185-190, 196-203, 208-213, discuss some of the rumors and the FBI tapes and pictures.

12. National Catholic Reporter (April 2, 1969), p. 6.

13. C. Eric Lincoln, ed., Martin Luther King, Jr.: A Profile (New York: Hill and Wang, 1970), p. xiii.

14. Ralph Abernathy, "My Last Letter to Martin," Ebony (July, 1968), p. 61. Reprinted as "Our Lives Were Filled with the Action," in Lincoln, p. 227.

15. I prefer to describe King's method as militant nonviolence, because it makes clearer the active character of the method, as well as the fact that the initiative for action often comes from the side of nonviolence. His method is more than a mere reaction or simple resistance, and I believe the name, militant nonviolence, brings that out more clearly. The name is borrowed from the subtitle of Erik Erikson, Gandhi's Truth: On the Origins of Militant Nonviolence (New York: W.W. Norton & Company, Inc., 1969).

16. There have been rumors and suggestions that King was becoming disillusioned with nonviolence and the nonviolent method and would soon have forsaken it had he lived. It is hard to see how he could have been more explicit in affirming the opposite. Martin Luther King, Jr., "A Testament of Hope," _Playboy_ (January, 1969) XVI, 1, p. 236.

17. Gunnar Myrdal, _An American Dilemma_ (New York, Evanston, London: Harper & Row, Publishers: 20th Anniversary Edition, 1962).

18. _Ibid._, lxxi. Italics omitted.

19. _Ibid._, lxxv.

20. See, for example, Stokley Carmichael and Charles V. Hamilton, _Black Power_ (New York: Random House, Vintage Books, 1967), p. 4-32; Charles E. Silberman, _Crisis in Black and White_ (New York: Random House, Vintage Books, 1964), pp. 9-10. Both these books rejected Myrdal's dilemma because they did not accept white America's commitment to the American Creed.

21. Myrdal's subtitle was "The Negro Problem and Modern Democracy."

22. Myrdal, p. lxxvii.

23. He does speak of "institutional segregation" in both the North and the South. _Ibid._, p. 628.

24. _Ibid._, pp. 3-5. Myrdal's conception of an American Creed has been taken up and refined by other sociologists. It is quite similar to what has been called America's civil religion. See Robert Bellah, "Civil Religion in America," _The Religious Situation: 1968_, ed. by Donald R. Cutler (Boston: Beacon Press, 1968), pp. 331-356, and more recently, _The Broken Covenant: American Civil Religion in Time of Trial_ (New York: The Seabury Press, 1975).

25. Myrdal, p. 1007.

26. _Ibid._, pp. 30-49.

27. _Ibid._, pp. 997-1024.

28. <u>Ibid</u>., p. 1021.

29. <u>Ibid</u>., p. 998.

30. For a review and a defense of these optimistic predictions see Arnold Rose, <u>The Negro in America</u> (New York: Harper & Row, Publishers, Harper Torchbooks, 1964), pp. xvi-xxxiv.

31. Myrdal, p. lxxi. The quote is from John Dewey, <u>Freedom and Culture</u> (New York: G. P. Putnam's Sons, 1939), p. 172. Hannah Arendt, <u>On Violence</u>, pp. 64-66, makes the same point in reference to charges of collective guilt and collective responsibility, particularly as it touches present racial tensions.

32. Details of King's life are taken from his biographers, all of whom agree on the major details. See David Lewis, <u>King: A Critical Biography</u> (New York, Washington: Praeger Publishers, 1970), pp. 17-21.

33. The one exception was King's conviction that capitalism had to go as America's economic system. <u>BU Coll</u>: XIV (41).

34. King, <u>Stride Toward Freedom</u>, pp. 173-174; <u>BU Coll</u>., I (11A); "Speech to the National Bar Association," August 20, 1959: "As we struggle for our freedom America, we are struggling to save your soul. We are struggling to prevent you from committing a continuous act of murder."

35. King, <u>Stride Toward Freedom</u>, p. 174.

36. The King papers in the <u>BU Collection</u> have few items later than 1962, and his later papers are only recently available for study. Even in the available material there are no letters or notes that are the least bit personal. James Baldwin pointed out King's reluctance to speak of himself in 1961. James Baldwin, "The Highroad to Destiny," in Lincoln, p. 91. The article originally appeared in <u>Harper's Magazine</u> (February, 1961).

37. Herbert Warren Richardson, "Martin Luther King -- Unsung Theologian," <u>New Theology No. 6</u>, ed. by Martin E. Marty and Dean G. Peerman (London:

The Macmillan Company, 1969), p. 184. The
article appeared originally in Commonweal
(May 3, 1968).

38. Martin Luther King, Jr., A Comparison of the
Conceptions of God in the Thinking of Paul
Tillich and Henry Wilson Wieman (Unpublished
Doctoral Dissertation; Boston: Boston Universi-
ty, 1955). Cited hereafter as King, A Compari-
son.

39. Richardson, p. 178.

40. Ibid., p. 180.

41. Ibid., p. 181. For Paul's command see Romans
12:17-21.

42. Ibid., p. 182. It may be a semantic quibble
with Richardson here, but theology has usually
been understood as faith seeking understanding.
A position that does not start from faith is not
theology; it is philosophy which would claim a
right understanding of reality apart from faith.

43. Ibid., p. 183.

44. Abernathy, p. 224.

45. Joseph R. Washington, Jr., Black Religion
(Boston: Beacon Press, Beacon Paperback, 1966).

46. Ansbro is repeatedly concerned to refute this
judgment; see e.g., pp. 273-275 ns. 135, 137,
140.

47. Washington, p. 3; this judgment is concurred in
and assessed positively by Carl H. Marbury, "An
Excursus on the Biblical and Theological Rhetoric of Martin Luther King," Cartwright (ed.),
pp. 14-28.

48. Washington, pp. 5-9.

49. Ibid., p. 13; Oates, p. 146, adopts this view of
the matter, but favorably, without attribution
to Washington.

50. Ibid., pp. 16-21.

51. Joseph R. Washington, Jr., _The Politics of God_ (Boston: Beacon Press, Beacon Paperback, 1969). The hardcover edition first appeared in 1967. The edition used here contains a new preface and a tribute to King.

52. _Ibid._, pp. 16-21.

53. Washington, along with others, was concerned to work out a theology of black liberation. His approach centered around the suffering servant theme of Isaiah. We will deal with the content of it later in this study. See _Ibid._, pp. 153-227, and more explicitly Joseph R. Washington, Jr., _Black and White Power Subreption_ (Boston: Beacon Press, 1969), pp. 123ff.

54. For one example, J. Deotis Roberts, _Liberation and Reconciliation: A Black Theology_ (Philadelphia: The Westminster Press, 1971), pp. 195-198. A useful collection of documents pertinent to black theology up to the present is Gayraud S. Wilmore and James H. Cone (eds.), _Black Theology: A Documentary History, 1966-1979_ (Maryknoll, NY: Orbis Books, 1979).

55. Lewis, p. 152.

56. Lincoln, p. vii.

57. Louis E. Lomax, _The Negro Revolt_ (New York, Evanston and London: Harper & Row, Publishers, 1962), p. 92.

58. Lincoln, p. xiii.

59. William Robert Miller, _Martin Luther King, Jr._, p. 91.

60. Lewis, p. 213.

61. _Ibid._, p. 349.

62. _Ibid._, p. 393.

63. _Ibid._, p. 375.

64. Williams, _op. cit._

65. _Ibid._, p. 103.

66. _Ibid._, p. 105.

67. _Ibid._, p. 183.

68. _Ibid._, p. 119.

69. _Ibid._, p. 211.

70. _Ibid._, p. 171.

71. _Ibid._, p. 192.

72. _Ibid._, p. 194.

73. _Ibid._, p. 211.

74. Carmichael and Hamilton, p. 50.

75. _Ibid._, p. 184.

76. This was the original orientation of the Student Nonviolent Co-ordinating Committee and became that of many Black Power advocates. See Lerone Bennett, Jr., _What Manner of Man_, 3rd rev. ed. (Chicago: Johnson Publishing, 1968), p. 114; Washington, _Black Religion_, p. 26.

77. This was and is the assessment of more radical black writers who tended toward separatism or at least a primary and almost exclusive concern for black unity. See Albert B. Cleage, Jr., _The Black Messiah_ (New York: Sheed and Ward, 1968), p. 210; Malcolm X, _The Autobiography of Malcolm X_ (New York: Grove Press, Inc, 1966), p. 183, and James H. Cone, "An Interpretation of the Debate Among Black Theologians," _Black Theology_, pp. 609-623.

78. Hanes Walton, Jr., _The Political Philosophy of Martin Luther King, Jr._

79. _Ibid._, p. 6. Walton is quoting Plato from B. Jowett, trans. _The Dialogues of Plato_, I, 4th rev. ed. (Oxford: Clarendon Press, 1964), pp. 335-336.

80. Lokos, _House Divided_.

81. _Ibid._, p. 460.

82. Ibid., pp. 460-461.

83. Reese Cleghorn, "Martin Luther King, Jr. Apostle of Crisis," Saturday Evening Post (June 15, 1963); reprinted in Lincoln, p. 121.

84. Time (January 3, 1964), p. 27.

85. Carl T. Rowan, "Martin Luther King's Tragic Decision," Reader's Digest September, 1967); reprinted in Lincoln, p. 213.

86. Baldwin, p. 91; pp. 104-105.

87. Bennett, p. 2.

88. King, Stride Toward Freedom, p. 97.

89. August Meier, "On the Role of Martin Luther King," New Politics, Vol. IV (Winter 1965), pp. 52-59.

90. Ibid.

91. David Halberstam, "The Second Coming of Martin Luther King," Harper's Magazine (August, 1967): reprinted in Lincoln, pp. 187-211, under the title "When 'Civil Rights' and 'Peace' Join Forces."

92. Ibid., p. 205.

93. Bishop, p. 215.

94. Ibid., p. 265.

95. The people who used this image were numerous. See, for example, V. Pillai, ed., Indian Leaders on Martin Luther King, Jr. (New Delhi: Inter-State Cultural League of India, 1968).

96. The language was not injected into the movement by King. He admits in Stride Toward Freedom, p. 67, that the first allusion to Gandhi came from a white woman in a letter to the Montgomery Advertiser. People from FOR and the Friends made the language popular within the movement.

97. King, Stride Toward Freedom, pp. 78-79.

64

98. Lewis, p. 99.

99. Walton, pp. 24-25.

100. Confer note 96 above. King devoted two pages to Gandhi and what he says there suggests inspiration more than any solid ideas or specific techniques. As we expect to show, there is no other evidence that Gandhi made a big impact on him. Mrs. King has admitted that as late as 1959, under the impact of the trip to India, King was asking himself whether he was in fact nonviolent. Coretta Scott King, My Life With Martin Luther King, Jr. (New York, Chicago, San Francisco: Holt, Rinehart and Winston, 1969), p. 179. Cited hereafter as My Life.

101. Mithrapuram K. Alexander, Martin Luther King: Martyr for Freedom (New Delhi: A New Light Publication, 1968), p. 24.

102. Ibid., p. 16.

103. Confer notes 95, 96, 100.

104. Milford Q. Sibley in Nonviolence After Gandhi: A Study of Martin Luther King, Jr., ed. by G. Ramachandran and T. K. Mehadevan (New Delhi: Gandhi Peace Foundation, 1968), p. 21; Ansbro, pp. 6-7, points out parallel ideas and valuations, but fails to show the causal influence he claims existed.

105. Eugene H. Maly, Prophets of Salvation (New York: Herder and Herder, 1967), pp. 15-20.

106. Robert G. Hoyt, Martin Luther King, Jr. (Waukesha, Wisconsin: County Beautiful Foundation, Inc., 1970), p. 14.

107. Ibid.

108. Coretta Scott King, My Life, p. 171; and "Creative Suffering: The Ripple of Hope," National Catholic Reporter (April 2, 1969).

109. Hoyt, p. 16.

110. Ibid., p. 49.

111. Genesis 37:19 and 20B.

112. James Bristol in <u>Nonviolence After Gandhi</u>, p. 60.

113. That was not the first time King used the dream imagery, but it is the most reknowned.

114. Abernathy, p. 224. For the explanation of the relationship of Caleb and Moses see Numbers 13:38, and Ecclesiasticus 46:7-12.

115. Cleage, p. 213.

116. <u>Ibid</u>., p. 208.

117. <u>Ibid</u>., p. 210.

118. <u>Ibid</u>., p. 183.

119. James H. Cone, <u>Black Theology and Black Power</u> (New York: The Seabury Press, 1969), p. 108.

120. <u>Ibid</u>., p. 109.

121. <u>Ibid</u>., p. 108.

122. James H. Cone, <u>A Black Theology of Liberation</u> (Philadelphia & New York: J.B. Lippincott Company, 1970), pp. 77-78.

123. See Coretta Scott King, <u>My Life</u>, p. 316; Deuteronomy 32:48-52, and 34:1-9.

124. Baldwin, p. 96.

125. Maurice Friedman in <u>Nonviolence After Gandhi</u>, pp. 12-21.

126. Maurice Friedman, <u>Problematic Rebel: An Image of Modern Man</u> (New York: Random House, 1963; rev. ed. 1970). The latter will be used here.

127. <u>Ibid</u>., p. 486.

128. Friedman, <u>Nonviolence After Gandhi</u>, p. 16.

129. <u>Ibid</u>., p. 17.

130. C. Wright Mills, The Sociological Imagination (New York: The Grove Press, 1961), p. 6, has characterized the task of social science as "to grasp history and biography and the relationship between the two within society," or to understand personal troubles as social issues and vice versa. This, it seems to me, is an alternate expression of what King did in his life as Friedman saw it.

131. Friedman, Nonviolence After Gandhi, p. 21.

132. King's own account of his "Pilgrimage to Nonviolence" in Stride Toward Freedom, pp. 72-88, is to be relied upon only with caution. It is very sketchy, and a good deal of the more substantive part owes a great deal to Bayard Rustin and his editor. See BU Coll., IV (10A). King's words there need to be weighed in the light of his deeds and words at a given time.

133. Coretta Scott King, "The Legacy of Martin Luther King, Jr.," Theology Today, XXVIII, (July, 1977).

134. King, Stride Toward Freedom, p. 74; Vincent Harding, "Amazing Grace," East West Journal (November 1982), pp. 25-31, stresses this unity in terms of the inner connection between spirituality and social responsibility, a unity which he attributes to King's vision or dream.

CHAPTER II

THE FAITH OF A MAN

To understand Martin Luther King, Jr. and his
vision of militant nonviolence, it is necessary to
consider several biographical features of the man.
He was a black man born and raised during the first
half of the 20th century in the southern part of the
United States of America, nurtured in a home where a
father's love, strength and encouragement,(1) and
Baptist Christianity(2) were the dominant influences.
He was personally intelligent and sensitive, and
believed in a God who was very much alive and very
personal. It is this faith in a personal God and its
implications that I will begin to explore in this
chapter, not because King's faith was the unique
thing about him, but because it was fundamental in
leading him to his understanding and justification of
nonviolence.

The sources for an understanding of the content
of King's faith are fortunately rather ample. The
King papers at the Mugar Library of Boston University
contain many of his class notes, term papers and
examinations from his studies at Boston University,
as well as a lesser number from his days at Crozer
Theological Seminary. His doctoral dissertation was
a comparative study of the concepts of God in the
thought of Paul Tillich and Henry Nelson Wieman.(3)
Since King disagreed with both men,(4) the study
reveals far more about King's own thinking than about
anything else. In addition, his published sermons(5)
make plain a good number of King's basic beliefs, and
gleanings of the same can be gathered from letters
and other published writings.(6)

A word on the method of interpreting King's
class notes and other papers would seem to be in
order here. Obviously King cannot be held account-
able for every idea or expression that appears in a
test or in his class notes. But such documents do
indicate the kinds of things he was thinking about,
the degree of his comprehension of them, and the
notes reveal, at a minimum, what he considered to be
important about a given subject. King was not much
of a doodler, to judge from his class notes, but the
notes do contain an occasional quotation or idea that
is clearly not germane to the subject matter at hand,

which indicates that he was thinking about something
else at the moment and judged it important enough to
be written down.(7) Neither do the class notes in
every instance allow for a clear analysis of the
actual temporal development of his thought.(8) But
they do permit a logical presentation of the content
of King's thought and faith which will shed light
upon his later convictions and activities.

The vast majority of King's class notes origi-
nate from his days at Boston University where the
personalist philosophy of Borden Parker Browne, Edgar
Brightman, Harold DeWulf, Albert Knudson and others,
was the dominant influence. This personalist philosophy and its accompanying interpretation of Christian
faith were significant contributors to King's intellectual development and to his own interpretation of
reality and Christian faith, along with the liberal
theology he was taught at Crozer. Such notions as
the centrality of personality in the understanding of
existence, the strong emphasis on love as man's
fundamental relationship and on ethics as the heart
of Christian faith, the softening or de-emphasis of
the radical character of sin and its effects on human
nature, are basic ideas both in this personalism and
in liberal theology, and will appear unquestioned and
unchanged in King's outlook. The whole basis of his
criticism of Tillich and Wieman in his doctoral
dissertation is nothing more than an application of
personalist ideas and categories to the thought of
the two men.

Rather than attempt a systematic exposition of
the personalist philosophy and its relevance to King,
however, I have chosen simply to present what appears
in King's own notes and writings and speeches, and
that for three reasons. First, King was not himself
a systematic thinker, so that a systematic presentation of personalism simply cannot be assumed to
represent his own views adequately. Second, the
presentation of King's views and beliefs offered here
highlights, more accurately than anything else would,
what he did in fact absorb from personalism and what
he understood its implications to be. In this regard
all the references to his class notes in the next two
chapters document the extent of personalism's influence on his own thinking, except where Crozer Seminary is explicitly mentioned, more concretely than
any secondary reference to the works of personalist
authors. Third, the procedure adopted here allows

70

for a critical analysis of King's own beliefs without getting explicitly involved in a critique of personalism itself either as a philosophy or a theology. I have tried to take King on his own word as much as possible, and I am not especially concerned with how fully or how accurately he understood Brightman or DeWulf or anyone else, except in so far as such analysis will make clear what he himself actually thought. In proceeding this way I do not mean to slight the personalist influence. It was undoubtedly the major intellectual force in King's world view, both in providing him with the categories and concepts in which he thought and in emphasizing the values which he most esteemed. Chapters II and III in a very specific way underline this influence.(9) But I do mean to question a methodology which first explains personalism or liberal theology, and then presumes that such explication represents King's views because such is what he was taught, or which attributes an intellectual influence to such explications for positions King reached for quite other reasons.(10) To say, then, that personalism was the major intellectual force in King's world view, is not necessarily to disagree with Joseph Washington's claim that such intellectual force did not run very deeply.(11)

The decision that King made in his junior year at Morehouse College to become a Baptist minister was not surprising for a boy of his background and upbringing. Yet the reasons for his decision have remained somewhat obscure. He himself tells us very little about them in his published account,(12) and the reasons have puzzled his biographers.(13) His difficulties with the emotionalism of the ordinary Baptist churches that he knew and with the lack of serious intellectual content in the sermons he heard there are well known. Psychologically, the influence of his father, and of ministers he encountered at Morehouse, particularly Dr. Benjamin Mays and Dr. George Kelsey,(14) was a powerful inducement to the ministry. The latter two men certainly provided an alternative to the emotional performances he so disliked. Yet their example alone is not sufficient to explain his decision.

While at Crozer, King wrote, apparently as an assignment, a paper entitled "An Autobiography of Religious Development," which runs to some fifteen hand-written pages.(15) In the paper he mentions as

important influences in his life an intimate family
relationship, "a saintly grandmother" (maternal) who
was especially dear to him, extraordinary health such
that he hardly knows what an ill moment feels like,
an above average I.Q., and a precocity both physical
and mental. "So it seems that from an hereditary
view nature was very kind to me."(16) He mentions a
great deal about his father, and in fifteen pages has
but one line about his mother. Above all he reveals
a spirit fundamentally at peace with itself and with
the universe. He writes:

> It is quite easy for me to think of a God
> of love mainly because I grew up in a
> family where love was central and lovely
> relationships were ever present. It is
> quite easy for me to think of the universe
> as basically friendly mainly because of my
> uplifting hereditary and environmental
> circumstances. It is quite easy for me to
> lean more toward optimism than pessimism
> about human nature mainly because of my
> childhood experiences.(17)

In the same document King goes on to comment on
the ordinariness of life. The church he looked upon
as a second home and he cannot remember ever missing
it on Sunday. He acknowledges a complete ignorance
of the meaning of what was taking place at his
baptism, and the best he can say for Sunday school is
that it helped him develop the ability to get along
with people. Nor did he ever go through a conversion
experience, or, as he calls it, "the so-called crisis
moment," the experience which is more commonly
called, in the evangelical tradition, making a
decision for Christ. "Conversion for me," he wrote,
"has been the gradual intaking of the noble ideas set
forth in my family and my environment, and I must
admit this intaking has been largely unconsci-
ous."(18)

King's mind apparently began to function critically as he reached his teen-age years, for he has
reported shocking his Sunday school class at the age
of twelve by denying the bodily resurrection of
Jesus. That started the doubts and they reached a
peak in a period of skepticism during his second year
at Morehouse when he began to regret his association
with the church. The doubts stemmed largely from the
fundamentalistic and unquestioning literal interpre-

tation of the Bible to which he had been continuously exposed. There can be little doubt that it was this skepticism, with the resultant inability to relate meaningfully to the root document of Christian faith, that deterred him from accepting what would appear to have been his natural inheritance, the ministry.

It was a course in the Bible at Morehouse that exposed him at last to modern biblical criticism and helped him over his doubts. "I came to see that behind the legends and myths of the Book were many profound truths which one could not escape."(19) One other kind of doubt also blocked his path to the ministry and it, too, required a college experience to resolve. That doubt was how he could love a race of people who hated him and had destroyed one of his closest childhood friendships.(20) The growing anti-white feeling that gnawed at his soul was only dissipated when he came in contact with white students while taking part in inter-racial organizations.

The call to the ministry had been pressing upon King from his latter high school days, but the doubts had caused him to put it off. His father, he reports, never talked to him about the ministry, but he could scarcely have been unaware of his father's hopes for him. In any case, with the doubts resolved, the call to the ministry returned and he answered it. What that call was is best described in his own words. "My call to the ministry was not a miraculous or supernatural something; on the contrary, it was an inner urge calling me to serve humanity."(21) If asked, but why the ministry as the vehicle of service, King would acknowledge his father's example: "He set forth a noble example that I didn't mine [sic] following. Today I differ a good deal with my father theologically, but that admiration for a real father still remains."(22)

The result of these early experiences was that King was ordained a Baptist Minister(23) and then entered Crozer to begin his formal theological training with the shackles of fundamentalism removed "from my body,"(24) and with a readiness to accept the liberal interpretation of Christianity. Ready he was indeed! Nowhere has King recorded any serious doubts or objections to that interpretation. Basically what he had upon entering the seminary was a lively faith in a personal God, very much in the image of his own father, and a deep attachment to the ethical ideals he had grown up unconsciously assimilating. He claimed that even in times of theological doubt he could never turn away from these ideals. Despite the lack of any striking conversion experience, religion was very real to him, very much part of life. "In fact," he wrote, "the two cannot be separated; religion for me is life."(25) The process of honing and refining this nebulous and loose conception of faith took place during his years at Crozer and Boston University.

The liberal interpretation of Christianity which King found himself so ready to accept was, for the most part, a product of European biblical and historical criticism with its roots extending back to the Protestant Reformation. While it was never the intention of either Luther or Calvin to set up every individual as his or her own interpreter of the Christian message, their challenge to the established authority of the Roman Church started individuals on the road of questioning and criticism. The impact that scientific method made upon Christian theology was enormous and often threatening - so enormous, in fact, that the major questions in Christian Protestant theology quickly became methodological. Just what was theology, what were the sources for it, the norm of truth it sought, and how did one go about the construction of a theology?(26)

The development of theological liberalism in Germany and then in France and its transfer to the United States has been recounted elsewhere, but its single most representative example may well be Adolf Harnack's What Is Christianity?(27) Harnack's answer to that question was a vast reductive generalization of Christian faith and doctrine to a slogan. The meaning of Christianity, Harnack suggested, is exhausted by the idea of the Fatherhood of God and the brotherhood of man. That slogan came close to exhausting the theological content of liberal Christianity, and became the guiding light of King's theological education.

In a series of short papers, which appear to date from his Crozer days and were probably outlines for sermons,(28) King included one paper on what a Christian should believe about himself. He wrote that the Christian is a member of a larger family of which God is the Father. And he mentioned explicitly that the Fatherhood of God and the brotherhood of man is the starting point of the Christian ethic.(29) In one of the very rare references to slavery in his notes, he applied this starting point to the preaching done to slaves - "you are not niggers, not slaves, you are God's children."(30)

This God who was the Father of humankind was quite real and personal to King. If one does not grasp just how alive and how central this God was in King's mind and heart, it is likely that he will never comprehend King's message of militant nonviolence.(31) The fact of the matter is that King believed - he entrusted himself to and staked his life upon the God in whom he believed. In writing about his years at Boston University and his study of personalist philosophy while there, he claimed that he had been strengthened in two convictions: "it gave me metaphysical and philosophical grounding for the idea of a personal God, and it gave me a metaphysical basis for the dignity and worth of all human personality."(32) Yet King's God was not the result of metaphysical construction, no product of philosophical investigation, although the terms in which he described the nature and activity of his God are derived from personalist philosophy. In the same set of outlines mentioned just above there is one paper on the character of the Christian God. This God is personal, by which King means self-conscious and self-directing, and is defined as "the personal spirit, perfectly good, who in love creates, sustains, and orders all."(33) He is perfectly good in that he contains in himself all the possible excellence that the human mind can conceive and still transcends in goodness the highest conceptions of the human mind. He is also the original cause of the universe, the perpetual cause that preserves everything in being, and the final cause or the one who governs and directs the universe to a deliberate end. God's motive in all this activity is what King called holy love, which is a combination of his perfect goodness and immeasurable self-giving. This holy love is the substance of God's character and the motive of all his activity in relation to finite existence. How do we know this about God? We learn this, not from empirical observation, not from philosophical analysis, not even from some kind of personal experience. We learn this, insisted King, from Jesus of Nazareth.(34)

That King's articulation of the nature and character of God was an articulation of a faith (theology) and not a philosophy is confirmed in the one piece of scholarly analysis and criticism that he ever undertook, his doctoral dissertation. This study reveals King's superb expository ability. He studied the conceptions of God in Paul Tillich and Henry Nelson Wieman, and his exposition of their thought is a model of clarity and completeness. It is his critical analysis of their thought, his agreements and disagreements, which makes clear his own ideas and his own limitations. To start with those limitations in briefest form, he simply did not understand what was at stake in the thought of either Tillich or Wieman. They were philosophers writing theological apologetics. King was a Christian believer seeking to articulate a faith and an experience.

In explaining the methodology he employed in his study of Tillich and Wieman, King proposed three methods of investigation: the expository, the comparative, and the critical. Under the third heading he presents two norms of critical evaluation. They are "(i) adequacy in expressing the religious values of historic Christianity; and (ii) adequacy in meeting the philosophical requirements of consistency and coherence."(35) The second norm is, of course, unexceptionable. It is altogether fair to ask any thinker to avoid illogic and contradiction. But the first criterion is another story. It is the guiding norm of the believing theologian who is already committed to a specific object of faith, who already knows, or thinks he knows, what those religious values are or where they are revealed. Both Tillich and Wieman were engaged in an effort to discover in the human condition points of contact with the historic symbols of Christian language and behavior in order to provide new meaning and validity for those symbols. They wanted to know about the validity of historic Christian values and to evaluate the meaning of historic Christian symbols. They were not interested in simply expressing something already known and accepted in new words. King knew this. He explains both men to this effect in his study.(36) But when he came to criticize their views it is another matter. He accused Wieman, for example, of trying "to eliminate faith and analogical reference from the quest for knowledge of God."(37) That was certainly exactly what Wieman was trying to do. But

76

King faulted him for this, not because his attempt was unsuccessful, but because "it would hardly be adequate for religion,"(38) since the religious man seeks a personal relationship with the object of his knowledge, not a detached scientific objectivity in regard to it. That this rather begs the question of the validity of the religious man's knowledge, which was Wieman's concern even on King's own accounting, seems to have escaped King altogether.

King's criticism of Wieman was based upon Tillich's distinction between philosophy and theology, a distinction which he accordingly approved.(39) Yet he proceeded to criticize Tillich because of the absolute character of this distinction - an absoluteness which Tillich never claimed to exist other than analytically. King's criticism was based on existential grounds and his appeal again was to religious experience and to the adequacy of a formulation of that experience.(40) In employing such a criterion he is missing the whole point of Tillich's enterprise, which was an apologetic one, to wit, to find something in human experience to validate or ground the claims of religious faith and experience.

The blindness of King to the fundamental problem of theology - the problem of the relationship between reason and revelation(41) - is shown even more clearly in his repeated dismissal of Karl Barth's radical rejection of reason, apologetics and natural theology, a rejection the rationale for which he had not a clue.(42) There are several references to Barth or the Barthian school in the dissertation,(43) but no indication that King knew Barth either directly or well. The references smack of survey knowledge. Even clearer indications of his ignorance of both Barth and the issue that was at the heart of Barth's position are contained in King's notes. He dismissed Barth's rejection of reason in favor of revelation with the altogether irrelevant and trivial comment that Barth had to use reason and concepts in working out his own theology.(44) It would appear, then, that King never understood the difference between theology and philosophy, nor was he at all clear about the sources and norms of knowledge of any kind.

The same point of view appears in some notes of King's on the Protestant Reformation. It was his

77

conviction that there was no theological question that was fundamental to the philosophy of the Reformation - a curious way of expressing the matter. He regarded freedom of religion and freedom of conscience to be the central issues. Thus, in his view, both the Catholics and the Reformers were wrong.(45) The issue for King was authority, an issue resolved for him by affirming that the only authority in religion is love and this was not perceived by the Reformers, but it was discovered by the people. This last notion suggests something of the romanticization of the masses, a tendency rather common in King. In another reference he mentioned that Luther's opposition to the peasant revolt was the end of his credibility, and the movement of reform passed from leaders to people.(46) Such views are certainly not surprising coming from a Baptist, but they do give rather short shrift to the issues of the Reformation.

King's own conception of God and his meaning for human beings can be further illuminated by the points he was most concerned to criticize in Tillich and Wieman, and by the grounds of his criticism. The points are two and they revolve around the question of the personality of God and the question of theodicy, or how to explain evil if God is all good and all powerful. Again and again King faulted Tillich for suggesting that there is an element of evil or destructiveness in God, for implying that in some way God is responsible for evil. For example, he wrote in a footnote, "Surely physical evil, pain and death are evils, and the fact that they are implicated in the finitude of all creaturely being does not help at all. For if creation is of finitude, and finitude is evil, then God is the creator of evil."(47) Or again in a note he commented, "In other words, God creates because he must, because that is how he is.... Now, if creation is inevitable, and if the result is inevitably bad (a 'fall'), then it follows that God contains a destructive principle."(48)

He also attacked Wieman in the same cause, although Wieman was so concerned to exempt God from any responsibility for evil that he insisted God is not the creator or source of all reality, but only of what is good.(49) But for King this limitation upon God raised more difficulties than it solved. He called it "an easy solution to the problem of evil," and suggested that it fails to deal completely with the problem of good, though why good is a problem or

78

what kind of problem it is he did not say. He found
Wieman's solution inadequate because it is a conception which threatens the ultimate triumph of good
over evil.(50)

On the question of the personality of God King
was equally critical of both men. Essentially both
Tillich and Wieman argued that God is above or beyond
the human concept of personality. Tillich, for
example, explained the attribution of the symbol,
person, to God as meaning "that God is the ground of
everything personal and that he carries in himself
the ontological power of personality."(51) But God
was not to be understood as a person beside or above
other persons. Wieman's concern was much the same.
He wrote that "God towers in unique majesty infinitely above the little hills which we call minds
and personalities."(52) Both men, in short, were
arguing that God transcends personality as it is
humanly conceivable, while both allowed that religious faith might well need to think of God as a
person in order to pray and worship.(53) It is a
somewhat delicate and arguable philosophic point
which the two men were trying to make, but King would
have none of it. Both men, he argued, present a
conception of God that is sub-personal or impersonal,
and that simply will not do. And why not? Because
"the religious man has always recognized two fundamental religious values. One is fellowship with God,
the other is trust in his goodness. Both of these
imply the personality of God."(54) Again: "True
fellowship and communion can only exist between
beings who know each other and take a volitional
attitude toward each other... Fellowship requires an
outgoing of will and feeling."(55)

Goodness, as well as fellowship, requires God to
have a personality. Goodness in any true ethical
sense requires both freedom and intelligence, so that
only a person can be good. And only a person can
love and be loved. "What we love deeply is persons -
we love concrete objects, persistent realities, not
mere interactions, and certainly not 'being-itself'
or the 'creative event'."(56) In sum, King's criticism was based on a norm that is neither philosophical nor even theological, but is a cry of the
human heart expressing what it needs to believe; it
is an affirmation of faith.

What King's criticism of Tillich and Wieman makes evident above all else is a characteristic of his own mind, a characteristic which we might call the both-and mind set, as opposed to an either-or mentality. It is based upon, or better, reflected in King's complete misunderstanding of the Hegelian dialectic,(57) a way of thinking which King rightly claimed to use in all his reading and studying.(58) King took this dialectic to mean "combining a partial yes and a partial no."(59) This mentality or style of thinking betrays itself in the repeated observation that "again we find Wieman and Tillich each overstressing one phase of reality while minimizing another."(60)

The high point of King's dissertation, the purpose of it, was to decide whether Tillich and Wieman were philosophical monists or pluralists, and whether they were qualitative or quantitative in their monism or pluralism. These terms of analysis and critique were designed to set off King's own position and conclusion about the nature of God and finite reality. He concluded that Tillich was both a qualitative and quantitative monist, while Wieman was a qualitative and quantitative pluralist. King's own position was entirely typical of him. "Here again the solution is not either monism or pluralism; it is both monism and pluralism."(61) King insisted that a position of qualitative monism and quantitative pluralism can be meaningfully held, and that it is a way to preserve both the oneness and manyness of experience. What he did not see was that all his solution achieved was a re-statement of the classical philosophical problem of the one and the many, or the articulation of the problem and the data of the problem in different words, without advancing one step toward its solution.(62)

Once again the foundation on which King rested his criticism of the two men is the most significant aspect. He objected to what he called Tillich's quantitative monism, which is almost certainly an unfair reading of Tillich, because it tends to pantheism. But the real danger he saw in it was that it will cause havoc to religious faith.

> True religion is not concerned about metaphysical union of the human with the divine, but with a relation of mutual understanding between them, a relation that

80

expresses itself in worship and love. Such
a relation is possible only between persons
who maintain their distinct individuality.
To make human personality a mere phase or
mode of the absolute is to render real
religious experience impossible.(63)

And as a summary statement he concluded, "Freedom
requires metaphysical otherness."(64)

King's difficulty with what he called Wieman's
qualitative and quantitative pluralism - a view which
is certainly fairer to Wieman than he was to Tillich
- was that it failed to satisfy the demand for unity.
King explained:

Certainly the quest for ultimate unity
haunts the religious man. One of the main
things that the religious worshipper is
seeking is a Being who is able to reduce
all multiplicity to unity. Wieman's
failure to discover this unity leaves him
with a conception of God that is both
religiously and intellectually inadequate.(65)

Once again the desires and needs of the religious
person are the final norm of judgment.

The foundation of King's criticism throughout
his dissertation was ostensibly his own personalist
philosophy which, in his own words, affirmed that
"the clue to the meaning of ultimate reality is found
in personality."(66) But more fundamental than any
philosophical truths or insights was the felt religious need for a God who is at once all good and all
powerful. Almost certainly one thing that attracted
King to a study of Tillich and Wieman was that he
read them to be emphasizing one or the other of the
two attributes: Tillich God's power and Wieman God's
goodness. King needed a God who was both good and
powerful, and in the last analysis the simple affirmation of a good and powerful God was the substance
of King's own position. He was no metaphysician.
Personality may well be a clue to the meaning of
ultimate reality but it is certainly not humanly
conceivable as ultimate reality. Nor did King try to
say anything about the intrinsic relationship between
goodness and power in God. In the long run power was
affirmed to be a metaphysical quality of a God who

just happened to be an ethical God. And the only explanation for how he knows that God is good and powerful which King could offer is that Jesus tells us so.

This conception of God is not confined to King's doctoral dissertation. It is the operative conception in all his sermons and is also at the root of his espousal of militant nonviolence. He had a variety of ways of expressing this conception of God, but the persistent affirmation that God is both good and powerful, that the two attributes meet in his personality, remained without explanation. The unity of goodness and power in God was based solely upon the oft-repeated slogan that Hegel said the truth is to be found "in an emergent synthesis which reconciles opposites."(67)   So, for example, God has a tough mind and a tender heart, he is austere and gentle, just and merciful: such combinations indicate the content of King's preaching. God is, he could say, "tough-minded enough to transcend the world; he is tenderhearted enough to live in it."(68) Or again, the faith that we are to have is "the faith that God is good and just."(69)   Or, "Christianity clearly affirms that in the long struggle between good and evil, good will eventually emerge as victor."(70)   King also expressed the same idea with a peculiarly Kantian ring to it.   "Would not this be a strangely irrational universe if God did not ultimately join virtue and fulfillment...",(71) and again, in a wildly optimistic view of human conscience, "God's unbroken hold on us is something that will never permit us to feel right when we do wrong or to feel natural when we do the unnatural."(72) Finally, the same idea was the basis for nonviolent resistance, which "is based on the conviction that the universe is on the side of justice," that in man's struggle for justice he has cosmic companionship, or that there is "some creative force that works for universal wholeness."(73)

CHRISTOLOGY

This conception of God as both good and powerful was for King the substance of what Jesus of Nazareth has revealed to humankind and it is through his life that we know this about God most definitively.   The place and the meaning of Jesus of Nazareth in King's view of human life is, therefore, quite important.

82

Once again his understanding of Jesus reflected very concretely the liberal theology which he had been so ready to accept. "Jesus is like God" was taken to be the basic affirmation of Christian faith, and Jesus' message was regarded as more important than his person: yet this message is to be derived not so much from his words as from the meaning of his person. In what can only be considered an amazing sentence, King had written the following words in the notes about Jesus. "He was a representative of the popular religious movement that emphasized liberalism in religion. He was a modernist of his day."(74) Again he offers us the idea that Jesus was not the founder of Christianity. Rather he stood in the midst of the development and gave himself for it. His genius was to take old techniques and give them new meanings. Although King's notes afford no examples to illustrate this genius, a marginal note suggests the reason behind these views. "No one," he had written, "is sufficient of himself to begin or end faith."(75)

Essentially King's theological comments on Jesus are a form of Arianism, the ancient heresy that declared Jesus to be a man like God in character, but who in no way was to be considered divine in being.(76) This charge of heresy would not have disturbed King, for he had a marginal comment in his notes to the effect that all through history "the heretics have been true to original Christianity."(77) The real importance of Jesus is simply his influence on persons which flows from the power of his example, the power of his personality. For King, Jesus was the most persistent, inescapable and influential figure that ever entered history. The spirit of his teaching was what was important, far more than the detailed form or content of it; hence it is important to interpret any one aspect of his teaching from the context of his whole life and message.(78)

King's approach to understanding Christ reveals the fundamental ethical concern of all his reflections. Jesus is both a model for human life and an inspiration for life. All other doctrines of Christianity are explained on this basis.(79) Jesus is portrayed as a rebel against the established order, while his relationship to God is declared to be completely similar in kind to that of every other man's relationship to God. The difference between

83

Jesus and us in this regard is simply one of degree. What Jesus did, thought King, we can do, if we submit our wills completely to God. The only kind of "divinity" King assigned to Jesus is an ethical divinity, which means that Jesus became God-like by the completeness and perfection of his obedience. It was his personality, not his body or his being, that was divine. His divinity, such as it was, was an ethical achievement.(80)

Further scattered comments about the man of Nazareth are also illuminating. King thought that Jesus was concerned in his life with the creation of a crisis in the minds of his hearers so as to change their way of thinking. Among the positive virtues of Jesus, King commended his integrity, his compassion for the masses, and, oddly, his willingness to give up a vacation.(81) The fundamental structure of Christ's life, his death and resurrection, or his humiliation and exaltation, was the key that God provided by which his sons and daughters might understand the design imprinted in all creation.(82) King found in Jesus, therefore, an inseparable union between religion and morality, not a substitution of ethics for religion. He also warned against the worship of Jesus, pointing out a two-fold danger in such a practice. Worship might become an end in itself rather than the means to an end, and we might put undue emphasis on the name of the teacher and forget his teachings.(83)

As with most of his theological and philosophical reflections, King did not advance the issues or questions with which he dealt, so much as he restated the problem in other words. As always with him, his own experiences and his unstated or unexamined beliefs were the guiding norm of comment and interpretation. It was only on rare occasion that he even tried to advance another kind of reason for his own position. His doctrine of salvation provides another indication of this tendency and brings us still closer to his reasons for embracing nonviolence.

SOTERIOLOGY

The overriding importance of Jesus in classical Christian faith has always been that he is looked upon as the Savior of humankind. The great Christological controversies over the nature of Christ which divided the Church so bitterly during the fourth and fifth centuries of our era all had this savior aspect at the heart of them. (84) The Protestant-Catholic battles of the sixteenth century were equally concerned with Jesus as savior and with his role in and contribution to human salvation. Like the Pelagian-Augustinian controversy in the fifth century, the emphasis was on what a person must do to be saved, but the guiding norm for deciding that question was always the role of Christ as savior and how that was understood. (85)

The fine distinctions that theologians have made over the centuries in order to find their way through this difficult maze were not to King's temper or interest. For a mind that consistently treated every difference of opinion by saying that you are right in what you affirm and wrong in what you deny, or alternately, the truth is not either-or but both-and, such controversies had little meaning or interest, and even less importance. That he did not understand what was at stake in the argument over salvation by faith or by works any more than he understood the reason-revelation argument, never seems to have crossed his mind. In this temper of mind he is in many ways quite similar to Mohandas Gandhi.

Salvation, King defined as "moral likeness to God leading to spiritual fellowship with him." (86) Jesus' role in this salvation was again understood to be largely inspirational. By his suffering and self-limitation Jesus awakens in other human beings their own noble possibilities. Or, the cross of Christ saves human beings because it attacks the moral and spiritual inadequacies in which people live and awakens them to higher possibilities. (87) But it is not really the cross of Christ that saves people, but their own cross. And the cross means, "speaking the truth, seeking the truth and defending the truth." (88) Such a view of salvation is a classical moral-influence theory of atonement, (89) and, as such, King explicitly embraced it despite the fact it is unorthodox. It was his conviction that all other theories demanded a change in God, presumably from anger to acceptance, or from alienation to reconciliation. (90) For King held that in Jesus God was trying to reconcile man to himself and not himself to the world. (91) His more fundamental concern in this regard, however, was what he thought a person needs in order to achieve moral likeness to God. Since human beings are growing out of an evolutionary past, they need an example to lead them on, to call forth their higher possibilities, to urge them to continue the process of development. It is the need for an example and an inspiration that led King to deny the classical Christian definitions of the nature of Christ. He thought they deprived Jesus of the quality of inspiration by putting him on an altogether higher and different plane than human beings.(92)

If one were to pick a name from the historical roster of atonement theories to denominate King's theological doctrine of salvation, it would most aptly be semi-Pelagianism.(93) Typically enough it is a theory which attempted to strike a middle ground between salvation by faith and salvation by works or moral effort. Or, as King would have expressed it, had he had to, it is not either God who saves people or people who save themselves, but both God and human beings cooperate in the work of salvation. The idea that the person is God's co-worker in the realization of God's purpose for the universe is a constant theme in King's thought, and he is most emphatic in his insistence upon the independent part human beings have to play in this enterprise. Humanism, he tells us, is an illusion because "man by his own power can never cast evil out of the world."(94) On the other hand, God will not and, indeed, cannot cast evil out of the world without human cooperation.(95) By giving human beings freedom, God imposed limitations upon himself and surrendered a measure of his own sovereignty. "Therefore God cannot at the same time impose his will upon his children and also maintain his purpose for man. If through sheer omnipotence God were to defeat his purpose, he would express weakness rather than power."(96)

King, therefore, was opposed to both humanism and to the Reformation doctrine of original sin which affirmed the human being's total inability to do anything on his or her own toward salvation.(97) But once again the reason for his opposition had nothing to do with the doctrine itself, which he did not trouble to understand, but was because of what he feared it led to in human experience, namely to an otherworldly religion that ignores social reform and looks upon prayer and good intentions as substitutes for work and intelligence.(98) "God," he proclaimed, "who gave us minds for thinking and bodies for working, would defeat his own purpose if he permitted us to obtain through prayer what may come through work and intelligence. Prayer is a marvelous and and necessary supplement of our feeble efforts, but it is a dangerous substitute."(99) That such a doctrine gravely imperils the ultimate triumph of good over evil by putting severe limitations on the omnipotence of God did not seem to concern King. He was involved in exhortation and the proclamation of faith, not in its philosophical or theological clarification and coherence.

ESCHATOLOGY

King's doctrine of eschatology was rooted in the same kind of liberal theology that we have been dealing with all along. Properly speaking, it is not a doctrine of eschatology at all, for King focused rather exclusively upon the single element of eternal life which was of great personal and theoretical importance to him.(100) Once more his arguments and explanations were not doctrinal or theological so much as experiential and inspirational. In some notes that date from his Crozer days he remarked that there is a widespread doubt about immortality and recommended some steps to counter this doubt.(101) The first step is to make people feel that life on earth is so rich and significant that it deserves to continue. What we need is a renewed faith in life. Secondly, he suggested we discover the possibilities for growth and progress which Jesus attributed to human beings, though he does not tell us where to look for such attribution. Thirdly, he thought that the power of example is very great in this regard, that some men make it easy to believe in immortality. The examples he offered are both curious and interesting: Lincoln, Dante, Shakespeare, David Livingstone, Jesus Christ.

In addition to the experiential arguments he also advanced Christian reasons for believing in immortality. The resurrection of Jesus, whether it be physical or spiritual, is a proof of it. The reasonableness of the universe supports it, and he referred to Darwin, of all people, in defense of his claim of reasonableness. The goodness of God demands it. We simply cannot conceive of God blotting out the choicest fruit of the evolutionary process, so that immortality really comes down to faith in a God who is not only the source of all values but the conserver of them as well. Finally, King offered an argument which is curiously reminiscent of Kant's 'proof of immortality' as a demand of practical reason.(102) Jesus has revealed to us, said King, capacities within ourselves and within others which require another life for their full expression. Our goodness on earth, if it be passionate and earnest, does not need a reward exactly, as the Kantian position argued; rather it needs a chance, an eternal chance, of being even better. Why a doctrine of re-incarnation would not do as well as one of immortality to satisfy this need is something King did not discuss. For him virtue would seem to be very much its own reward. The real value of human beings lies not in what they are or do, but in what they become, in their possibilities which would seem to be without definable limit.(103)

The other three topics traditionally treated in eschatology, heaven, hell and judgment, received little attention from King. What happens after death, he thought, is that the spirit leaves the body and passes on to new scenes of activity. He admitted that we cannot prove this, but he argued that personality, ideas, love and truth are also invisible, yet they are the deepest forces of human life. What happens to the rogues of the earth, the people who have not realized their potentialities for good, is not at all clear. King rejected - or more accurately, perhaps, stood aloof from - the traditional Christian notion of a final judgment. Instead he offered his own personal interpretation of the judgment. There are, he insisted, certain eternal laws established by God in the very fiber of the universe which confront every man. "There is an eternal and absolute distinction between right and wrong."(104) But what happens to the person who fails to recognize these laws or who rejects their authority was not very definite. Presumably vice brings its own punishment just as virtue brings its own reward. King's personal interpretation of the judgment shed no real light on the question.

> The highest court of justice is in the heart of man when he is inspired by the teaching of Christ. Rather than being the judge, Christ is the light in which we pass judgment on ourselves. The truth is that every day our deeds and words, our silence

88

and speech, are building character. Any day that reveals this fact is a day of judgment.(105)

What underlay most of King's convictions about Christian teaching was his perception of what the personal God of power and goodness is about in this world. He is working, according to King, "to bring goodness to pass and...through human beings is striving to achieve a social order that is moral in its nature and capable of expressing love."(106) That was one meaning he attributed to the symbol of the Kingdom of God. King took a spiritual rather than an apocalyptic view of the Kingdom. Indeed, he rejected the latter view on the grounds that it is inconsistent with a God who saves man through love rather than by force. So the Kingdom for him was both a present and a future reality. As a present reality it can exist as an inner possession in history.(107) "Wherever the love of God is sovereign in a man [sic] life, there is the Kingdom of God." As a future reality it is the idealized social order as expressed immediately above. Every progress of human life toward that idealized order is an expression of the power of the Kingdom in history.(108) The God of goodness and power has committed himself in truth and love to bringing about the moral transformation of humankind. His "final purpose is the building of a regenerated human society which will include all mankind in a common fellowship of well-ordered living."(109) The goal of a person's individual existence is the sonship of God while the goal of collective existence is the reign of God's law within society.(110) The Kingdom of God will come on earth. We must never lose faith in God's power to achieve His purpose. "God chose this world as a site on which to build a wonderful structure, a global union of real brothers sharing in his good gifts, and offering all achievement as a form of worship to him."(111) If one has faith and cooperates with God, he or she will soon be able to see the Kingdom in this world. In years to come, however, this enthusiastic faith of King's was to be tempered somewhat. Hard experiences modified the immediacy of the coming of the Kingdom to a still optimistic but more cautious hope.

Even though all progress is precarious, within limits real social progress may be made. Although man's moral pilgrimage may never reach a destination point on earth, his never-ceasing strivings may bring him ever closer to the city of righteousness. And though the Kingdom of God may remain not yet as a universal reality in history, in the present it may exist in such isolated forms as in judgment, in personal devotion, and in some group life.(112)

FAITH, HOPE, LOVE

Given this overall theological and philosophical conception of the nature and meaning of Christian faith, it is possible to specify the concrete content and ground of King's faith, hope and love. Jesus of Nazareth was not the object or the content of King's faith, but he was the ground of faith in as much as in him God has revealed both his plans for mankind and the basic structure of the universe; in addition his example provides the model and the inspiration for human activity. It might be said that King believed on Jesus but not in him. What he believed in was the power and the goodness of a personal God who has irrevocably committed himself to achieving his plan for humankind, and in the potentiality for goodness in every human being, a potentiality put there by God which nothing can destroy. To believe in one is to believe in the other. So much is this true that King could write, "Christianity is the belief in the potential good in human nature.... The basis of Christianity rests in dealing with man not for what they are [sic] but for (what) they may become."(113) That latter is a sentiment that would surely prompt Luther and Calvin to leap out of their graves in stern protest.

As an act of a human being, faith was understood to be of two kinds. There is the faith that such a good and powerful God exists, and there is the faith in such a God, a trusting faith which involves the commitment of the heart to a person. To know God the second type of faith is required.(114) Theoretical faith in God is not unimportant, but the good of humanity is far more fundamental in Jesus' teaching, so that the quintessence of religion is devotion to the highest ideals,(115) and it is far better for "a man to be a committed humanist than an uncommitted Christian."(116) What saves this devotion from being purely humanistic is the recognition that one is

90

dependent upon and must adjust to God for the realization of these ideals. What saves this devotion
from being Utopian, or merely wishful thinking, is
the experience of success that follows correct
adjustment to the divine will. This experience of
success, thought King, may be called salvation or
revelation, and it is precisely this experience of
success that one sees in Jesus.(117) Therefore, as
an act of a human being, faith may be defined for-
mally as "a rationally grounded conviction of the
truth of beliefs not wholly proved,"(118) or more
personally as "devotion to those rationally grounded
ideas believed to be real yet not wholly proven to be
so."(119)

King's faith, therefore, had elements of intellectual content and personal commitment. It was also
a power(120) which enabled a person to "accept that
which cannot be changed, to meet disappointments and
sorrows with an inner poise, and to absorb the most
intense pain without abandoning our sense of
hope...."(121) The rational grounds of his faith
were experiential, not logical, practical, not
theoretical. Faith was to be judged by its fruits,
by the consequences it produces in a person's character. At its best Christian faith was more than a
mere relation to the deity: it was also an ethical
religion.(122) King had numerous ways of expressing
what he meant by such a statement. "If loyalty to
God does not make for devotion to highest ideals
in our lives then he might as well be dismissed."(123) Again, in a series of notes on mysticism, King applied the same pragmatic test. "The
final test for the validity of mysticism lies in the
fact that it produces men who are beneficial to
society."(124) He rejected outright the notion that
contemplation is the person's highest good. Ideals,
he insisted, are to be embodied, not gazed at, an
observation which is certainly true, but one which
misunderstands completely the nature of mystical
union and prayer.(125)

King's observations on mysticism are interesting
for the light they throw on his basic temper of mind
and on his own personal experience. His whole
understanding of union, communion and unity was
ethical; the sole foundation for unity between God
and man, man and man, was deliberate choice. This
understanding, as we shall see, colored greatly his
understanding of faith and love. He made the remark-

able statement that alcohol maintains its hold on mankind because it undoubtedly has the power to stimulate man's mystical faculties.(126) He further misunderstood the nature of mystical union and experience when he claimed that the mystics were mistaken in speaking of God as ineffable. What he thought happened to them was that their experience was ineffable and they falsely concluded that the object of that experience was also ineffable. The real value of mystics, claimed King, was that they afforded a transcendental interpretation of human institutions. One reason that they are often criticized is that they attempted to undermine both the Bible and the Church, though he gave no examples to illustrate this claim.(127)

Behind these views of King was his conception of what constitutes valid religious experience. It requires two elements: the experience of the ethical which is the content of God, and the experience of the numinous which is the form of God.(128) The knowledge that is gained in such experience is personal knowledge. It is this knowledge which causes us to trust or believe in that which cannot be proved, and it is also such knowledge which is the basis for love. The validity of such knowledge and experience is to be judged by the fruits that it produces in the human character. Beyond this test there is one final test of the truth of faith. In his notes on William James, King had a quotation which he approved. "A thing may be untrue, but one may make it true by having faith."(129) Faith, therefore, is its own justification, its own validation, in so far as it realizes in action its own claims.

Hope and love in King's perspective closely followed upon faith. The form of hope is that God will bring to realization what he has committed himself to do in the world in Christ. The content of that hope is a world in which every individual is free and encouraged to develop his or her own personality to the fullest degree.(130) The ground of hope is three-fold. There is, first, what God has done and is doing as a consequence of who he is. Concretely under this heading one could list creation, the great events of salvation history recorded in the Scripture, most especially the life of Jesus of Nazareth. The second basis for King's hope, but only in relation to the first, is what the human being is, i.e., potentially good, having the capacity to achieve what is highest and most noble in himself or herself. Concrete signs of hope under this heading are the moral progress of the human race, for example, the abolition of slavery. The third basis for hope is really a combination of the first two grounds brought into the present. As such it defines what King understood by the work of the Holy Spirit in the world. The formal expression of this ground of hope is that God is at work in the world today through his Spirit, by which King simply meant the living God is present among us.(131) The tangible evidence for this claim can be seen in humankind's growing understanding and control of the world through science and technology. Even if people fail to recognize the presence and power of God in their achievements, they are nonetheless being led by the Spirit of God. More importantly, however, is the moral progress of the human race, to be seen in the rising demand among peoples for justice, for freedom, for a world at peace. It is the Spirit of God who helps human beings differentiate between right and wrong and encourages them to choose the right. The Spirit of God is seeking humankind and hopes people will seek him. Thus the achievement of the good life is the work of both God and human beings. "All good that appears in men grows up under the fostering care of the Holy Spirit."(132) All this is to say that the ground of King's hope is most simply his faith, as is always the case in theology and human life.(133)

Love was a far more problematic element in King's thinking than any other single element, and it became increasingly problematic with the passage of time. His by now well-known analysis of love, using the Greek words eros, philia and agape, was borrowed from Paul Tillich, and first appeared in King's doctoral dissertation in greater fullness than it later received.(134) There he included libido as a fourth type or mode of love. In his analysis of Tillich's understanding of love, King criticized him for making love an ontological concept. Although Tillich speaks of God as love, said King, "on closer scrutiny we discover that love is just the dialectical principle of the union of opposites."(135) For King this was little more than an attraction of elements one for another. In his own understanding of love there was simply no metaphysical basis. It was altogether an ethical concept.

Love was projected in King's understanding as an instrumental reality, therefore, as a means not an end. It was a power and a weapon, an instrument for achieving other, and presumably higher, goals. So, according to King, "love is the most durable power in the world." "It is a creative force," and the most potent instrument available in mankind's quest for peace and security."(136) Or again, "unarmed love is the most powerful force in all the world."(137) The love King spoke about in this way is, of course, the Greek _agape_ which he defined as "understanding, redeeming good will for men."(138) It is, he told us, "purely spontaneous, unmotivated, groundless and creative. It is not set in motion by any quality or function of its object."(139)

Yet King was not always consistent in this understanding of love. In one of his more famous sermons he proudly announced that he had discovered what has been the chief quest of ethical philosophy throughout the ages, the quest for the summum bonum. That highest good is love.(140) Love, he proclaimed, is the clue to the meaning of ultimate reality; it is the principle at the center of the cosmos. Unfortunately, the quest of ethical philosophy for a summum bonum was not a quest for an ethical principle or an ethical concept, but for something that would ground and guide an ethic, for something not itself to be done but that could serve as the ultimate norm for what ought to be done.(141) It was not a quest for a means but for an end, not for an ideal but for something already realized in some way. Furthermore, King could speak of _agape_ as spontaneous and unmotivated and in the same breath claim that it springs from or is called forth by the need of the other person.(142) So God loves us because we need his love. The good Samaritan loved the battered Jew on the road to Jericho because he needed the Samaritan's love. "The Negro must love the white man because the white needs his love to remove his tensions, insecurities and fears."(143)

On the whole, then, love was seen to be an instrument toward the achievement of something else. It was the reality or the act which moves human beings from what they potentially are to the actuality. Most fundamentally, by loving our enemies we become sons and daughters of God and thus can experience the beauty of his holiness. Love at its best is forgiving love after the perfect model of Jesus'

94

prayer of forgiveness on the cross.(144) As such it is the bridge between words and results, between what is and what ought to be. It is both an attitude and an action, a freely adopted motive and a free act. King's rejection of any metaphysical basis for love was rooted in the perception that "nature does not and cannot forgive."(145) Only persons can. Forgiveness is the main hallmark of this love, and forgiveness is entirely a category of freedom, not of reason.(146)

More concretely, love was thought to do three things. It drives out its opposite which is hate, in King's view the arch evil. This had a two-sided importance. Hate brings damage to those who are its victims, whether that hate be expressed in the form of war, segregation, or some other form of injustice. It also damages the one who hates. It destroys his or her sense of values and objectivity. It leads one to perceive the beautiful as ugly and the ugly as beautiful, the true as false and the false as true. Most of all it causes one to be blind to the human person as the imago Dei. In both cases there is a destruction of the human personality, a warping of the selfhood of persons. Only love can drive out hate so that personality can develop and realize its full potential.(147)

A second effect of agape is that it is the only power that can achieve reconciliation between enemies, that can create and preserve community and mutuality between people.(148) It is the only cement of human relationships, the one force capable of holding people together in peace and justice.(149) In this conception human community is the highest good and love is the instrument for achieving and preserving that good. King argued that love, as he understood it, is based on a recognition of the inter-relatedness of all human life, the recognition that one person cannot be fully what he or she potentially is, unless and until his brother or sister is also fully what he or she potentially is.(150)

The two ends which love achieves are quite inter-dependent. Since personality is, in fact, the highest good for King, and since personality is a social reality, the fullest development of one individual's personality requires mutuality and ordered community among people. Indeed, King could

95

write that the aim of Christianity is "the fullest development of every human personality through the cooperative creation of a world wide community of persons."(151) Some notes of King's which again appear to date from his time at Crozer, on the religious development of personality further clarify what he meant by this fullest development of every personality. The aim is not the saving of the soul for heaven. "But the aim is to develop the personality to its fullest possibilities in terms of the principles of Jesus, so that he can feel a degree of status and feel that what he is doing has cosmic significance."(152)

The third effect of agape, which again indicates its essentially instrumental value, is that it recognizes and overcomes a human being's intellectual and spiritual blindness. Evil is perpetrated and spread not only by human badness, but also, and perhaps more commonly, by human blindness and ignorance. Jesus was crucified by those who knew not what they did.(153) The system of slavery in America was perpetuated by people who were sincere but spiritually ignorant.(154) "Millions of Negroes have been crucified by conscientious blindness."(155) This is a matter about which King felt very strongly. "Nothing in all the world," he writes, "is more dangerous than sincere ignorance and conscientious stupidity."(156) In order for a person's head to be right, in order to avoid the blindness and ignorance which are so perilous, it is necessary that the person's heart be right. For the heart to be right means that the person loves as Christ loved, that the person achieves the knowledge that is available only through love, that one first must set his or her heart, desire, and will upon the truth in order that he or she might come to know the truth.

The ground of possibility for the love that King advocated was once again his faith, what he believed about God and man. Concretely, the possibility of love was based on two convictions: that an element of goodness is to be found in every person, or that every person is made in God's image. Therefore, there is that in every human being which is lovable, and the potentiality to love is but the active side of that image etched in the person by God.(157) Secondly, the human person is free; he or she can choose to love and he or she can recognize that forgiving love is an absolute necessity for spiritual

growth and maturity.(158)   It is the instrument by
which a person grows into the fullness of selfhood.
Love is what frees life in human beings, illuminates
life and humanizes it.(159)   The <u>imago Dei</u> in others
which is the ground on which one can love them is
also the ground in oneself which enables a person to
love, for the <u>imago Dei</u> simply means that a person is
free and able to choose his or her own ethical worth
and dignity.

SCRIPTURE AND REVELATION

     One final element in King's theological perspec-
tive requires some elaboration.   This concerns his
understanding of scripture and revelation, or of what
are generally considered to be the sources of Christian   theological   knowledge   and   reflection.   It
touches upon such questions as how do we know what we
know about God, and what is the norm for judging the
validity of our knowledge?   We have touched upon such
points above, but only in passing.   A more precise
consideration of them will be helpful.   As has been
mentioned,   King   embodied   the   basic   attitude   of
liberal theology in his approach to an understanding
of Christian faith.   For him this meant two factors
determine theology: personal religious experience
and the pressure of the environment in which one
lives.   Liberal theology appealed to him because he
considered it to start with experience and to return
constantly to experience to check out what it affirmed.   Just whose experience he meant is something
he did not specify.(160)   In an interesting inversion
of the more common assumption, a thing which was
common in King, he regarded fundamentalism as basically a form of intellectualism.   He saw it as holding
that one must accept this or believe that in order to
be saved.   Liberalism, on the other hand, he saw as
more emotional and personal, holding that one must
feel this or experience that for salvation.(161)

     The authority of the Bible was somewhat vague in
King's understanding of it, as it is in liberal
theology in general.   He had a marginal comment in
some notes on the gospels to the effect that "we
should read scripture with our brains rather than
with our eyes,"(162) which is certainly a criticism
of the literalism on which he was raised.   He approved the Reformation stress on the authority of the
Bible over the authority of the Church, but there is

no indication of what he understood either authority to claim for itself or even how they differ.(163) In some notes from a course on the history of Christian Doctrine he commented favorably on Clement of Alexandria urging men to study philosophy and logic if they would understand the Bible well.(164) Since he also called Clement a good Hegelian in the same notes, one wonders just what was going on in his mind at the time. Possibly Clement appealed to him in this way because of his insistence on both Christ and culture as fundamental responsibilities of the Christian life.(165) At times he took both Barth and Niebuhr to task for forced and outdated exegesis of Scripture, but without any specific reference or example.(166)

On the more affirmative side King held the Bible up as a spiritual guide to finding God, a sacred book which contains the progressive self-revelation of God and which tells us how human beings have thought of God, what they have done for Him and how they have experienced Him. As such, it puts us in touch with these people and encourages us to believe that we can do what they did and shows us how to do it. Most important, it makes us acquainted with Jesus and informs us that God is like Jesus and Jesus is like God. For King, that was the heart of the Christian faith.

When we come to a more specific understanding of the contents of the Bible, King insisted that it was necessary to recognize that not every book is equally valuable. In order to comprehend the progressive revelation of God, a knowledge of the progression of the great ideas of human beings is required. What is important to grasp is that the Bible is both literature written in literary language and is also a book of life, growing out of experience in a vivid way. Looked upon in this way, it can help us realize afresh some of the perennial convictions of Christian life. Among these are the love of God, the Lordship of Jesus, the reality of sin and our need for redemption, the power of the Spirit and the hope of immortality. It can also clarify our thinking about right and wrong by showing us what great persons in the past have thought and done. Finally, it can deepen and purify our emotional life, helping to bring order into the often discordant realm of our hopes, fears and affections.(167)

98

King treated the Bible just as he treated everything else, from an essentially practical perspective. He claimed the Bible itself puts action before belief, the first question always being, "What must I do."(168) That the answer always given to the question in the New Testament is "repent and believe" did not enter into his horizons. Yet his exposure to biblical criticism does not seem to have been very radical. His notes dated all the gospels before 70 A.D., with Mark dated the earliest at 40 A.D. The notes also mentioned that all gospels were written originally in Aramaic and accepted the Q document hypothesis for the composition of Matthew and Luke. In addition there was mention of the severe limits of form criticism and talk about the possibility of finding the ipsissima verba Jesu.(169) King had no doubts about the historical reality of Jesus and disliked the distinction between the Jesus of history and the Christ of faith.(170) Indeed, the problem of reason and revelation out of which the distinction grew simply did not exist for King. He seemed to think that reason can demonstrate the nature and existence of God, and Joseph Washington was certainly correct in saying that there was no real understanding in King of the difference between philosophy and theology, or between what one knows in faith and what one knows apart from faith.(171) Revelation was not meaningful to King apart from reason; reason was the presupposition of revelation, which meant to him that scripture, theoretically at least, is not the norm and standard of Christian truth.(172) The only authority King recognized is love or practice, or what he called the absolute authority of God's truth, which latter is quite unexceptionable but rather begs the question.

Essentially, then, the Bible is regarded as a book of inspiration and moral example, a book containing ethical principles and models of the highest nobility, a book which communicates the basic convictions of Christian faith. It is a book to be inspired by and acted upon, but it is not to be idolized or made normative for knowing truth. If it has any exclusive claims, it is only that it puts us in touch with Jesus who is the example for human beings of ideal personality. King's attitude toward theology and philosophy and the ticklish problems their relationship has posed for academic theologians was summed up in a marginal comment in his notes. One doesn't know whether it was written in impatience and boredom in a classroom, or in excitement and relief, but in either case it has nothing to do with the subject matter of the notes. Nor does it throw any light on the problem. But in what would one day come to be recognized as typically Kingian rhetoric he wrote, "We need the fresh breeze of philosophy blowing through the musty halls of theology." (173)

The foregoing analysis of King's theological and philosophical convictions lays bare several features of importance, features which touch upon both the temper of his mind and the content of his thought. For all his analytical and expository brilliance, King's mind was neither disciplined nor terribly subtle or profound. Several of his professors have testified to his fondness for large ideas, (174) his zest for intellectual discussion and his ability in philosophic debate. (174) That testimony may well be accurate, but his mind was basically eclectic, pragmatic, and syncretistic. His entire orientation to ideas, to truth, was ethical and pragmatic, falling just short of being utilitarian. The two norms he consistently used in judgment are experiential and consequential. Does such and such an explanation adequately describe feelings and needs; does such and such an idea lead to consequences beneficial to human development? In a more classical philosophic formulation, truth for King was a function of the good, good was not a function of the truth. The unity of truth and goodness was not a metaphysical unity but only an ethical unity. Faith was not itself true, but it could make truth. (175) What saved him from complete utilitarianism and relativism was the stern conviction that there are absolute moral laws.

A second feature of his temper of mind was that it was remarkably undogmatic, despite the fact that he thought he knew a lot more than he actually did know, and indeed a lot more than is knowable. (176) He was impatient with, and usually blind to, the meaning of fine distinctions, and so often missed the theoretical problem involved in an issue. Such distinctions often seem to have struck him as mere quibbles about nothing and as a way of avoiding the real issue which is "What am I going to do?" One of his favorite phrases, often used as an admonition, catches this attitude perfectly: "the paralysis of analysis." (177) Hence, if he missed a theoretical issue, he rarely missed the practical moral one. His constant tendency was to assume all ideas under a more comprehensive umbrella, or to combine in a very precarious synthesis ideas which were often simply not compatible. The one criticism he most often made was that a theory or an explanation contained an over-emphasis on one side of an issue or the other. He repudiated excess even to the extent of criticizing Aristotle, the greatest exponent of the golden mean, for not being sufficiently moderate about his moderation.(178) Yet for all that, he did know and was most definite about what was simply unacceptable.

When it comes to the content of his thought, the most noticeable and significant feature about it was the action-orientation which he gave to every idea and concept. Jesus is a model for action and an inspiration to action. We can do what he did. The human person is important, has dignity and worth, is lovable because of his or her potentialities. Faith, hope and love are all future-oriented, having their ground in potentiality and their content and form from what they can achieve. Revelation is knowledge of what humankind's higher possibilities are. The Bible is inspiration for and a pointer to those possibilities. Immortality is a dictate of human possibilities. Even God himself is faced with the continuous need to do good, since his goodness and love are purely ethical qualities with no metaphysical basis.

It is this disjunction of love and power, of being and value in God which is the most salient feature of King's thought and which became in time the most questionable feature in his understanding of nonviolence. For God's love does not really do anything or effect anything other than God's own character. It does, to be sure, afford human beings hope, inspiration and encouragement, but it leaves the realization of potentiality to the action of these same human beings. It creates and preserves values, but values that are only ideal and need to be achieved. It promises humankind salvation and creates the possibility for it, but it is a salvation that is achieved not by the cross of Christ but by a person's own cross. Most difficult of all, God's love puts absolute limits on his own power to achieve his purpose. To be good would, therefore, seem to be in sharp contradiction to being effective. For this reason the form and content of King's ethics become the most important and distinctive feature of his message. What is a person to do in this world and why? And what are the chances for success? It is to a consideration of these questions that we turn in the next chapter.

NOTES: CHAPTER II

1. The dominating influence of King's father is recognized by all his biographers. See especially Louis E. Lomax, To Kill a Black Man (Los Angeles, CA: Holloway House Publishing Co., 1968), pp. 47-51.

2. Ibid., pp. 31-33; Washington, Black Religion, p. 3.

3. King, A Comparison.

4. Coretta Scott King, My Life, p. 92.

5. Martin Luther King, Jr., Strength To Love (New York: Pocket Books, 1964).

6. Especially King, Stride Toward Freedom and Martin Luther King, Jr., The Trumpet of Conscience (New York, Evanston and London: Harper & Row, Publishers, 1968).

7. Most of King's doodling involved German words and forms when he was getting ready for his language exams, and the use of ornate adjectives in sentences, at times incorrectly. He was apparently getting himself the big words he vowed to acquire one day. See Lewis, p. 12.

8. Few of King's class notes are clearly dated. I have inferred the time from the maturity of his thought, as well as the content of the notes when measured against the transcript of courses he took at Boston University and Harvard.

9. For the philosophy of personalism see Borden Parker Browne, Studies in Christianity (Boston and New York: Houghton Mifflin Company, 1909); Philosophy of Theism (New York: Harper & Brothers, 1887); Personalism (Norwood, Mass: The Plimpton Press, 1936); Edgar Sheffield Brightman, Religious Values (New York: Henry Holt and Company, 1928); Person and Reality (New York: The Roland Press Company, 1958); Is God a Person (New York: Association Press, 1932); A Philosophy of Religion (New York: Prentice Hall Inc., 1940); Harold DeWulf, A Theology of the Living Church (New York: Harper and Brothers, 1953); The Case for Theology in Liberal

Perspective (Philadelphia: Westminster Press, 1959); Albert C. Knudson, The Philosophy of Personalism (Boston: Boston University Press, 1949). For an effort to apply personalist thought directly to King see Lois Diane Wasserman, Martin Luther King, Jr.,: The Molding of Nonviolence as a Philosophy and Strategy, 155-1963 (Unpublished Doctoral Dissertation: Boston University, 1972), pp. 37-56.

10. This is my fundamental criticism of the work by Smith and Zepp cited above, Intro.; n. 72. The fact that King studied Niebuhr and Rauschenbusch doesn't necessarily mean he understood or embraced their views. The same methodological flaw is present in Ansbro's work, though he succeeds in tracing the personalist themes in King's writings and speeches rather well. One example of this flaw will suffice. Ansbro, pp. 279, n. 36, accused the present writer of charging King with a failure to examine his religious beliefs and attributes that mistake to my neglect of DeWulf's writings. I did not accuse King of that. I pointed out, as I do in this chapter, that King's intellectual criteria were practical and experiential, not theoretical, pastoral not theological.

11. See Chapter I, p. (50). That King had greater personal force than intellectual force may well be due to the role he had in the civil rights struggle and not to intellectual inadequacy.

12. King, Stride Toward Freedom, pp. 72-73.

13. See Lewis, pp. 20-24; Bishop, pp. 91-95, Bennett, pp. 17-22; Miller, pp. 5-15.

14. BU Coll., XVI (7); "I could see in their lives the ideal of what I wanted a real minister to be."

15. Ibid., XIV (29).

16. Ibid.

17. Ibid.

18. Ibid.

19. Ibid.

20. Ibid.,; also King, Stride Toward Freedom, pp. 4, 72.

21. BU Coll., XIV (29).

22. Ibid.

23. Lewis pp. 24-25.

24. BU Coll., XIV (29); King's phraseology is of interest here. One would ordinarily expect the phrase "from my mind," but the phrase as he actually wrote it suggests his orientation to action. His doubts had literally rendered him inactive and once resolved, he was free to go into motion.

25. Ibid.

26. For a history of the development of liberal theology and some of the problems raised for theology by this development, see Alan Richardson, The Bible in the Age of Science (Philadelphia: Westminster Press, 1961); Frederick C. Baumer, Religion and the Rise of Skepticism (New York: Harcourt, Brace and Company, 1960); Karl Barth, Protestant Thought: From Rousseau to Ritschl (New York: Simon and Schuster, A Clarion Book, 1969); and the opening pages of Hermann Diem, Dogmatics (Edinburgh and London: Oliver and Boyd, 1959); James M. Robinson and John B. Cobb, Jr. (eds.), The New Hermeneutic (New York, Evanston and London: Harper & Row, Publishers, 1964); Owen Chadwick, The Secularization of the European Mind in the Nineteenth Century (London, New York, Melbourne: Cambridge University Press, 1975).

27. Adolf Harnack, What is Christianity? (New York and Evanston: Harper & Row, Publishers, Harper Torchbooks, 1957); another excellent example of liberal theology is Ernst Troeltsch, Christian Thought: Its History and Application (New York: Meridian Books, 1957).

28. BU Coll., XIV (75).

29. Ibid.

30. _Ibid_.

31. King, _Strength To Love_, pp. 90-94; this was equally true for Gandhi. See N. B. Parulekar, _The Science of the Soul Force or Mahatma Gandhi's Doctrine of Truth and Non-Violence_ (Bombay, 1962), p. 24. "He or she must have a living faith in non-violence. This is impossible without a living faith in God. A non-violent man can do nothing save by the power and grace of God."

32. King, _Stride Toward Freedom_, p. 82.

33. BU Coll., XIV (75); it is possible that these notes date from his Boston University days. The dating is problematic.

34. _Ibid_.

35. King, _A Comparison_, p. 8.

36. _Ibid_., pp. 12-13, 39-40.

37. _Ibid_., p. 60.

38. _Ibid_., p. 62.

39. _Ibid_.

40. _Ibid_., p. 64.

41. On this question see Frederick Herzog, _Understanding God_ (New York: Charles Scribner's Sons, 1966), pp. 11-64, 130-141; Langdon Gilkey, _Naming the Whirlwind: The Renewal of God-Language_ (Indianapolis and New York: The Bobbs-Merrill Company, 1969), pp. 3-29, 73-106.

42. Emil Brunner, "Nature and Grace," and Karl Barth, "No! Answer to Emil Brunner," in _Natural Theology_, trans. Peter Fraenkel (London: Geoffrey Bles: The Centenary Press, 1946), especially pages 67-128.

43. King, _A Comparison_, pp. 26, 61, 279, 318, _et alibi_.

44. BU Coll., XIV (55).

45. Ibid., XIV (71).

46. Ibid., XIV (27).

47. King, A Comparison, pp. 134-135, n. 4.

48. Ibid., p. 128, n. 2.

49. Henry Nelson Wieman and Walter Marshall Horton, The Growth of Religion (Chicago: Wilet, Clark and Co., 1938), p. 267; quoted in King, A Comparison, p. 215.

50. King, A Comparison, p. 308.

51. Paul Tillich, Systematic Theology I (Chicago: The University of Chicago Press, 1951), p. 245; quoted in King, A Comparison, p. 156.

52. Henry Nelson Wieman, "God is More Than We Can Think" Christendom I (1936), p. 432; quoted in King, A Comparison, p. 234.

53. King, A Comparison, p. 265.

54. Ibid., p. 202.

55. Ibid., p. 272.

56. Ibid., p. 274.

57. For King's explanation of the dialectic as he understood it, see King, Stride Toward Freedom, p. 77; in saying "reflected in," I mean to affirm that King misread Hegel's dialectic because of his own both-and mentality, not that he developed that mentality or way of thinking as a result of reading or misreading Hegel.

58. Ibid.; "rightly" means that King did use his understanding of the dialectic in all his study, not Hegel's understanding.

59. Ibid.

60. King, A Comparison, p. 297.

61. Ibid., p. 313.

62. For a clear explanation of the problem of the one and the many see Frederick Copleston, S.J., A History of Philosophy I, 1 (Garden City, New York: Image Books, 1962), pp. 64-70; from a different perspective William James, Pragmatism and Other Essays (New York: Washington Square Press, Inc., 1963), pp. 57-72.

63. King, A Comparison, p. 311.

64. Ibid., p. 312.

65. Ibid., pp. 310-311.

66. King, Stride Toward Freedom, p. 82.

67. King, Strength To Love, p. 1.

68. Ibid., p. 8.

69. Ibid., p. 60.

70. Ibid., p. 72.

71. Ibid., p. 104.

72. Ibid., p. 111; for additional examples see Ibid., pp. 124, 127, 132, 141, 144, 153.

73. King, Stride Toward Freedom, p. 88.

74. BU Coll., XIV (75).

75. Ibid., XIV (64).

76. For an explanation of Arianism see J. N. D. Kelly, Early Christian Doctrines, 2nd ed. (New York: Harper & Brothers, Publishers, 1958), pp. 226-231, 280-289; A. Grillmeier, Christ in Christian Tradition (New York: Sheed and Ward, 1965), pp. 183-192; Adolf Harnack, History of Dogma, IV (New York: Dover Publications, Inc., 1961), pp. 7-49.

77. BU Coll., XIV (27).

78. Ibid., XIV (75).

79. For the soundness of King's insight in basing everything on his Christological understanding

as a fundamental theological principle see Karl Rahner, "The Hermeneutics of Eschatological Assertions," _Theological Investigations_, IV (Baltimore: Helicon Press; London: Darton, Longman & Todd, 1966), pp. 323-346, especially p. 335. This procedure is a fundamental break with liberal theology. See Harnack, _What is Christianity?_, pp. 144, 184.

80. _BU Coll._, XIV (55). It might be noted that, had King been completely systematic, his claim here would be fully orthodox. For, if the personality is the ultimate metaphysical reality, and it is the personality of Jesus that is divine, then he has more than an ethical divinity. King would then have a problem of explaining how Jesus is also human.

81. _Ibid._

82. _Ibid._, XIV (47).

83. _Ibid._, XIV (41).

84. For the savior aspect of the Christological controversies see Kelly, p. 375; Grillmeier, pp. 488-495; "Now these formulas clarify only one, albeit the decisive, point of belief in Christ: that in Jesus Christ God really entered into human history and thus achieved our salvation.", p. 493.

85. For the history and inter-relatedness of these theological issues and controversies see L. Richard, _The Mystery of the Redemption_ (Baltimore: Helicon Press, 1966); Karl Rahner, "Current Problems in Christology," _Theological Investigations_, I (Baltimore: Helicon Press, 1961), pp. 149-200; Gustaf Aulen, _Christus Victor_ (New York: Macmillan Paperback Edition, 1969), pp. 2-12, 36-60, 123-142.

86. _BU Coll._, XIV (33).

87. _Ibid._

88. _Ibid._, XIV (27).

89. Aulen, pp. 146-157.

90. BU Coll., XIV (33).

91. Ibid. It is hard to know who holds the opposite view from the one King proposed here. He was merely quoting Paul, 2 Corinthians 5:19.

92. BU Coll., XIV (33).

93. For an explanation of semi-pelagianism see Kelly, pp. 375-372; Harnack, History of Dogma, V (New York: Dover Publications, Inc., 1961), pp. 245-261.

94. King, Strength To Love, p. 147.

95. Ibid., p. 154.

96. Ibid., p. 79.

97. Ibid., p. 148.

98. Ibid., p. 149.

99. Ibid., p. 150.

100. BU Coll., XIV (29).

101. Ibid., XIV (75).

102. Immanuel Kant, Critique of Practical Reason and Other Works on the Theory of Ethics, ed. and trans. by Thomas Kingsmill Abbot (London: Longmans, Green & Co., 1889), pp. 229-239; Kant, Critique of Practical Reason and Other Writings in Moral Philosophy, ed. and trans. by Lewis White Beck (Chicago: University of Chicago Press, 1949), pp. 223-227.

103. BU Coll., XIV (75).

104. Ibid., XIV (67).

105. Ibid.

106. Ibid., XIV (75).

107. Ibid., XIV (75).

108. Ibid.

109. _Ibid._, XIV (75).

110. _Ibid._, XIV (32).

111. _Ibid._, XIV (75).

112. King, _Strength To Love_, p. 78.

113. _BU Coll._, XIV (33).

114. King, _Strength To Love_, p. 152.

115. _BU Coll._, XIV (46).

116. King, _Strength To Love_, p. 148; for a similar notion which relates closely to King's conception of freedom see John G. Milhaven, "Be Like Me! Be Free," _America_ (April 22, 1967), pp. 584-586.

117. _BU Coll._, XIV (46).

118. _Ibid._, XIV (57); King attributes the quote to Georgia Harkness without any citation.

119. _Ibid._

120. King, _Strength To Love_, pp. 103-104.

121. _Ibid._, p. 105.

122. _BU Coll._, XIV (32).

123. _Ibid._, XIV (46).

124. _Ibid._

125. _Ibid._, XIV (31).

126. _Ibid._, XIV (34).

127. _Ibid._, XIV (31).

128. _Ibid._, XIV (46).

129. _Ibid._, XIV (55).

130. _Ibid._, XIV (46).

131. _Ibid._, XIV (75).

132. Ibid.

133. Faith is more than logically prior to hope and love. In King's case hope and love follow only upon the actual commitment of faith.

134. King, A Comparison, pp. 147-151; the analysis of love also appears in shorter form in Strength To Love, p. 44; Stride Toward Freedom, pp. 86-88; The Trumpet of Conscience, pp. 72-74. For the original source see Tillich, Systematic Theology, I, pp. 277-282.

135. King, A Comparison, p. 158.

136. King, Strength To Love, p. 149.

137. Ibid., p. 164.

138. King, Stride Toward Freedom, p. 86.

139. Ibid.

140. King, Strength To Love, p. 163.

141. John Passmore, The Perfectability of Man (New York: Charles Scribner's Sons, 1970), pp. 13-27; James M. Gustafson, Christ and the Moral Life (New York, Evanston, San Franciso, London: Harper & Row, Publishers, 1968), pp. 2-8.

142. King, Stride Toward Freedom, p. 87.

143. Ibid.

144. King, Strength To Love, p. 30.

145. Ibid., p. 132.

146. Forgiveness may well be a category of freedom, but it is also, as Rollo May has pointed out, a category of grace beyond the simple exercise of human freedom. May, Power and Innocence, p. 256. Forgiveness is also not without rational and social significance as Hannah Arendt has pointed out, for it alone enables imperfect human beings to have a future together. Hannah Arendt, On Revolution (New York: The Viking Press, 1965), pp. 77-89.

147. Ibid., p. 45.

148. Ibid., p. 43; King, Stride Toward Freedom, p. 87.

149. King, Stride Toward Freedom, p. 88.

150. Ibid.

151. BU Coll., XIV (46).

152. Ibid.

153. King, Strength To Love, p. 34.

154. Ibid., p. 36.

155. Ibid., p. 37.

156. Ibid.; James T. Burtchaell, Philemon's Problem (Chicago: ACTA, 1973), pp. 65-83, has some eloquent illustrations of this same point.

157. Ibid., p. 43; here is a metaphysical basis for love, but King seems not to have averted to the fact.

158. Ibid., p. 32.

159. Ibid., p. 140.

160. BU Coll., XIV (64). A discussion of the problem of experience and theology can be found in David Tracy, Blessed Rage for Order (New York: Seabury, 1975) and is resumed in The Analogical Imagination (New York: Crossroad, 1981), pp. 3-82.

161. Ibid., XIV (29).

162. Ibid., XIV (59).

163. Ibid., XIV (71).

164. Ibid., XIV (56).

165. H. Richard Niebuhr, Christ and Culture (New York: Harper & Row, Publishers, 1951), pp. 125-128. "Clement's Christ is both the Christ of

culture and the Christ above all culture,"
p. 128.

166. BU Coll., XIV (55).

167. Ibid., XIV (75).

168. Ibid., XIV (47).

169. Ibid., XIV (38).

170. Ibid., XIV (58). See James M. Robinson and John B. Cobb, Jr., (eds.), New Frontiers in Theology: Vol. III Theology as History (New York, Evanston and London: Harper & Row, Publishers, 1967).

171. Washington, Black Religion, p. 3.

172. BU Coll., XIV (67).

173. Ibid., XIV (54).

174. Ibid., XIV (7).

175. See note 129.

176. The only way to document this would be to cite all of King's notes, especially those dealing with the history of Christianity.

177. King, Strength To Love, p. 21.

178. BU Coll., XIV (54).

CHAPTER III

THE VOCATION OF A MAN

Martin Luther King, Jr. described his vocation
to the ministry as a call to serve humanity and as a
way of implementing his devotion to the highest
ideals. Service to humanity, devotion to the highest
ideals, are vague and elusive notions, claimed alike,
often enough, by tyrants and martyrs, millionaires
and paupers, poets and pornographers. It is the
concrete determination of just what service is being
rendered, what ideals are being implemented and why,
and in what way such activity benefits real people,
that enables us to put lofty humanitarian claims into
perspective. It is this more concrete determination
of what King understood service and the highest
ideals to mean which this chapter seeks to accom-
plish. The various images of King which were re-
viewed in the opening chapter are suggestive ways of
pinpointing what King's service to humanity actually
was. But we are seeking here for a less symbolic,
less impressionistic indication of King's service,
and for a more substantive and direct explication of
it. In short, this chapter seeks to know specifically what King thought was of service to humanity,
what he thought the highest ideals were, how he
thought they were to be implemented, and why he
thought as he did.

If Martin Luther King had an ethical theory that
was unique and proper to himself, it will have to be
discovered in his deeds far more than in his words.
But his words do provide a useful introduction to the
search. It was noted in the preceding chapter that
King took the liberal slogan, "the Fatherhood of God
and the brotherhood of man," to be the starting point
of the Christian ethic.(1) But it is not at all
clear what he meant by calling it the starting point,
nor how it could function as a starting point. For
if all people united as brothers and sisters under
the acknowledged Fatherhood of God is taken to be the
highest ideal, the summum bonum, the final goal of
human life, then it can hardly be proposed as the
beginning and the basis of present human activity,
nor does it shed much light on the more specific
moral questions of day to day living in which people
strive to implement the ideal or achieve the goal.
On the other hand, if the slogan is taken to describe

a given fact of human life, as King sometimes attempted to establish,(2) then it may suggest certain fundamental moral attitudes we should have toward one another, but it can hardly serve as the highest ideal or final purpose of human life and activity. In other words, if the common brotherhood/sisterhood of human being is something to be achieved, it cannot serve as the reason or the concrete ground either of why it ought to be achieved or of how it should be achieved. If, however, this common unity of persons is already a fact of faith, or of the human biological, social or metaphysical condition, then it cannot be proposed as the highest ideal and the final purpose and goal of human life. Additionally, it is hard to see why an ethic that would start from such a point should be called Christian at all, since it does not start from Christ or with Christ. As a matter of fact, King did not start with the liberal slogan, as was indicated in the previous chapter,(3) and Jesus was central to his ethical understanding.

A more accurate assessment of King's ethical perspective would take its starting point from an expression King himself used to describe the aim of his studies at Crozer Seminary. It was there, he wrote, that he began "a serious intellectual quest for a method to eliminate social evil,"(4) social evil being understood to be, concretely, racial and economic injustice. A method to eliminate social evil summed up, in King's mind, the quest of all ethical thought, while the actual implementation of the method, using the method, summed up the content and meaning of ethical life.

This strategic approach to the subject of Christian ethics was a reflection of King's essential pragmatism and it appeared very early in his educational career. Reverend J. Pius Barbour, with whom King had many close and informal contacts during his Crozer days, was editor of the National Baptist Voice during the period of the Montgomery bus boycott, and he had more than a little to reveal in its pages about King and his past. While Barbour's testimony is not always consistent with other evidence, and is certainly not dispassionate, it is blunt and to the point. In the March, 1956 issue of the magazine, writing in the editorials and opinions section, Barbour offered some reminiscences of King at Crozer.

The battle he is fighting now, we have
fought many a Sunday afternoon in my parlor.
Never did he nor I ever dream that the
battle would shift from my parlor to the
streets of Montgomery, Ala. I considered
little Mike a calm ivory tower philosopher
that was as far removed from a field general
as possible.(5)

Yet, despite this ivory tower impression, Barbour
goes on to relate that he had heard King and Walter
McCall(6) discuss "CHRISTIAN STRATEGY"(7) over and
over again. And he adds: "All Mike has to do is
reach in his note book and pull out the blue
prints."(8)

It is also Barbour's testimony that King had
read and re-read books on Gandhi,(9) and had argued
all through the night at times in favor of Gandhi's
methods as opposed to Barbour's theories of coercion
and violence. "Mike has always conterded that no
minority can afford to adopt a policy of violence.
Just a matter of arithmetic, Dr., he used to say. He
is moving according to plan."(10)

If such discussions, indeed, took place in the
way Barbour remembered them, he himself was not
convinced by King's arguments or eloquence and King
either forgot or lost the blueprints.(11) In a
letter to King at the end of 1954 Barbour wrote:

The trouble with you fellows from Univer-
sities is you think that there is only one
type in the World...the Socratic. But
history records Attilla the Hun as well as
Jesus; Stalin as well as Paul. And by the
way I never heard of Attilla drinking the
Hemlock or Stalin's going to the cross.
Don't believe that mess about the Pen is
mightier than the sword. Give me the
Sword.(12)

And during the outbreak of violence in Montgomery
following the Supreme Court decision outlawing
segregation on public transportation, Barbour sent
King a one-sentence telegram. "Can you overthrow a
social system without violence."(13)

Barbour's deepest insight into King, however,
appeared in some additional comments he wrote in

117

March, 1956, openly addressed to King himself. "I was thrilled when I heard your remarks: 'We must not fall so low as to allow our enemies to make us hate.' I have heard you say that many a time. I thought you were just carrying on an intellectual argument. BUT YOU REALLY MEANT IT."(14)

This stress on effective strategy and the pragmatic seriousness of King in his ethical attitude make of his ethical ideas more a spirituality which supports a method of social change, than an intellectual theory of good and evil. That is to say, his was not a search for universal or generally valid principles of behavior or norms of activity, nor for an inter-related set of rights and obligations. Rather it was a search for the personal and concrete meaning and application of such principles and norms to himself and his world (a method of social change), as well as a quest to learn how to find what such an application should mean for him (a spirituality).(15) King thus accepted for his own personal life and for society the plain implications of the word "ought," one of which is change, difference, newness, growth, an implication which, however obvious, is often glossed over or even denied by advocates of peaceful change. A second implication of "ought" is evil, elimination, ought not. Thus the ethical problem was how best to change what clearly needed to be changed in himself and in society. What shaped his ethical thinking, therefore, were almost exclusively methodological considerations which spoke to processes, means, the dynamics of change, rather than a purpose for living. In simplest terms, King was not concerned with what one ought to do but with how to do what one clearly ought to do, how to render practical and concrete what was ideal and general. In more formal ethical language, King was not concerned with the nature of the good, but with the moral self or how to become good, and with the more immediate and concrete norms of how to know the good in specific situations.(16)

In rendering an account of his "pilgrimage to nonviolence," King detailed the intellectual influences which fed his concern for social change. It is both interesting and instructive to note carefully the contributions he ascribed to the men who he felt most influenced him. Henry David Thoreau, through his famous essay, "On the Duty of Civil Disobedience," put in King's head the idea of refusing to cooperate with an evil system, an idea that was to become a central one for him.(17) Walter Rauschenbusch, the greatest exponent in America of the so-called social gospel, gave King "a theological basis" for the social concern he already had.(18) The great social and ethical philosophers from Plato to John Locke contributed nothing which he can specify.(19) Karl Marx and other un-named communist authors had a mainly negative impact on him in that King rejected their materialism, ethical relativism and depreciation of individual freedom. But he liked their expressed concern for the poor and agreed with their repudiation of extreme economic individualism.(20) But none of this was new to King. He scarcely needed to read Marx or Lenin to reach or solidify such views, nor did he grasp the philosophical, economic, or social meaning of Marxism.(21) Nietzsche challenged but failed to destroy King's "faith in love" by his glorification of power.(22) If he influenced King at all, it was unwittingly in his confirmation of the radical separation of power and love in King's outlook. To Gandhi King attributed a method of social reform that emphasized love and nonviolence, and in it he claimed to have found a moral and an intellectual satisfaction which he had singularly failed to find in utilitarianism or communism.(23) But he did not explain more concretely what he understood by the method, and it would seem that Gandhi's example simply kept alive in him the social relevance of an ethic of love. Niebuhr contributed a sense of realism, a sense of the complexity of human motives, and a good analysis of the complex relationship between morality and power. He also served as a critical foil for Rauschenbusch's optimism and Gandhi's nonviolence.(24) Boston University afforded him a renewed optimism about human nature and a metaphysical basis for a personal God and the goodness of human beings.(25) Finally, Hegel impressed King with the insights that growth comes through struggle and that truth is to be found in the whole or in a total view of reality.(26)

If one were to ask what all this amounts to, either as a comprehensive ethical theory or as a theory of social change -- or as a combination of the two -- I would suggest that it comes down to this. The Christian gospel is concerned with the total person, so that the establishment on earth of a just economic and social order is a primary purpose of God and so a primary ethical task for human beings. For a theological defense of this position King would have us consult Rauschenbusch. What blocks or stymies the creation of this order of justice are certain evil structures, attitudes and habits: a lack of concern for the poor, an excessive economic individualism represented in capitalism, a practical materialism, an ignorance of the real situation of others. But it is possible in various ways to refuse to co-operate with these structures and attitudes. The communist emphasis on a classless society and the concern for social justice are healthy reminders of our real situation and a useful pointer toward what needs to be done. Yet the means of change, the method for moving from injustice to justice, must be a moral method. To rely on coercion, or force, or power is tempting, but wrong. It is wrong because it will not work. Thoreau had indicated by word and example a way man can avoid contributing to injustice and Gandhi had afforded an example of nonviolent resistance as a more positive form of action most in keeping with the gospel emphasis on love which is also a method that works. But there is no place here for a false optimism. Human beings are capable of both good and evil, and Niebuhr has reminded us of how complex human motives are and how prone human groups are to injustice. On the the other hand, we must not over-emphasize human sinfulness. Human beings are capable of good and real progress is possible. Change is admittedly a struggle, but it is through this struggle against evil that human persons grow and moral progress is made.

The above paragraph does not contain a theory of great depth, originality, power or persuasiveness. Trite as it is and true as it may be, it is surely not adequate to account for bodies freely submitted to beatings and incarceration, nor hearts and minds bearing abuse, insult and hatred without retaliating in kind. It in no wise indicates, as Le Roi Jones once asked, "what kind of mind shift I would have to undergo, for instance, so that I would be convinced, as these rednecks were working me over, that I was doing something to break Charlie's back."(27)   To make more sense of King's views, to see more clearly the depth and power of his convictions, it will help to look first at the more formal elements in his ethic and then to specify the contribution of various thinkers to the more concrete aspects of it. In this way it will become clear just where and why King derived his views on nonviolence and what precisely the strengths and weaknesses of his theory are.

Despite any and all protestations about love, the highest good in King's perspective, the aim and purpose of all human activity, was the fullest development of every human personality.(28) From his religious point of view Jesus was the ideal of human personality, the model of human development, the concrete embodiment of what the development of personality meant as well as the actual proof of such a possibility. So King's ethic might be called an ethic of the imitation of Christ, in that the human person is intended to grow into the fullness of personality that was Christ's or to share his ful- fillment. From a philosophical point of view the ideal of personality as the highest good means that all choices should be made in terms of what the individual self is capable of becoming individually and socially.(29) From this perspective it is clear that the imitation of Christ is not intended to be any kind of external mimicking, but rather a personal recapitulation in one's own concrete situation of the meaning of Jesus' life, or a life lived in accord with his Spirit. The content, then, of what human development meant for King, or the norm of a person's individual and social capacity, is seen to involve a combination of three elements which are held together in a somewhat precarious synthesis.

The first element comprehends one's own unique- ness or the individual dimension of human life.(30) Every individual ought to develop himself, ought to realize his potential, ought to come to a healthy self-love. This would require the active development of an individual's unique talents to the highest point of excellence.(31) It is the quality of one's activity that counts, not the objective social usefulness of one's gifts or efforts. The worth of one's talents is not to be judged against another's gifts or by how much they contribute to society, but solely against one's own capabilities.(32) Indi- vidual excellence in this sense is understood to be a moral achievement as well as a technical one. While the effort to be excellent is qualitatively single in all persons as regards its character, the result of that effort is quite obviously not. A person could become morally excellent without being technically excellent, though the opposite is also true but for quite different reasons.(33)

The second element involved in contributing
content to the highest ideal of full human development is the social good of the individual, or what
King variously called the breadth of life as opposed
to the length,(34) or the personalistic law of
altruism.(35) This meant that a person ought to
choose to co-operate with other persons in the
achievement of value, or that one ought to be concerned with the welfare of others equally with one's
own. This element of a person's social good is not
an altogether separate element over and above or in
addition to one's individual good. For the self, in
order to be a self and to reach its own fulfillment,
needs other selves with who to interact, to share and
to love, to have communion. What must be opposed,
therefore, is the false doctrine of individualism
which afflicts so much of western culture. The
individual is the self concerned with itself. It is
the grasping self, the self blind to or indifferent
to others, and so to its own potential. It is the
private self which Le Roi Jones has seen embodied in
"White North American culture [which] is committed to
individualism, ego satisfaction and personal gain...
at the world's expense."(36) The individual, in this
understanding, is not limited to a single human
being, but could include a family, a class, a race, a
nation.

On the other hand, what is to be affirmed is the
person, the self concerned with others, the giving
self who has his or her being and meaning in and
through others, who recognizes the inter-dependence
of all persons and the inter-relationship of all
reality. Every person should suppose that the whole
community of Persons is more important than any one
person. This, insisted King, is only rational.(37)
In addition to being a demand of reason, he also
considered it a requirement of world Christianity
that there be an all-inclusive love that embraces all
persons.

The third element that goes into making up the
one ultimate norm of ethical judgment is the need for
a person to adjust the self to God's will, or the
ultimate allegiance due the eternal Being who is the
source and ground of all goodness, or the need to
relate oneself to a cause larger than time and
humanity.(38) For King, since "God is Christlike,...
by committing ourselves absolutely to Christ and his
way, we will participate in that marvelous act of

faith that will bring us to the true knowledge of God."(39)

Each of these three elements or dimensions of life needs painstaking development if a person is to realize his or her true self.(40) King did not attempt to show whether there is any intrinsic relationship between these dimensions of life or whether they are quite distinct and independent of one another. He wrote as if it were possible to realize one's individual potential without any concern for the breadth and height of life, or to realize the first and second dimensions without any concern for the third. But they are only combinations he referred to. At times it appears that he conceived human life to be all of one piece, fully unitary; at other times his conception of human life seems to have been quite compartmentalized. On such occasions King's picture of man was very much like a potential three-room building. The first, second and third rooms are all potentially present in the foundation of a human being's given biological and social existence. But any of the three rooms may be built at any time and in any order, without having any effect on the other rooms. Each one enlarges the structure of the person, but no one room qualitatively changes the structure of the whole or has any intrinsic impact on any other room.(41) A simpler and cruder image of the same idea would be that a person could become a master plumber, but the dimensions of social good and of adjustment to the divine will would make absolutely no difference one way or the other to his or her individual excellence.

To set up as the highest good and ultimate norm of right conduct the fullest development of every human personality is, of course, to base one's ethical position on an understanding of the human. The passage from what is to what ought to be was made for King by affirming that what a person can be he or she ought to be, at least in so far as human personality was concerned. So the question, what is the normative human, in fact as well as _in potentia_, was central to King's ethical perspective.

Wrote King:

Man is man because he is free to operate within the framework of destiny. He is free to deliberate, to make decisions, and

123

to choose between alternatives. He is
distinguished from animals by his freedom
to do evil or to do good and to walk the
high road of beauty or tread the low road
of ugly degeneracy.(42)

The theologians' _imago Dei_ in the human person, or
that which the philosophers look for and label as the
specifically human, was situated for King in human
freedom, in the innate possibility for judgment,
decision, and action that is both self-initiated and
self-controlled. It was the ability the human person
has to create by his or her own choice and activity
the ethical quality of one's own personality.
Furthermore, this freedom which is the person's
unique and specific characteristic King regarded both
as a limitation upon God's omnipotence as well as the
ground of the possibility of evil. "The price of
freedom is the possibility of the perversion of
freedom."(43)

Human freedom, while genuine, is not absolute,
not without determinations, limits, controls.(44) It
operates within what King called a framework of
destiny, by which he seems to have meant the natural
laws written into the structure of the universe by
the Creator. These are the laws which dictate or
necessitate that life will work only in a certain
way. They are the givens of existence. As they
touch upon man's moral life, King had in mind here
what he called the moral absolutes, by which, presumably, he hoped to distinguish natural moral laws
from physical laws such as gravity. Human beings are
free to ignore or to defy the moral absolutes. But
no matter what their stance toward them, if human
beings disobey them by acting contrary to or outside
of the framework such laws establish, the absolutes
will break them. To act in defiance or contradiction
of the moral absolutes is to do evil. The forces of
evil may prevail in human life for a day or a season,
but evil always contains the seeds of its own destruction, for it has within itself no possibility of
solid growth or permanence. It is, then, not so much
the moral absolutes which break the person who defies
them, as it is evil which will destroy the person or
let him or her down. Justice triumphs in the long
run because injustice is self-destructive; truth
overcomes falsehood because falsehood is without
stability or permanence.(45)

When King spoke of cosmic companionship, or of God's power, or of God's will to which persons must adjust themselves, it was these moral absolutes he had in mind. But exactly what such moral absolutes are is not very clear. They seem to operate at the highest level of abstraction where by definition alone no one could take serious exception to them. In King's reaction to what is called communism's ethical relativism, he insisted upon a divine government, an absolute moral order, and fixed, immutable principles.(46) A further reading suggests that two such fixed principles would be that the end cannot justify the means and that every person is an end and should always be treated as an end in himself or herself.(47) Other passages in his writings suggest that he regarded truth and justice as such immutable principles, albeit they are values and not principles. He was fond of quoting poets and preachers to such effect.(48) This view also represented his interpretation of Christ's death and resurrection.

> The belief that God is on the side of truth and justice comes down to us from the long tradition of our Christian faith. There is something at the very center of our faith which reminds us that Good Friday may occupy the throne for a day, but ultimately it must give way to the triumphant beat of the drums of Easter.(49)

Love, despite its instrumental character, would also seem to qualify as a fixed and immutable principle for King, in as much as its opposite, hate, is, like injustice and untruth, ultimately self-destructive. "He who hates stands in immediate candidacy for non-being."(50)

The picture of human life which King presented might be represented metaphorically as a journey along a network or relationships, a network whose basic structure has been created and is preserved in being by a personal God, but a network which has also been supplemented and expanded by human activities. Some of the strands of this network lead persons to a fuller and fuller realization of their inherent capacities and potentialities. They are the strands which can be trusted to support us on life's journey for their origin is God. Other strands are deceptive for, while they promise freedom, they in fact lead us to prisons of futility and despair. These latter strands of the network have been produced by human beings who used their freedom in disregard of or in defiance of the basic structure laid down by the Creator. To trust them is, therefore, a form of idolatry, a substitution of what is only human for what is of God.

What marks out the difference between the productive and the destructive strands in the one network of life is not any arbitrary designation of good and evil by the creator, nor any determination or purpose of human beings. The difference is rather to be found in the very nature of human freedom, which is the key to the meaning or the nature of the human person, as well as to what he meant by nonviolence. The clearest way of developing this aspect of King's thought is to consider what he understood by evil - or in theological terms, sin, and how he accounted for it and suggested we deal with it.

The presence of evil in the universe King took to be an obvious fact, a "stark, grim and colossally real"(51) force which touches every level of human existence. The human story is a history of the struggle between good and evil.(52) To account for the existence of evil King offered no metaphysical theory, and he was further convinced that there is no theological explanation for the origin of evil. Be the choking weeds of evil a result of the machinations of Satan or of human beings misuse of their own freedom, the weeds are the work of an enemy and for King that was sufficient. The power of evil he felt was as real as the power of good. He saw the ugly reality of evil expressing itself in lust, in inordinate selfishness, in the sacrifice of truth to self-interest, in imperialism resulting in social injustice, in wars that leave people physically and morally destitute.(53) On a more individual level he glimpsed the power of sin in slavery to drink or to untruthfulness or to impurity or to selfishness.(54) What makes all these things evil is that they destroy a person's character precisely by preventing the development of the person's capacities and freezing his or her potential for growth. Evil, then, represented for him the is of life and not the ought, it represented the actual and not the possible.(55) A clear hallmark of evil and its essential weakness he found to be that it cannot permanently organize

126

itself.(56) This characteristic of evil is what King called the checkpoint in the universe and it is why he considered human beings to have cosmic companionship in their struggle to overcome evil and do the good. He offered no explanation for the attraction that evil holds for humans other than that freedom holds the possibility of its own abuse. He rejected the optimistic doctrine that the human person is inherently good, just as he rejected the Reformation doctrine that the person is inherently corrupt. His both-and mentality would have no traffic with the subtleties or reasons for either position. For him both positions were simply overemphases. The human person has a capacity for good and a capacity for evil, and that was enough. Nor would he have any traffic with the notion that evil is to be explained by our social condition or by our inherent selfishness, and thus the solution to evil was either to transform the social situation or the human soul. Again the solution was not an either-or but a both-and. There was no dichotomy between the life of a person's soul and a person's life in society, between the secular and the sacred, between religion and life. Both individual lives and the social situation required transformation.

Yet King was steeped enough in the Christian faith to insist upon the sinfulness of human nature and human beings' inability to save themselves or to eliminate evil by their own efforts. He did not discount the very real advances that come from the development of scientific understanding and technological achievement. He was enthusiastic in his praise of the transition "from the stagnating valleys of superstition and half-truth to the sunlit mountains of creative analysis and objective appraisal."(57) But knowledge alone, he was convinced, will not and cannot save us or drive out evil. For, writes King, "that ignores fundamental facts about our mortal nature."(58)

On the other hand, King was equally insistent that God will not and, indeed, cannot save human beings or eliminate evil from human life in despite of themselves. God is not a despot, a tyrant, an omnipotent czar nor even an absolute monarch. He does not force anything upon humans or give them gifts they will not receive. It is precisely in this respect for human freedom that God reveals His infinite goodness. No army of angels, no avenging thunderbolt will appear to blast away evil. Such an expectation or belief that God will do everything is not faith, said King, but a lack of faith, a superstition. For the real effects of sin upon human nature are impaired vision and weakened strength of soul. Evil has warped but not destroyed our vision, pride has enfeebled but not paralyzed our free disposal of ourselves. What we need to eliminate evil from our lives is a clear light to recognize the trustworthy and solid strands of life's network and the power to choose to walk exclusively on those strands. In an alternate formulation, human beings require a clear grasp of the inherent relationship between the end of human life and the means to realize the end. Or to put the same idea in a religious form, neither God nor the human person exclusively will bring about human salvation - the elimination of evil. But together, in a unity of purpose which comes from God's free gift of himself in love to us and our perfect openness to the gift and our response to it in obedience, human beings and God can transform the human network and drive out the sickness of sin and evil.(59)

This process of divine-human cooperation is what the Pauline doctrine of justification by faith meant to King.(60) Despite his rejection of the Reformation view of man's sinfulness and inability to believe, King's teaching was in all respects but one(61) essentially the same as the doctrine of both Luther and Calvin, as well as that of the Roman Catholic Church as articulated at the Council of Trent and further interpreted by her contemporary theologians;(62) about neither teaching was King particularly knowledgeable in any academic way.(63) But what King understood very clearly was the difference between a faith that was only a theory and a faith that was centered in a person and involved a devotion of the heart, a surrender of the self that staked one's very existence on a vision of human life, a commitment of one's energies to making true human persons' highest ideals and purposes, because one trusted God absolutely to bring about his purpose for human life. For King this latter kind of faith took on a more concrete form in the commitment to oppose evil wherever it showed itself.(64)

It is, perhaps, ironic that the great proclaimer of love and human brotherhood should produce an ethic that was, in its central features, essentially negative in as much as it could tell people what to oppose and what not to do far more readily than it could offer positive suggestions or affirm concrete programs. It was an ethic that sought justice by opposing unjust situations and conditions, that sought freedom by opposing specific limits put upon freedom, that sought to extend love by refusing to hate. At heart, therefore, it was an ethic that was really a faith in practice, for it did not and could not assure one about the results of a given action nor could it guarantee how justice would be achieved but only that it would be someday. Such words as justice, freedom, and love were not at all specific in this ethic. It was simply not possible to say all that these words signify. But it was possible to say rather specifically what they do not mean, and hence to oppose certain deeds and situations that are clearly antithetical to the good.(65)

It is also ironic that the champion of nonviolence and peace should find his teaching best explained through the language of war, battle, conflict, struggle. But most ironic is the fact that this man who had a dream of the end and goal of human existence should for that reason have become a defender of a means and should have seen his dreams go up in smoke(66) because the means he championed was so misunderstood and found to be unacceptable. But the irony - or paradox, if that be the more accurate description - is only the irony of his Christian faith which has rejected law to live by the Spirit and consequently always finds it far easier to say concretely what is not of the Spirit than to say what is.(67) This again points to the faith character of King's ethic in that it asked for a commitment to a means or a process and assured the end, but could not explain how the process would achieve the end.(68)

During the days of his Crozer training King wrote a short exercise on how a Christian overcomes evil.(69) This early effort throws light on the paradoxical notion that the way to do good is by opposing evil. The series of steps which King listed as essential to overcome evil also throws light on his whole ethic and later practice. The first step is to discover by careful examination what is worst in us, what sin it is to which we are most frequently tempted, and then admit it and call it by its right name. So the step calls for a direct and open honesty about the actual situation and condition of the self. For example, America had to call its practice of racism by the proper name and acknowledge that it was the major contradiction that lay at the heart of its social existence. The second step is to ask God's help in overcoming the evil and to conduct a daily examination on how well one is doing. For the elimination of evil involves a process and a struggle, not a single act or deed, which is one reason why violence cannot be effective.(70) Thirdly, the way to eradicate evil is to concentrate on the cultivation of its opposite. Goodness is not passivity in the face of evil, but rather it is activity in the opposite direction. Evil is not to be attacked directly, but indirectly, for evil can only be driven out by the expulsive power of something good. Again this argues against violence which is destructive by nature, and is hardly activity in the opposite direction of violence. King offered two stories from classical mythology as examples of the difference. The story of Ulysses and the Sirens is, he thought, an example of eradication, while the story of Orpheus and the Sirens is an example of cultivation.

While this strategy of King's is rather unexceptional in practical terms, in theory it tends to define good in terms of the absence of evil, reversing the classical metaphysical explanation of evil as having no metaphysical reality, being solely the absence of a due good. This inversion had its clearest manifestation and most significant import in King in his definition of agape, which he often called the highest good. Agape he defined as forgiving, redeeming love. For such love to exist it is altogether dependent upon evil, upon something to forgive, upon someone to redeem. Once evil is overcome or eliminated, this love has no positive value, indeed, there is no possibility of its worth or even of its existence. Thus, the human good in King's thought must be seen as pure potentiality without any specific content.

Before developing this last point any further and indicating how it led King to embrace militant nonviolence as an absolute moral imperative, it will be helpful to pull together the main strands of his thought that bear directly on the question of nonviolence. These elements may be briefly stated. King believed in a personal God, a powerful being who freely chooses to be good and who, by his own free choices and deeds, effects his own moral perfection. This God has created human beings and the world in freedom and out of love. This act of creation is both a deed of goodness and a self-imposed limitation on the ethically neutral power of God. Human beings are made in the image of God, which is to say that they have the capacity to effect their own moral goodness by their own choices and deeds. One inevitable and necessary consequence of this capacity is that they may also choose evil. Evil is anything that is opposed to the continued ability of a person to choose his or her own ethical goodness; it is whatever enslaves human beings, whatever denies or restricts their capacity for the free disposal of their own attitudes and actions. For that reason evil is self-defeating or self-destructive. It does not have the inherent capacity for continued development, or, in King's own phrase, the ability to organize itself permanently. Hence evil is not capable of anything new; it can only repeat itself. This is an inevitable law of evil and it is an inexorable as the physical laws of nature. Either you build the house on a foundation that can hold it, or it will collapse, be it sooner or later. But in such a case, it is much easier to say what will not work than to say what will. For goodness is a creative reality, containing ever new and unlimited possibilities. Evil is a static reality; it is fixed and its possibilities are finite and determined.

To illustrate the meaning of this claim, we might take examples of evils that touch the physical, psychological, intellectual, social and spiritual dimensions of the human self. A man who loses both his legs suffers a physical evil. The loss is evil because it puts a severe limitation upon the choices available in regard to the man's physical freedom, on his mobility and the possibilities of free movement. To have legs does not specify the direction and the purpose or even the fact of human movement. It only affords possibilities. Not to have legs severely restricts these possibilities. It is not, however, an ultimately decisive evil for through technical means new possibilities for movement can be created. Or we might consider a man with an emotional problem, a psychological evil. Such a condition once again limits the man's possibilities for action, frequently subjecting him to compulsive and repetitive behavior. Freedom from the psychological disorder does not specify the direction and development of the man's life, but only affords possibilities that would otherwise be absent. Ignorance, or false knowledge, e.g., an opinion that the world is flat, imposes similar restrictions on human possibility, as does, for example, the social institution of slavery or segregation. The absence of such evils does not specify any particular practice or behavior, but only makes choice possible. It might also be noted that in these examples, the limitations do not affect just some people, to wit, those suffering them directly. The limits rather come to define everyone's existence and possibilities.(71)

Finally, as an example that touches directly human spiritual or ethical existence,(72) we might take King's favorite opposites, the choice to love or to hate. If a woman succumbs to hatred, she has severely limited the possibilities of her own development as well as the development of all who stand in some kind of relationship to her. Should hate become the exclusive feature of her moral attitude, she would truly be, as King says, a candidate for non-being, or in Christian terminology, she would be in hell. Love, the opposite of hate, specifies only the openness of a relationship, the possibilities for growth and continuous development, but not the direction or the precise content of such a relationship. Love preserves her freedom. Hatred simply cannot do so.

The foregoing examples are intended to illustrate the formal meaning of good and evil in King's thought. They also make plain the formal meaning of truth, justice, freedom, of what it means to say that a person is an end in himself or herself. All of these words were used by King to describe a situation and a condition of a person in which there are no inner or outer barriers to the continuing development of human personality. The stress in his idea of freedom, therefore, was on neither "I will" nor on "I may," but on "I can," a stress that is fundamentally in accord with the New Testament idea of freedom as that is given to the believer through faith in Christ.(73) The same stress also points to the incompatibility of freedom with violence, since the latter arises out of weakness, is a sign of incapacity or inability and has the character of necessity about it.(74) Violence, therefore, as something essentially destructive and marked by must rather than can, is in fundamental contradiction to the pure potentiality that is the good.

It should be noted, however, that while King's picture of human life was idealist in both the philosophical and common sense meanings of the word, the meanings that he assigned to such realities as truth, justice and freedom are not ideal in either sense. The development of the human personality is dependent upon a very concrete and specific set of relationships, the relation of a personal self to his or her own unique talents, to other living persons, to a living God, and also to existing evils. Indeed, it is the relationship to evil, a relationship of active opposition, which defines and directs the other three relationships. Despite the impression mentioned earlier of the human person as a house of three unrelated rooms, King held fundamentally to a completely unitary view of human life, a view in which a person's truth is not one or another of these relationships, but the well-ordered and mutual dependence of all of them in a single whole.

Such was the formal structure of King's ethical understanding, and as such it is also the formal meaning of his call to serve humankind. That call, which he originally described as service to humanity, he later specified and developed when he wrote that during his studies he searched for "a method to eliminate social evil."(75) Although his undoubted concrete concern was for a means to eliminate the burden of segregation from the black American, King's concern was richer in content and wider in scope than the abolition of Jim Crow laws, or the ameliorization of a social problem. From a social and humanitarian perspective, King was concerned with the transformation of persons and society. In a religious sense this was translated into a concern for obedience to the will of God. King was not posturing when he wrote that "the end of life is not to be happy or to achieve pleasure and avoid pain, but to do the will of God, come what may."(76) While there remain certain inconsistencies and several inadequate formulations in his overall position, the substance of that position displays a remarkable unity and a faithfulness to traditional Christian orthodoxy. The truth about human beings and their condition and the power to live in accord with their best selves come from God to humans through faith in Jesus Christ. The enemies of God which afflict human life are a consequence of the human's refusal to accept and live by the truth that God has created and revealed. King offered no speculation to explain or to account for this basic perversity in human beings. He was simply content to point to and to name the enemies, and to declare all out war upon them.

The more specific content of King's ethical understanding of human life, the concrete problems of human choice and action with which he found himself confronted, also played a large part in leading him to embrace militant nonviolence as the method of Christian living and acting. Indeed, the concrete evils he faced in his own life preceded the more sophisticated and formal effort to ground his inner convictions. In this development of his vision there were four dominant influences, one of which was largely inspirational, one which was his very life's blood, and two which were more intellectual or academic influences and which strongly reflect the wrestlings of his mind and heart. King himself has told us about three of these influences. We referred above to the impact of the two theologians, Walter Rauschenbusch and Reinhold Niebuhr, upon King. These two men define the intellectual poles of King's quest and set the terms or sides for his own intellectual debate. Mohandas Gandhi was undoubtedly something of an inspiration and model for King, but his influence grew with King's successes and failures and is certainly not by way of intellectual or spiritual content. The un-named but dominant influence upon King was the black experience in America which he lived and suffered and shared with those he most knew and loved. In the following chapter we will turn to an analysis of the contribution and impact of these four influences in the final shaping of King's version of militant nonviolence.

NOTES: CHAPTER III

1. Cf. *supra*, pp. 86-88.

2. *BU Coll.*, XIV (75).

3. Cf. *supra*, p. 96.

4. King, *Stride Toward Freedom*, p. 73.

5. *National Baptist Voice* (March, 1956), p. 4; *BU Coll.*, X (37). King's family and friends called him Mike, not Martin. See Lewis, p. 4.

6. Walter McCall was a Crozer classmate and friend of King's.

7. The capital letters are Barbour's; *National Baptist Voice*, p. 4.

8. *Ibid.*

9. *BU Coll.*, XIV (7).

10. *Ibid.*, X (37); such a pragmatic consideration is very foreign to Gandhi and is inconsistent with King's own accounting of nonviolence in *Stride Toward Freedom*, p. 83. "If one uses this method because he is afraid or merely because he lacks the instruments of violence, he is not truly nonviolent. This is why Gandhi often said that if cowardice is the only alternative to violence, it is better to fight."

11. See King's own account of his perplexity and unreadiness at the start of the Montgomery boycott in *Stride Toward Freedom*, pp. 44-46.

12. The letter is dated 12/21/54; *BU Coll.*, VIII (16).

13. *Ibid.*; the telegram is dated 1/11/57.

14. *National Baptist Voice* (March, 1956), p. 5; *BU Coll.*, X (37).

15. By a spirituality I mean the personal and concrete application to oneself (individual or communal self) of what is held to be true in a universal or abstract way. Such a process is

held to be ethics in the mainstream Protestant
tradition. Franz Bockle, <u>Law and Conscience</u>
(New York: Sheed and Ward, 1966), pp. 91-94,
106-111. I have elaborated on this claim in my
article "Militant Nonviolence: A Spirituality
for the Pursuit of Social Justice," <u>Horizons</u>
(Spring 1982), pp. 7-22.

16. Gustafson, pp. 2-8.

17. King, <u>Stride Toward Freedom</u>, p. 73; Henry David
Thoreau, "On the Duty of Civil Disobedience,"
<u>Civil Disobedience and Violence</u>, ed. by
Jeffrie G. Murphy (Belmont, California: Wadsworth Publishing Company, Inc., 1971), pp. 24-
28.

18. King, <u>Stride Toward Freedom</u>, p. 73.

19. <u>Ibid.</u>, p. 74.

20. <u>Ibid.</u>, pp. 74-77.

21. There is a letter to King from Melvin Watson in
<u>BU Coll.</u>, XV (5), dated Aug. 14, 1952, which is
a critique of a King sermon on the challenge of
communism to Christianity, in which Watson
points out King's misunderstanding of communist
materialism and communist social structure. No
one would ever claim that King was any kind of
an economist. See also King, <u>Strength To Love</u>,
pp. 114-123.

22. King, <u>Stride Toward Freedom</u>, pp. 77-78.

23. <u>Ibid.</u>, p. 79.

24. <u>Ibid.</u>, pp. 80-81.

25. <u>Ibid.</u>, p. 82.

26. <u>Ibid.</u>

27. Le Roi Jones, <u>Home: Social Essays</u> (New York:
William Morrow & Co., Inc., 1966), pp. 201-202.
Mr. Jones has since changed his name, but I cite
him here as his name was at the time of publication.

28. BU Coll., XIV (75); XIV (46); XIV (33); and numerous other places. This, of course, is pure liberalism in its classic form. See John Stuart Mill, "On Liberty," The Essential Works of John Stuart Mill, ed. Max Lerner (New York: Bantam Books, 1961), p. 266.

29. Ibid., XIV (54).

30. King, Strength To Love, p. 85.

31. Ibid., p. 86.

32. This is a very biblical idea; Galatians 6:4-5, and again reflects the distinction between a spirituality or concrete ethic and a moral theory.

33. King's ideas on excellence are quite classical. See John W. Gardner, Excellence: Can We Be Equal and Excellent Too? (New York and Evanston: Harper Colophon Books, Harper & Row, Publishers, 1961), especially pp. 127-144. If a person does his or her best, he or she may not achieve technical excellence, but will achieve moral excellence in King's sense. They have done their utmost. On the other hand, a person may become technically excellent and yet not be morally excellent; he or she may use this technical ability for bad ends.

34. King, Strength To Love, p. 87.

35. BU Coll., XIV (54).

36. Jones, p. 219.

37. It is certainly not only rational, though it may be a clear and reasonable conclusion of faith. Arendt, On Violence, p. 78; "ultimately because of the human condition of mortality, the self qua self cannot reckon in terms of long-range interest, i.e., the interest of a world that survives its inhabitants....To expect people who have not the slightest notion of what the res publica, the public thing, is, to behave nonviolently and argue rationally in matters of interest is neither realistic nor reasonable."

38. King, Strength To Love, p. 90.

39. *Ibid.*, p. 93.

40. *Ibid.*, p. 94.

41. See, for example, *Ibid.*, pp. 96-98.

42. *Ibid.*, p. 110.

43. *BU Coll.*, XIV (54).

44. King, *Strength To Love*, pp. 109-110.

45. *Ibid.*, p. 112.

46. King, *Stride Toward Freedom*, p. 74.

47. *Ibid.*, pp. 74-75.

48. King, *Strength To Love*, pp. 15-16, 18, 74, 129, are but a few examples.

49. King, "Address to the First Annual Institute on Nonviolence and Social Change," (December, 1956), *BU Coll.*, X (29).

50. King, *Strength To Love*, p. 163.

51. *Ibid.*, p. 71.

52. *Ibid.*, p. 72.

53. *Ibid.*

54. *Ibid.*, p. 153.

55. *Ibid.*, p. 145.

56. *Ibid.*, p. 73.

57. *Ibid.*, p. 148.

58. *Ibid.*

59. *Ibid.*, pp. 152-155.

60. *Ibid.*, p. 153; Romans 3:25-30; Galatians 3:1-9.

61. The one respect in which King's doctrine differs was not the result of deliberate intent, but simply of lack of appreciation for the precise

theological issues involved. King was ostensibly a semi-pelagian, as explained, because he would not treat of the precise relationship between God's grace and man's deeds. On the level of social action it was not particularly urgent for him to stress that every good intention, motive and deed, even the desire for God's grace and help itself, is already a gift of grace. He gave the impression, but only the impression, that man's goodness has a certain independence of God's grace, and a number of his unhappy formulas only strengthened this impression.

62. See, most typically, Hans Küng, Justification: The Doctrine of Karl Barth and a Catholic Reflection, trans. by Thomas Collins, Edmund E. Tolk, and David Granskou (New York: Nelson, 1946); Karl Rahner, "Questions of Controversial Theology on Justification," Theological Investigations IV (Baltimore: Helicon Press; London: Darton, Longman and Todd, 1966), pp. 189-218; Böckle, op.cit.

63. In all of King's class notes there is simply no treatment of these issues in any clear or systematic way. The notes contain largely impressions that liberal theology has of various thinkers in terms of its own interests. King's interest was consistently inspirational and practical.

64. King, Strength To Love, pp. 152-153.

65. Herbert McCabe, What Is Ethics All About? (Washington, Cleveland: Corpus Books, 1969), pp. 20-22.

66. King, The Trumpet of Conscience, pp. 75-76.

67. For this common difficulty see Paul's Epistles, especially 1 Corinthians 6:9-10 over against 13:4-8, or Galatians 5:19-21 against 5:22-26.

68. Vernard Eller, The Promise: Ethics in the Kingdom of God (Garden City, New York: Doubleday and Company, Inc., 1970), pp. 22-26.

69. BU Coll., XIV (75).

70. Arendt, _On Violence_, pp. 79-80. "Since when we act we never know with any certainty the eventual consequences of what we are doing, violence can remain rational only if it pursues short-term goals." In direct opposition to this view is Georges Sorel, _Reflections on Violence_, pp. 47-48; "To examine the effects of violence it is necessary to start from its distant consequences and not from its immediate results ....We are not comparing two kinds of reformism, but we are endeavoring to find out what contemporary violence is in relation to the future social revolution."

71. This idea of King's reflects quite closely Hegel's famous master-slave dialectic. Yet, for all his liking of Hegel, it does not seem that this particular aspect struck King enough for a place in his notes or books.

72. As King writes and speaks, ethical and spiritual are equivalent words.

73. Eller, pp. 31-47; Rudolph Schnackenburg, _The Truth Will Make You Free_ (New York: Herder and Herder, 1966), p. 36; Rudolph Schnackenburg, _Christian Existence in the New Testament_, 2 vols. (Notre Dame, Ind.: University of Notre Dame Press, 1969) II, pp. 31-53. "What is at issue here is not a new attitude of mind but a new power given us by God the Spirit of life...," p. 45.

74. King, _Where Do We Go From Here_, pp. 52-56; Arendt, _On Violence_, pp. 47-51; Ellul, pp. 127-131; Rollo May, _Power and Innocence_, pp. 14-15, 20-27.

75. King, _Stride Toward Freedom_, p. 73.

76. King, _Strength To Love_, p. 162.

CHAPTER IV

THE MOLDING OF A MAN

The historian, Louis Lomax, who was both a personal friend and a critical observer of Martin Luther King, has suggested that one of the keys to King's strong determination to commit himself as a leader of militant nonviolence is to be found in an incident which took place quite early in the Montgomery bus boycott.(1) King himself selected the incident as an especially memorable one to report in Stride Toward Freedom,(2) and though an examination of King's private papers does not add any new evidence for the importance of the incident, as Lomax suggested it would,(3) the event itself is highly illustrative of King's deepest convictions and orientations.

At the second negotiation session between the MIA leadership and the Montgomery city officials on December 17, 1955, one of the members of the Mayor's citizens committee, a Dr. E. Stanley Frazier, then minister of St. James Methodist Church and known to be an outspoken segregationist, upbraided King and his associates for providing leadership in the boycott. What especially incensed Dr. Frazier was that the boycott leaders were Christian ministers and he made his objections pointedly clear. To continue the report of the incident in King's own words:

> The job of minister, he averred, is to lead the souls of men to God, not to bring about confusion by getting tangled up in transitory social problems. He moved on to a brief discussion of the Christmas story. In evocative terms he talked of "God's unspeakable gift." He ended by saying that as we moved into the Christmas season, our minds and hearts should be turned toward the Babe of Bethlehem; and he urged the Negro ministers to leave the meeting determined to bring this boycott to a close and lead their people instead "to a glorious experience of the Christian faith."(4)

Dr. Frazier was, to be sure, personally unacquainted with King at the time, but had he known him intimately for two lifetimes, he could not have said

141

anything in that situation more provocative or more contradictory to all that King held to be true and holy. In King's eyes a position like Dr. Frazier's was, as Lomax expressed it, "a total prostitution of the Christian ethic,"(5) and hence, as we have seen, a complete denial of his Christian faith. Though King himself would not have used the word, he was faced quite simply with the gravest kind of practically heresy(6) which called into question not only the rightness of the bus boycott, but his own calling and integrity as well as the truth of his faith. What was at stake for him here was much more than the racism and arrogance of one Methodist preacher. I have recounted in a previous chapter his early wrestlings with his doubts about the significance of his faith and his church, his revulsion from the emotionalism and lack of content in so much of the preaching he had heard.(7) In Dr. Frazier's admonition he came up against all that he had rejected and despised. King had settled in his own mind and heart that religion is life or it is empty. He would not and could not allow the Jesus he believed in and loved to be pushed out of this world to some ethereal and unthreatening place of private ecstasy.

His own response to Frazier's charge sets his personal position in the clearest and most definitive opposition to any privatization or spiritualization of the Christian gospel. He, too, he insisted, knows the Jesus that Frazier refers to; he, too, has had an experience of him and he will not yield in his commitment to the revelation of God in Jesus Christ. But there is no contradiction between that commitment and the boycott. On the contrary, King insisted that there is a necessary connection between the two. "If one is truly devoted to the religion of Jesus he will seek to rid the earth of social evils. The gospel is social as well as personal."(8)

This conflict between King and Frazier is, in principle, no less momentous, no less basic for the life of Christian faith and the integrity of the Christian Church than any of the other controversies that have torn apart the body of Christ throughout its long history. Unlike many of the controversies in the Church, from Paul's struggles with the Judaizers(9) through Gnosticism, the Christological and Pelagian controversies up to the still unresolved debate over the nature of the Church,(10) this conflict is not one that can be settled by a Council

142

or the discussion of theologians and the reformulations of doctrine. A practical and lived heresy bears far more the character of sin than of error; it cannot be removed or overcome through words and conceptual understanding. It can be conquered only in a concrete way, through action effecting change. In a very real sense, therefore, King's agenda for life can be seen in this brief, almost accidental encounter. In such a context, then, it will be useful to examine the four specific influences that had molded this conviction in him, that led him to become a champion of militant nonviolence as the concrete, lived way of overcoming what can only be called a Christian heresy of American life.

The first of these influences, not first in time or even in importance but in terms of a priority of conscious awareness, was the theology of Walter Rauschenbusch. It is not to the point here to provide an extended discussion of Rauschenbusch's views, for his influence on King was not that determinative, systematic, or complete. King himself mentions but one work of Rauschenbusch that made an impact upon him, and being a completely eclectic thinker, he simply chose those points that appealed to him and seemed relevant to his interests. The points he selected, or better, perhaps, imbibed, are simply related. First, the gospel deals with human beings' total life, their material and social existence as well as their spiritual well-being. Or in a more religious formulation, Jesus Christ is Lord or our bodies, our history and social organizations as well as of our souls. There are, then, ways of organizing human economic and social life that are simply incompatible with Christian faith. Human beings can and do sin, not only in their private and personal affairs, but in their collective actions as well. Repentance on one level is neither adequate for fidelity to Christ nor sufficient for the health of one's soul.(11)

To put this insight into the context of a more contemporary discussion, it is necessary to recognize that there is social sin as well as personal sin, or to understand that sin is both a condition of human existence and an act of human beings. In such a perspective it becomes meaningful to speak about sinful social structures, sinful institutions and sinful systems, all of which by their very nature contradict and violate human dignity. Correlatively one can also speak about social salvation and social grace.(12) The point of such terms is not merely to allow Karl Marx his due, but more fundamentally to take seriously the solidarity of human beings in sin, in much the same way that the doctrines of creation, providence and the universal salvific will of God emphasize the mutual interdependence of human beings in grace. The usefulness of such concepts in heightening human consciousness and moral sensitivity on a broad scale remains to be seen, but it is clear that they have strongly influenced theologians and church leaders to a more direct concern for social justice. Rauschenbusch and the social gospel influenced King in this direction at an early date.

A second point imbibed from Rauschenbusch concerns the possibility of real moral progress. Though King faulted Rauschenbusch for succumbing to the nineteenth century cult of inevitable progress,(13) he shared with him an evolutionary view of human moral development which left him with the conviction that qualitative progress could be made, that certain evils could finally be eliminated from human life, that not every aspect of human life and action had to be infected by sin. It is true that Rauschenbusch, at least before the First World War, displayed what to us today would be an incredible optimism about human nature which King rightly called superficial.(14) This optimism had an immediate connection with Rauschenbusch's understanding of the traditional Christian doctrine of original sin, a doctrine which Rauschenbusch rejected on the grounds that he did not find it practical or effective. To quote from one of his discussions of the topic:

> The traditional doctrine of the fall has taught us to regard evil as a kind of unvarying racial endowment, which is active in every new life and which can be overcome only by the grace offered in the Gospel and ministered by the Church. It would strengthen the appeal of the social gospel if evil could be regarded instead as a variable factor in the life of humanity, which it is our duty to diminish for every young life and for every new generation.(15)

This conception of evil as a variable factor in the life of humanity means, of course, that it does not necessarily touch all human enterprises, nor does it necessarily affect every individual. Sin, for Rauschenbusch, in the sense of original sin, was transmitted socially; hence different forms of social organization could block the transmission of sin and, indeed, thus eliminate sin and evil from human lives. While King was not nearly as optimistic about the ease with which sin could be eliminated from human life as was Rauschenbusch, his basic conception of social sin or social evil was the same as Rauschenbusch's, and King's optimism was of a high order. His ostensible success in his first public campaign only highlighted that optimism,(16) and it took the events of the next ten years to temper and reduce his sunny mood to more realistic and hard-headed proportions.(17) Indeed, it was precisely this optimism which caused a good deal of disillusionment with and a rejection of King's teaching. For a key element of King's faith was that white Americans had a conscience, and, once challenged nonviolently, that conscience was capable of repentance and change. Malcolm X was not the first nor the only black leader that felt such optimism was the sheerest of fantasies.(18)

A third key element in King's outlook which he derived from Rauschenbusch and modified only partially was the strong identification he made between Christianity and democracy.(19) King criticized Rauschenbusch for coming perilously close to identifying the Kingdom of God with a particular social and economic system.(20) Rauschenbusch did more than come perilously close to doing this. He did do it, and King was not far behind him.(21) Although King was far more critical of the concrete American society in which he lived than Rauschenbusch ever was, King could and did use the terms "democracy," "Christianity," and "the philosophy of nonviolence" interchangeably.(22) He could quite naturally call upon America to return to its Christian principles, and then be genuinely surprised to receive a letter from a Jewish American suggesting that such a plea was both offensive and inaccurate.(23) It is an important insight to realize how fully King was immersed in the early Protestant conviction that the United States of America was the closest thing on earth to a new chosen people and how completely he accepted both the Declaration of Independence and the Constitution of the United States (as duly amended) as embodying the fundamental principles of Christian faith.(24)

Like Rauschenbusch, King thought America's weakness to be its economic system, capitalism, which represented the social institutionalization of greed and selfish individualism. As early as 1948 King was convinced that capitalism had failed and had to be replaced by a more cooperative and more humane economic system.(25) To this extent he considered himself an economic Marxist, which certainly did not mean he was a communist or even inclined in such a direction. King knew as little about Marxian economics as he did about capitalist economics. As an aside, it might be added that the efforts to portray King as a communist or even as a sympathizer involve either the rankest ignorance of the man and his beliefs and actions, or the most malevolent kind of perversity. Although the Poor People's March on Washington was the last conception and dream of his life, King's concern with economic injustice and exploitation was one of the first concerns of his life. It is a concern reflected in his notes at Crozer and Boston University far more than any other social concern. In this he was one with Rauschenbusch.(26)

The tendency to identify social structures as Christian in a normative, ethical sense is an unhappy one. All such efforts are fundamentally flawed, not because Christian faith does not provide some guidelines for the ordering of social existence, but because the only realization of Christian faith and values is a material one, never a purely formal one. This has, I suggest, been perceived somewhat more clearly and realistically, in theory if not always in practice, by the Catholic tradition of social thought. This is reflected in its persistent refusal to sanction any one economic or political form as intrinsically best or normative. It is understood that the material realization of general political and social principles and values is possible in a variety of forms and dependent upon specific historical and cultural conditions.(27) Even the right to private property, a right often staunchly defended in the Catholic tradition, has never been held to be an absolute right and must always receive a situational as well as a principled defense.(28)

Rauschenbusch's influence on King in this regard, even as tempered by Niebuhrian relativism, was unfortunate. While normative social structures are by no means essential to the nonviolent position, they do hold out a false hope and often distracted King and others from the real issue. Hannah Arendt has shown the unhappy consequences that come from confusing the issues of freedom and poverty and from arguments about communism or capitalism as the better economic system.(29) When inflated claims are made for systems, they are quickly absolutized or identified with the Kingdom of God or Utopia, or even more modestly referred to as Christian institutions or structures. The danger in this is that they then become ends in themselves and men and women are slaughtered to preserve capitalism or establish socialism. This is fundamentally contradictory to King's whole emphasis on the centrality of personality, on the human person as an end in himself or herself, and on any system as no more than a means.

A fourth point derived from Rauschenbusch had to do with King's view of the Christian church and its function in society. We will have to discuss this at greater length in a later chapter, but for the moment it will suffice to say that for Rauschenbusch "the Church is the social factor in salvation. It brings social forces to bear on salvation."(30) For King the Church is the "guardian of the moral and spiritual life of the community,"(31) and "the conscience of the state."(32) The two conceptions differ mainly in the wording and are early adumbrations of the increasingly common belief that the Church does not exist for its own sake but to serve the world.(33) Both Rauschenbusch and King, being Baptists, had a conception of the Church that was somewhat vague and elusive. The key elements of the Church for both were fellowship and mutual support, but with the added dimension of the social gospel, the Church was given the additional responsibility for amending society's ills.(34) What remains a troubling mystery in this conception of the Church is where the Church gets either the power or wisdom to execute this particular task, a mystery as impenetrable as who or what the Church concretely is. The practical difficulties that this conception entails and the consequences of it will also be dealt with later. But for both men the conception implied a theory of social change that was mainly ethical in character, one that stressed the good will and conscience of human beings, presumed upon their openness to truth and their desire for goodness, and their capacity to choose both at will. For nonviolence it also suggested the fundamental importance of a community of some kind. The nonviolent way of life was not something to be lived alone, was not an individual enterprise, but rather the task of a gathered group.

On the whole Rauschenbusch's attraction for King was far more a matter of a temper of mind and the verbalization of a common concern than of a profound and systematic grasp of issues and ideas. As Rauschenbusch himself wrote in his interpretation of Jesus, "Jesus' interest was practical and not speculative, religious and ethical and not philosophical."(35) And again, "the social gospel is above all things practical. It needs religious ideas which will release energy for heroic opposition against organized evil and for the building of a righteous social life."(36) No words could have caught more accurately King's own concerns and convictions. It is little wonder that he saw in Rauschenbusch a kindred spirit.

The second major influence which shaped King's thinking was the theology of Reinhold Niebuhr. Indeed, Niebuhr was something of a persistent challenge and annoyance to King, and his influence on King was, as Lois Wasserman has attempted to show,(37) and as Smith and Zepp have confirmed,(38) far more significant than had been previously realized. King's class notes and papers reveal more work on Niebuhr than on any other author,(39) except the personalist philosophers with whom he dealt at Boston University. In addition, there was the running debate he seems to have carried on with Professor Kenneth Lee Smith while at Crozer defending his allegiance to Rauschenbusch against the Niebuhrian position of his mentor.(40) Niebuhr's analyses of man's nature, history and social life were, of course, noticeably more profound and complex than any Rauschenbusch ever offered, and for a bright young mind like King's, they could not be simply ignored or dismissed. King himself attested to the impact Niebuhr had upon him, admitting that he was so impressed that he "almost fell into the trap of accepting uncritically everything he wrote."(41) While it would be difficult to fit such an experience into King's life chronologically, it is an accurate reflection of the challenge Niebuhr offered to his thinking. Even when he was preparing the manuscript for Stride Toward Freedom, he was still wrestling with Niebuhr and felt the inadequacy of his own response to Niebuhr's criticism of Gandhian nonviolence. He had to be warned off by Bayard Rustin from trying to deal with Niebuhr at any depth. Rustin bluntly wrote to King that anything he could say would be too difficult for the popular reader and would remain unsatisfying to scholars and academics.(42)

Niebuhr, then, more than any other intellectual influence, became the foil against which King had to test his hopes and ideas. But even in this matter it was the temper of his mind and his attitude more than the substance of his thought that led King to chafe against Niebuhr. Once again his interest was not theoretical or academic, and this led him to pass over the finer distinctions and insights which Niebuhr laboriously unfolded, in order to select the warnings and suggestions which moved King, as he thought, closer to his goal of a method of social change. He was forced to yield to Niebuhr's scathing criticism of the sentimental optimism of much of liberal Protestantism as represented by Rauschenbusch,(43) and to give him credit for his profound analyses of the complexity of human behavior and motivation. He was deeply impressed by the thesis of Niebuhr's Moral Man and Immoral Society,(44) and a great deal of his own optimism rested on the thesis of this book, that people in groups tend to behave rather worse than they do as individuals because of their blindness to and lack of understanding of social reality and collective evil. He was equally moved by the suggestion Niebuhr made about the possibility of the American Negro using nonviolent tactics to achieve civil and other liberties.(45) Indeed, a cardinal purpose of the demonstrations King was later to mount was to make clear to white Americans the collective evil they (unwittingly, as he thought) perpetrated through their laws and institutions, in the fond expectation that they would change social reality to accord with their personal moral convictions.(46) King also attributed to Niebuhr's theology the power to remind us of the reality of sin on every level of human existence, but from this reminder he drew the pedestrian conclusion that human beings are capable of evil as well as good.

Niebuhr's meaning was far more profound and telling than that.(47)

Above all else, however, King was troubled by Niebuhr's critique of pacifism. On his own accounting, King had already been excited by Gandhi and his achievements in South Africa and India when he faced Niebuhr's critique and it posed a sharp challenge to any extension or absolutizing of nonviolence. Although he reported that he found many things lacking in Niebuhr's theology, he did not tell us what these things were.(48) Rather he faulted Niebuhr for two things: first, for wrongly thinking that nonviolent resistance as practiced by Gandhi was passive and not really resistance at all; and secondly, that it was based on a naive belief in the power of love. This, however, was not at all the point of Niebuhr's criticism.(49) Rather Niebuhr emphasized the failure of responsibility in nonviolent resistance when one knows, or has every reason to believe, that it will be ineffective in resisting evil.(50) King felt this charge more than he explicitly expressed it. He knew, both then and later, that militant nonviolence had to work, actually had to achieve the result of checking or eliminating evil to be a viable doctrine, and for more than political reasons.(51) His was not the traditional pacifism of being a witness to peace, of having a special calling to represent in one's own life and flesh a sign and a direction of hope.(52) King wanted to affirm two things about militant nonviolence as he understood it. First, it was the better way or at least, in concession to Niebuhr's critique, the lesser of two evils in any circumstance. Second, it did, in fact, get results; it was more than a noble gesture or a simple stand for integrity of conscience. The difficulty with saying either of those two things is that they are, at least in part, empirical judgments and will not serve as universal ethical principles, no matter how one defines "evil" and results."(53)

At the heart of Niebuhr's criticism of nonviolence, as King rightly perceived, was his theological understanding of the nature of the human person which he based upon his interpretation of the reformation doctrine of justification by faith.(54) As was pointed out above,(55) King never grasped the subtleties of this ancient controversy, and in any case his own Baptist faith and theological education hardly prepared him to be favorably inclined toward

Niebuhr had he understood them fully. But he felt the force of Niebuhr's view continually and his life experience tended to confirm Niebuhr and to challenge his own hope. For this reason it is worth looking at Niebuhr's position in greater depth to see just where it rubbed against King's hope and why King resisted it so mightily even under the strongest pressures to despair.(56) It is in King's resolution of the challenge posed by Niebuhr that one finds the ultimate theological ground of militant nonviolence.

Reinhold Niebuhr was a forceful exponent of the ambiguity of all moral choices, especially in regard to social matters.(57) In his view there was something to be said in favor of every concrete choice available to human beings and no one could be certain with any firm knowledge that he or she had chosen the best or wisest course. People must do the best they can to analyze the factors in a given situation and then choose what appears to be the most promising and least evil course of action. In every choice, therefore, we have no recourse but to appeal to the mercy of God, for every choice involves loss of some kind to someone. Be it war, or some government regulation, or an economic decision, in every social choice, while some people will benefit, someone stands to die, to suffer coercion, to lose a job or whatever no matter what decision is made. This is simply the human situation and the human dilemma. It cannot be avoided by inaction or by good intentions or by withdrawing from society, for that would be to abandon responsibility, the responsibility that humans have for the regulation of social affairs. Nor can human beings control all the results and consequences of their decisions and actions. No one has sufficient foresight to perceive the total outcome of any course of action. Intended or not, the consequences are produced by human actions and are, therefore, a human responsibility. Hence, when Niebuhr pointed to the reality of sin at every level of human existence, he was saying much more than that people are capable of both good and evil. He was affirming that they do evil as well as good in all their social deeds. There was no possibility of a grace-given perfectionism that, as King quoted him, "actually lifts man out of the sinful contradictions of history and establishes him above the sins of the world."(58) Even when human beings do their duty to the best of their ability and wisdom, their

righteousness depends not on the goodness of their
own deeds but upon the mercy of God.

For Niebuhr the effort to avoid or to deny this
fundamental human condition was to deny that humans
are justified by faith, and he was convinced that in
practice it led either to an irresponsible kind of
perfectionism in which one fled the burdens and
responsibilities of social decision and action, or to
an equally irresponsible and far more dangerous
self-righteousness in which human beings pridefully
and sinfully did what they wanted, oblivious to or
indifferent to the real harm they did to others.(59)
Essentially, then, all moral choices come down to
choosing the lesser of two evils, the least harmful
of alternatives as best that may be determined. This
conception of the human moral situation was reflected
clearly in Niebuhr's famous aphorism about democracy
as a form of government. "Man's capacity for justice
makes democracy possible; but his inclination to
injustice makes democracy necessary."(60) Note that
the subject of the two clauses is the same. There is
no division between some good people who make democracy possible and some bad ones who make it necessary. The capacity and the inclination are in all
alike. There is no imminent dialectical process, as
in Hegel and Marx, which will eventually dissolve the
human dilemma into some higher synthesis beyond good
and evil. Only God's mercy, or justification by
faith, can resolve the human dilemma. Quite simply
human people cannot eliminate evil from their social
life.

Niebuhr's insight and basic concern in this
regard are paralleled in a secular way in a surprising passage in Herbert Marcuse's Eros and Civilization which appears near the end of his controversial
study of Freud.(61) It will serve to illustrate the
key point in King's wrestling with Niebuhr.

Reflecting upon the last and most definitive
enemy of human life, death, Marcuse has written:
"Not those who die, but those who die before they
must and want to die, those who die in agony and
pain, are the great indictment against civilization."(62) Even though he believed that even death
can one day be made rational and painless, that even
death can one day become a "token of freedom,"
Marcuse saw that even such a final liberation would
continue to cast a shadow over Utopia. "But even the

152

ultimate advent of freedom cannot redeem those who died in pain. It is the remembrance of them, and the accumulated guilt of mankind against its victims, that darken the prospect of a civilization without repression."(63) This is a remarkably frank observation by an author who continually points humankind toward a secular utopia, yet recognizes that there exists no secular dynamic to remove human guilt or to forgive us our sins. Not even a final establishment of justice and freedom for all living persons can make just and right the deeds and processes by which Utopia is achieved. In short, it would seem to be impossible for us to eliminate the shadow of evil from the human condition.

In a very similar way Niebuhr conceived the human social condition and human behavior to be confronted with the same problem. His faith, of course, led him to some quite different ethical judgments than Marcuse makes, but the process and calculus of decision-making in both men is not very different, even though their language is.(64) Most importantly, however, is that there is and can be no place for concrete absolute norms or prohibitions in regard to social action. So, at best, a strategy or tactic of nonviolent resistance can only be an empirical decision, the result of a calculation that it is the way to effect an end with the least evil consequences in a specific situation. It may be, in a given situation, the way to minimize evil and do good. But it also may not be.

This sort of moral ambiguity and moral calculus did not appeal to King. Despite his vivid perception of humankind's solidarity such that one person's freedom is restricted by another's lack of freedom,(65) the picture painted by Niebuhr was too gloomy for his taste. As a consequence his only reply to Niebuhr was that his view of human nature was too pessimistic, that he over-emphasized human corruption.(66) With the swiftness of his both-and mentality, King sought to balance human corruption with the divine goodness and to offset Niebuhr's diagnosis of human sinfulness with the remedy of God's grace. Again this is not argument but affirmation. It tells us that King disagreed with Niebuhr, but it does not tell us why Niebuhr was wrong or why King was right. What it does reveal above all else, however, is the exact point at which Niebuhr's theological convictions most challenged King's own faith and hope. There had to be moral progress, people had to be able to eliminate evil from the world without at the same time adding to the weight of evil already in the world. There had to be some dialectical process which could enable human beings to rise above the intermingling of good and evil, grace and sin, in their lives. King appreciated Niebuhr's analysis and he saw the dilemma that Niebuhr set down at the center of human life. He would not accept the fact that it was without resolution in this world.(67)

Some students of Niebuhr have felt that his ethical teaching leads to a conservative attitude toward political and social action and that Niebuhr himself grew increasingly conservative politically as he advanced in years.(68) Whatever the truth may be about Niebuhr himself, his position, while it could be so employed, does not necessarily lead to social or political conservatism, nor was it Niebuhr's intention that it do so. Nor was it the possibility of this conservative direction that bothered King about Niebuhr's views. King himself, by temperament, was not a hasty or impetuous man as a rule, but careful, even cautious about what he thought and did.(69) On occasion he said things out of hand that had to be withdrawn or forgotten and he joined at times in movements that lacked adequate preparation. But the only truly hasty deed in his life was proposing to his future wife after one date.(70) If one had to label him politically, August Meier's description of him as a "conservative militant" is probably the most accurate.(71) It was not political action or theory that was at stake in his wrestlings with Niebuhr. It was rather his faith. For King believed that through the grace and power of God, he, too, could become like Jesus and do what Jesus had done; that through God's grace human efforts were of some avail in overcoming social evil and eliminating it from human life; that human life could be rendered more just and peaceful, human dignity and worth could be honored and allowed to flourish. He correctly read the plain implication of his own faith in God and His Christ to be a corresponding "deep faith in the possibilities of human beings when they allow themselves to become co-workers with God."(72)

This faith in human beings as a corollary of faith in God did not mean to King that human beings could be free from moral dilemmas or that somehow, magically or mystically, they could be raised above the travails and struggles of history. But if the realization of human possibilities depended upon becoming co-workers with God, then the most important task in life was to discern the will and work of God in human history and in one's own life situation and to obey that will. That is not, of course, a unique insight. It has fairly wide backing among a number of theologians.(73) But King read the implications of it more deeply than most. For the effort to do this changes one's emphasis and concern from theory to practice, from a general ethic to a concrete spirituality, from the ends or consequences of action to the means of action, from future hopes to present responsibility, from the goal of activity to the process of it, from faith as either belief in doctrine or hope in the future to faith as trust in present guidance.

This transition was not to become clear to King until he was actually engaged in the Montgomery bus boycott, when, as he tells us, "living through the actual experience of the protest, nonviolence became more than a method to which I gave intellectual assent; it became a commitment to a way of life."(74) Nor did he ever articulate this transition in his speeches and books. I dare say it was a difference of which he was consciously not fully aware. Nonetheless, he did find and articulate the truth that the intellectual ambiguities about nonviolence as a theory or as a universal ethical principle were resolved for him in the sphere of practical action. That happened, and could happen, quite simply because militant nonviolence, as King grasped it, is not a theory at all but a concrete spirituality, a valid, specific way for a person so empowered to respond to mystery, to truth, to God. It is a way of living a faith, a discipline for faithful living. Or in terms of some modern Christian theologians, it is not a universal ethic, but an ethic for Christians alone in so far as they are more than Christians in name only.(75) To be altogether accurate, King himself would never have said this. It would have been foreign to him both theologically and temperamentally; and there were also practical reasons for not putting it in this way. But such, I maintain, is the character of militant nonviolence and it points to the third major influence on King, the example and the achievements of Mohandas Gandhi.

155

According to King's own account of his personal pilgrimage to nonviolence, his encounter with Gandhi took place during his days at Crozer and before he felt the sharp challenge of Niebuhr. The facts of his biography and the evidence of his classnotes do not permit such a clear temporal distinction. He certainly was engaged with Niebuhr at Crozer in a serious way,(76) while in all of his numerous class notes I found exactly two references to Gandhi, one of which mentions Gandhi's concern for the plight of the untouchables in India,(77) the other of which mentions in passing Gandhi's concern to remedy economic injustice.(78) Such evidence, or lack of evidence, does not, of course, allow the conclusion that King did not read about Gandhi or that Gandhi was unimportant to him.(79) But along with the fact that Gandhi and nonviolence were never even thought of by King during the Montgomery boycott until the comparison was made in a letter to a newspaper,(80) the evidence does suggest the nature of Gandhi's influence on him.

To understand the nature of this influence it must be remembered that King was in search of "a method to eliminate social evil." There are three key elements, however, in that expression: a method, eliminate, and social evil, all of which were qualified in King's thinking by certain implicit understandings. There is, first, the question of what he understood social evil to be, both in formal and material terms. Concretely for King social evil meant segregation, the second-rate status afforded America's black citizens, and economic injustice, the simple disparity between the rich and the poor, the fact that some men had more than enough while others went hungry or homeless.(81) In a formal sense social evil comprehended those institutional elements which put restrictions upon or distorted the development of human personality. With this understanding, therefore, there is the immediate implication that what is being sought is political and social change. The final term of King's quest, then, was external, real, objective and common. Faith for him had its realization or its truth in some new situation outside the subjective experience and attitudes of individuals. Whatever interior changes of attitude and affections this might require, faith demanded more than a new heart and a new attitude. It demanded a new situation, a new person that could be seen and evaluated. Truth was to be found in doing,

and the only test of faith was the quality of the
activity and the actor.(82)

Second, there is the element of elimination.
King was not looking for a tool with which to restrain evil or to limit the effects of social evil or
to control or counterbalance its influence. He
wanted to get rid of it altogether. This was a very
radical ambition, certainly as radical as the aims of
a Marx or a Mao or others who genuinely claim the
name of revolutionary. More conservative minds
perceived this in King, and while the charges of
anarchism and communism were quite mistaken in his
regard, there was a certain affinity between the
radicalness of hope and purpose that was King's and
that endemic to anarchist and communist ideology.
Because elimination is the goal or the end for King,
certain results of human activity ordinarily considered good might not qualify as success in his
view. Certain achievements might appear to be
victories and not be so simply because they did not
permit development or growth, because they did not
lead anywhere. Since evil is that which cannot
permanently organize itself, that which bears the
seeds of its own destruction within itself, the
quality of an achievement must be such that it can be
built upon if it is to count as good or as successful.(83)

The third element is that of method which
translates into the question of means. The qualifications here are numerous. Aside from the obvious
qualifications of effectiveness and suitability put
upon any means by the end, there were two additional
and crucial qualifications in King's mind. He was
not after just any means or method, but a moral
method, which to his religious mind meant a method in
keeping with the Christian emphasis on love, or
philosophically looked at, a method capable of
producing good as explained in the preceding paragraph. For this reason he simply could not move in
the direction of communism or accept the glorification of power, however tempting or plausible such
options appeared. Secondly, the test of method is
empirical, not theoretical. One may argue forever
about the suitability and practicality of a particular means, but, finally, only an example, a test-case
is truly persuasive and convincing. In keeping with
an old adage of scholastic philosophy, a esse ad
posse valet illatio; conversely, a posse ad esse non

valet illatio. To render the adage somewhat loosely,
an argument is valid it if proceeds from what is the
case to what could be the case. But it is not valid
to argue from what is possible to what actually is.
And that is exactly what Gandhi meant and did for
King. He was the example, the test-case, the empirical proof of a method which, in King's case, was also
a confirmation of a faith.(84) King did not, and did
not need to, know very much about the complexities of
Gandhi's thought or the intricate discipline of his
life. The importance of Gandhi to King was simply as
a reality; he was the missing fact which, when
finally discovered and appreciated, solved the
mystery. The solution awaited testing and depth and
confirmation. But it was in existence in King's mind
and heart. Gandhi has proved the method worked. In
this sense Dr. Barbour may be quite correct in his
estimation that all King had to do in Montgomery was
to open his desk and roll out the blueprints. For,
as the facts indicate, he actually, if unconsciously,
did something very like that.

It will be worthwhile here to look carefully at
both some similarities and differences between King
and Gandhi in order to understand King's version of
militant nonviolence. A great deal of misunderstanding has resulted from easy comparisons of the two
men, or from regarding King as a disciple of Gandhi.
While for both men a deep belief in a living, loving
God was central, King was not a disciple of Gandhi.
He was a disciple of Jesus Christ, while Gandhi was
not. King admired Gandhi and was impressed by him in
the same way that Gandhi admired and was impressed by
the Jesus of the New Testament without becoming a
believing Christian. Both men were religiously and
practically oriented with few speculative or theoretical interests. Their orientations were highly
moral, and both men sought God and human perfection
through action aimed at improving the social condition of man.(85) In this sense they were kindred
spirits, but King did not learn any of this from
Gandhi, nor were his mind and heart formed by the
disciplines developed by Gandhi.(86).

Gandhi was a religious seeker in a sense that
King was not, and his interests and experiments were
far more extensive and thorough than anything King
ever imagined. The streak of pragmatism in King
which some authors attribute to the influence of
Niebuhr(87) is more simply due to King's American,

Christian background as opposed to the Hindu background of Gandhi. Gandhi was a complex man with a deep sense of his own importance as a mahatma; he was paternalistic and elitist.(88) King, on the other hand, was a simple man, dazzled and often dazed by his prominence; and he was a thorough-going democrat.(89) Gandhi's doctrine and practice of nonviolence was a slowly developing thing, a many-faceted discipline derived from his own experience and his experiments with life.(90) He was constantly working out on paper and in his life the implications of his ideas, relating the results of his, at times bizarre, experiments to his over-all quest for truth, and then moving on to new areas of experiment. Gandhi's words rarely ran ahead of his experience and to that extent he was not a believer in the way that King was.

Martin Luther King, Jr., on the other hand, was not an experimenter with life and his words almost always outstripped his experience. He was a believer and he proclaimed a faith, a faith so real and obvious to him that he scarcely knew that it was a faith. It had none of the complexity of Gandhi's doctrine, nor did it undergo any notable development in the twelve years he was given to preach it. Mrs. June J. Yungblut and her husband, members of the Society of Friends, were knowledgeable Gandhites and associates of King. They worked at Quaker House in Atlanta from 1959 on and knew King personally. In a short appreciation of King written after his death, Mrs. Yungblut reported that King had been deeply influenced by Gandhi's work and witness to the truth of nonviolence, and that he had imbibed this influence from Dr. Allen Knight Chalmers at Boston University. What impressed and surprised her about King was the immediateness of his conviction. She writes: "Totally dedicated to nonviolence, his articulation of his faith sprang full blown, the faith of the once-born man."(91) Her reference to his faith springing full blown points to the first speech King delivered as head of the newly formed Montgomery Improvement Association, a speech which King has told us he had about fifteen minutes to prepare.(92)

Mrs. Yungblut was quite correct. In the most fundamental sense King's first speech was his only speech. It contained his message, the only message he ever delivered, in as much fullness of content as he would ever achieve. The speeches and sermons and books that followed in the years to come grew more sophisticated, more complex. King was forced to propose specific social programs and concrete political actions in order to flesh out the skeleton of his dream. The speeches picked up new quotations, employed new figures of speech and new images, and added historical illusions and a dash of statistics. But in reading King's speeches one is most struck with their similarity, their repetitiveness of image and language and illustrations as well as content. One encounters here not the ranging mind of the intellectual examining new ideas and unfolding their richness and implications, but the heart of the preacher proclaiming the one saving faith, exhorting his hearers to believe and obey, directing their spiritual energies toward the realization of the one truth.

In time, undoubtedly Gandhian influences took on a greater importance for King, and for the movement as a whole. The philosophy of nonviolence had to be further articulated and explained, disciples had to be developed, training sessions organized and conducted, leaders prepared. For all of this work Gandhi's language and practices proved useful. Much had already been adopted and adapted to the American scene by groups like CORE, FOR, and the Society of Friends, and members of these groups were quick to descend upon Montgomery with offers of assistance and practical suggestions.(93) But most of this work was left to other hands than King's.(94) Even the articulation of the elements central to the philosophy of nonviolence which appeared in King's Stride Toward Freedom owed a good deal to Bayard Rustin.(95)

As King himself felt the increasing weight that his leadership role imposed upon him, he also discovered certain specific claims upon his own personal life that were roughly similar to Gandhi's experience, most notably the claims for detachment from family and material goods.(96) But these claims never took on the importance in King's mind and practice that they occupied in Gandhi.(97) To the end, therefore, Gandhi remained for King a source of inspiration and a large-scale model and test-case that proved the truth of what he believed and proclaimed. Once again there was far more a kinship of attitude and aspiration between the two men than anything else.

The fourth great influence that shaped King's mind and heart was a largely unspoken one in his own writings, but was undoubtedly, I believe, the most fundamental and important one. It was also the influence which sheds the most light upon his own commitment to nonviolence as well as upon what is at stake in the whole issue of violence-nonviolence. Since King's death it has been increasingly recognized by black authors and has been taken as the very touchstone of their theology, history, and social practice. The documentation for such a claim seems to me too important to be relegated to a foot note and I invite the reader to consider the following views. Among theologians James Cone has posed the issue most sharply. "My identity with <u>Blackness</u>, and what it means for millions living in a white world, controls the investigation. It is impossible for me to surrender this basic reality for a 'higher, more universal' reality."(98) Among historians Vincent Harding has put the issue clearly. "Black History is the constant demand that the cancerous state of American be seen and known. Sometimes it hopes, as Martin King used to hope, to expose the sore and thus move to its healing."(99) The well-known book, <u>Black Power</u>, spoke about social practice. "It is a call for black people in this country to unite, to recognize their heritage to build a sense of community. It is a call for black people to begin to define their own goals, to lead their own organizations and to support those organizations."(100)

The influence I refer to is King's personal experience which may be simply stated as the experience of living as a Black man in the United States of America in the middle of the twentieth century. Once again it is not the point here to treat this experience in all its complexity or in exhaustive detail. The literature on it grows increasingly voluminous and it may be some time yet before a complete and balanced picture will emerge.(101) Nor does the present writer have any personal wisdom to share about it. Rather it will suffice to identify the salient points in the experience as they touched King and his commitment to militant nonviolence.

These salient points in the black experience were four, though, of course, they were completely inter-related in King's experience. There was, first, the experience of being a member of a distinct and visible minority with no credible chance of becoming a member of the majority. This was true not only in terms of numbers, but also as regards wealth, position, skills, status and so on.(102) Second, there was the experience of being placed in that minority by an unchangeable factor of one's own person, the color of one's skin, about which it is impossible to do anything. This, of course, is an experience of irrationality, of being assigned a place in a free association on the basis of a natural factor. Third, there was the common experience of evil, of being discriminated against, of constantly and arbitrarily being at the mercy and whim of white people. However varied the concrete forms of this experience may have been, however mildly or cruelly one had suffered because of it, to be black in King's America was to know it, and not merely to know about it, but to know it in one's flesh and inmost being. For one black person to look upon another was to know that he or she was beholding a fellow sufferer, no matter what one's class or station in life. It mattered not at all how this experience was articulated nor on whom the blame for it was placed, nor the solution for it that may have been proposed. The experience was common and known to be so. It mattered not at all that the subtle and hidden indignities of the North were harder to understand than the more overt insults of the South. To be black in America was to be completely vulnerable and, indeed, already wounded.(103)

Fourth, and I would suggest most important, there was the experience of a common hope - a hope that one day things would be different. This is not to say that there have not been some black Americans who embraced the status quo because they had found a place in the political or economic or even criminal establishments which afforded them personally a measure of satisfaction, security and welfare. Nor is it to suggest that there were not many black Americans who had given up any practical hope of change and who looked upon every new movement of reform with a skepticism and even a fear that it would only make things worse. It is to suggest, however, that the hope was somewhere in some form in every black person's heart, and that no more incredible question to any black person could have come from white lips than the question: "What more do you people want now?"

162

Living the black experience in American provoked
many different responses from the individuals who
endured it, as any common experience always does. It
evoked bitterness and compassion, apathy and heroic
activity, broken lives and genius, illiteracy and
artistic brilliance, hatred and love. The various
psychological, social, economic and religious factors
that would account for any one particular success or
failure are too numerous for discussion here.(104)
The point rather is that the black experience became,
because it was made to become, the quintessential
factor of every black person's life, a factor that
had to be dealt with in some way, and thus a factor
that became the touchstone for the success or failure
of the individual's life as a human being.(105)

To arrive at this level of personal experience
where one's own humanity is at stake - not merely
physical survival, but the human quality of a life -
is essential in order to understand the choice posed
by nonviolence. At any other level of experience
nonviolence makes little more than occasional tactical sense. If considerations of violence and
nonviolence remain only at a superficial utilitarian
level, if the discussion of nonviolence is limited to
pragmatic questions about means to an end, the
central point at issue for King is missed. The chief
question was what had to be done to make a success of
my humanity, of my manhood or womanhood under the
specific conditions of my particular place in history. There was, in this concern, to be no forfeit
of the individual to society, nor any rebellious
individual set over against society. Rather the
point was to find a happy combination of individual
and common destiny, to join in harmonious unity
self-fulfillment and social service, to combine a
vision of peace with practical steps toward the
realization of the vision.(106)

Martin Luther King was no different in this
regard than any other black American. The eloquence
and the passion with which he described something of
this experience in his famous Letter From Birmingham
Jail(107) testify to this fact. It was the way King
responded to the four factors of this experience,
however, which indicate his genius and creativeness.
For quite literally these factors set the agenda of
his life, and because he responded altogether truth-
fully and openly to the concrete reality that beck-
oned him and surrounded him, his own personal

163

response has a universal and profoundly human significance.(108)

In the first place King did not deny or hide from the experience he was enduring. He accepted and acknowledged the fact of his blackness. He did not hate himself or his black brothers or his white brothers for it.(109) It was an irradicable part of who he was and who they were and he affirmed it gladly. Black is beautiful was not a slogan of King's making, but it was altogether in keeping with his own self-acceptance and his love for his people. King was also able to accept the history of his people on American shores and found no need to create a mythology of black achievements, like the Black Muslims,(110) so as to take pride in the contributions of black people in the creation of the American civilization. The story of the black involvement in America is as proud a story as any people can tell. It is also a story, like the story of any people, full of failure, disappointment, slavery and fear of freedom. King was not afraid of or ashamed of the truth in it.(111)

Secondly, the common experience of pain and evil was not one he would attempt either to flee or ignore. It was something that had to be dealt with directly, and while he had great understanding and compassion for those who sought refuge from it in drink or drugs or other kinds of fantasy, ideology and myth, he saw quite clearly that such escapes brought only personal destruction and no social improvement. It was not King's way to theorize about the black condition, but the present interpretation of some black theologians that marks the black American as the suffering and chosen people of God(112) would not have been alien to his perspective. He had accepted the mission implied in that condition long before the theologians started to unfold it as an idea.

Thirdly, King recognized the minority situation he faced and let it play an important part in his thinking and acting. His life and the life of his people had to be played out in the context of whom and what they were. Not for him was the flight back to Africa, nor the hopeless counsel of despairing revolutionaries for armed assault.(113) He accepted the minority situation of America's black population as charting their God-given mission on earth. One did not have to have Messianic delusions to perceive the salvific role that the American black had been given in the life of the American nation. In time King came to perceive that this role had a scope and a significance that ran far beyond American shores, but the place and the time for beginning was here and now. (114)

Fourthly, there was the matter of common hope. Only lately are some white Americans coming to know of the persistence and depth of this hope in the history of black Americans. The history of black thought and religion is, indeed, the story of the articulation of strategic possibilities for realizing this hope. Students of black religion and black preaching have demonstrated how deeply this hope took root in and gave content to the concepts of Christian faith that were embodied in hymns and spirituals and sermons. (115) If for a time the peace and joy and freedom of the gospel promise had only a psychological and other-worldly realization, still the social content of the promise was never completely lost to view. The privatization of salvation and the extreme individualism of the Christian ethic that was set forth in so much of Southern Christianity was never wholly embodied in black Christianity. (116) If many of the outer forms of expression and content were identical in black and white churches, the inner content of the black man's hope remained alive, though hidden from white eyes and, doubtless, from some black ones. (117)

This common hope was for King both a reality to which he could appeal and a task to be undertaken. The hope, or better, the persistence of the hope was rooted in the promise and power of God, and so it was more than wishful thinking or impossible aspiration. It led him to have a dream, but the dream did not serve as an ideal or an escape for him, but as God's will which claimed his life and energies. The hope was also a task, something to be realized in practice, and so it required a method, a means by which the hope might be realized, but which must equally be in accord with God's will. This, no ideology could do, no elevation of God's promise over God's commandment, no justification of the means by the end. For King, God was as much to be trusted and obeyed in the choice of the means as he was for the achievement of the end. Since it is God, in Christian understanding, who achieves peace and creates community, the goal of human activity is not altogether dependent on human means, nor is its realization entirely a human responsibility.(118)

That a commitment of this kind might require heroism on occasion is indubitably true. But King took his God seriously and saw no reason why God could not and would not ask ordinary people to do something out of the ordinary. Karl Rahner has expressed this possibility for any one who takes moral goodness seriously in a way quite consistent with King's personal response to his experience. I quote him at length as he asks whether it is true that:

> the world stands under the <u>sign of the cross</u> to which God himself has been nailed? That it follows logically that God's commandment may demand even the death of a person; that there is no bitterness, no tragedy, no despair in the world which would be to high a price for God's eternal promise; that one may do no evil in order to reach the good; that it is an error and a heresy of "welfare ethics" to think that the moral good cannot put man in a tragedy which offers no outcome within the limits of this world; that, on the contrary, the Christian must expect, as almost a matter of course, that his Christian existence will bring him sooner or later into a situation in which he must give up everything so as not to lose his soul and that it is not up to man always to keep out of a "heroic" situation..."(119)

At the end of the narration of his personal pilgrimage to nonviolence King offered six principles, or more accurately six points, which he considered essential elements of the "philosophy of nonviolence."(120) As a way of summarizing the ideas discussed to this point and of focusing on the key aspects of nonviolence, a discussion of these six points is in order. Yet the concrete testing of King as a man and of his doctrine as a viable way of life began in Montgomery, Alabama in December of 1955 and ended in Memphis, Tennessee in April of 1968. The concrete application of his faith to practical situations raised many questions that could not be foreseen and resolved many ambiguities that could not

166

be clarified other than through experience. Among these questions and ambiguities four seem to be deserving of special attention in order to assess the worth and the validity of militant nonviolence from an ethical and theological standpoint. In order to clarify these questions in a concrete way, we will attempt to examine them as they are raised in the actual setting of one or another of King's protest movements. The following chapter, therefore, will discuss the six basic points of King's philosophy of nonviolence. Chapter six will deal with the question of means and ends in militant nonviolence and the implications of King's position as they appear in the Montgomery boycott. Chapter seven will raise the question of civil disobedience to law as that is manifested in the campaigns at Birmingham and Selma. This issue will also involve a consideration of the relationship between power and love, and moral persuasion and coercion. Chapter eight will consider the emphasis King put upon self-suffering, particularly as that is seen in King's life from his efforts in Chicago, his opposition to the war in Vietnam, and his death in Memphis. Finally, chapter nine will consider King's dream of the beloved community, and accordingly the relationship between the church and society, what exactly human freedom means in his vision, and will attempt a final assessment of the man and his teaching.

1. Lomax, <u>To Kill A Black Man</u>, pp. 44-45.

2. King, <u>Stride Toward Freedom</u>, pp. 97-98.

3. I agree with Lomax, at least about the symbolic if not psychological importance of the event. In the entire <u>BU Coll.</u> I could find no reference to it, no comment about it, beyond what was related in <u>Stride Toward Freedom</u>.

4. <u>Ibid.</u>, pp. 97-98.

5. Lomax, <u>To Kill A Black Man</u>, p. 45.

6. The notion of "practical heresy" is one for which I am indebted to Dr. Frederick Herzog of Duke University. It is an idea he developed at some length in his classes in the graduate department of Religion. See also Richard McBrien, <u>Do We Need the Church?</u> (New York: Harper and Row, 1969), p. 224; Karl Rahner, "What is Heresy"," <u>Theological Investigations V</u> (Baltimore: Helicon Press, 1966), pp. 468-512; "The Christian attitude towards heresy...is sustained by the basic conviction that truth as such is significant for salvation and...by the conviction that the discovery of the truth or the failure to find it has a fundamental moral quality...", p. 475.

7. Cf. <u>supra</u>, p. 83.

8. King, <u>Stride Toward Freedom</u>, 98; this conviction came to be shared by the bishops of the Roman Catholic Church as expressed in the Synod of Bishops Second General Assembly: "Action on behalf of justice and participation in the transformation of the world fully appear to us as a constitutive dimension of the preaching of the Gospel...." Cited from "Justice in the World," <u>The Gospel of Peace and Justice</u>, ed. Joseph Gremillion (Maryknoll, NY: Orbis Books, 1976), p. 514.

9. Gal. 2:1-5:12.

10. Avery Dulles, S. J., <u>Models of the Church</u> (Garden City, NY: Doubleday and Company, Inc., 1974).

11. King, <u>Stride Toward Freedom</u>, p. 73; Walter Rauschenbusch, <u>Christianity and the Social Crisis</u> (New York: The Macmillan Company, 1912), pp. 203-209; <u>A Theology for the Social Gospel</u> (Nashville, New York: Abingdon Press, n.d.), p. 95.

12. Patrick Kerans, <u>Sinful Social Structures</u> (New York, Paramus, Toronto: Paulist Press, 1974); <u>Soundings: A Task Force on Social Consciousness and Ignatian Spirituality</u> (Washington, D.C.: Center of Concern, 1974).

13. King, <u>Stride Toward Freedom</u>, p. 73; Rauschenbusch, <u>Christianity and the Social Crisis</u>, p. 421, "the hope surges up that perhaps the long and slow climb may be ending."

14. King, <u>Stride Toward Freedom</u>, p. 73; Rauschenbusch, <u>A Theology for the Social Gospel</u>, pp. 61-68 for an amazingly optimistic view of sin.

15. <u>Ibid.</u>, p. 43.

16. King, <u>Stride Toward Freedom</u>, p. 161; "Accord among the great majority of passengers is evidence of the basic good will of man for man and a portent of peace in the desegregated society to come."

17. By way of contrast, King, <u>The Trumpet of Conscience</u>, pp. 3-17; "Today when progress has abruptly stalled and hope withers under bitter backlashing...," p. 4.

18. For some examples see Floyd McKissick <u>Three-Fifths of a Man</u> (London: The Macmillan Company, 1969), p. 133; James Farmer, <u>Freedom- When?</u> (New York: Random Houses, 1963), p. 79; Carmichael and Hamilton, <u>Black Power</u>, p. 76; Jones, <u>Home: Social Essays</u>, pp. 200-205.

19. A good example of King's tendency to do this is "Paul's Letter to American Christians," <u>Strength to Love</u>, pp. 156-164, especially p. 158;

Rauschenbusch, <u>A Gospel for the Social Awakening</u>
(New York: Association Press, 1950), pp 43-52.

20. King, <u>Stride Toward Freedom</u>, p. 73.

21. Whether it was Rauschenbusch's intention to do
    so and whether it is a fair representation of
    his overall position is another matter, but his
    language leaned that way. See Walter Rauschen-
    busch, <u>Christianizing the Social Order</u> (New
    York: The Macmillan Company, 1912); some
    examples will be in order: "large domains of
    our social life have come under the sway of
    Christ's law in their spirit and their fundamen-
    tal structure, and these are by common consent
    the source of our happiness and the object of
    our pride....," p. 123; "The largest and hardest
    part of the work of Christianizing the social
    order has been done.", p. 124; examples he gave
    were the family and the Church, p. 139; educa-
    tion, p. 142; political life, p. 147; "In spite
    of all failures we can assert that our political
    communities are constitutionally on a Christian
    footing.", p. 153. King settled for the Consti-
    tution of the United States as the only "Chris-
    tian Structure" in the nation.

22. A good example is the annual "Presidential
    Address" given by King at the First Annual
    Institute on Nonviolence and Social Change on
    Dec. 3, 1956; <u>BU Coll.</u>, X (29).

23. <u>BU Coll.</u>, VII (39); the letter was dated
    9/17/61, and was addressed to a Mr. M. Bernard
    Resnikoff. "When I referred to America becoming
    a Christian nation, I was not referring to
    Christianity as an organized institutional
    religion. I was referring more to the prin-
    ciples of Christ, which I think are sound and
    valid for any nation and civilization...So let
    me assure you that when I speak of America
    rising to the heights of noble ethical and moral
    principles...."

24. H. Richard Niebuhr, <u>The Kingdom of God in
    America</u>(Chicago, New York: Willett, Clark &
    Company, 1937), pp. 79-81, 174ff.

25. <u>BU Coll.</u>, XIV (41); "I am convinced that capi-
    talism has seen its best days...not only in

America, but in the entire world. It is a well known fact that no social institution can survive when it has outlived its usefullness [sic]. This capitalism has done. It has failed to meet the needs of the masses."

26. Compare Rauschenbusch, <u>Christianity and the Social Crisis</u>, pp. 369-411 and King, <u>Where Do We Go From Here: Chaos or Community</u> (Toronto, New York, London: Bantam Books, 1968), pp. 164-194.

27. Jean-Marie Paupert, <u>The Politics of the Gospel</u>, trans. Gregor Roy (New York, Chicago, San Francisco: Holt, Rinehart and Winston, 1969), esp. pp. 136-154 makes this case but on grounds that I find somewhat dubious, evangelical indifference to worldly authority. The case is more clearly and adequately made for the economic order by Pope John Paul II in his encyclical <u>Laborem Exercens</u> (On Human Work), cited here from the <u>Catholic Free Press</u> 31, 38 (September 18, 1981), no. 7 & 8, p. A3.

28. <u>Laborem Exercens</u>, no. 14; See also Jacob Viner, <u>Religious Thought and Economic Society</u>, eds. Jacques Melitz and Donald Winch (Durham, NC: Duke University Press, 1978), pp. 9-150; Alexander Gray, <u>The Socialist Tradition: Moses to Lenin</u> (New York, Evanston, London: Harper & Row, 1968), pp. 42-60.

29. Hannah Arendt, <u>On Revolution</u> (New York: The Viking Press, 1965), pp. 53-61, 219-221. The Russian relationship to Poland in 1981 is a prime illustration.

30. Rauschenbusch, <u>A Theology for the Social Gospel</u>, p. 119.

31. King, <u>Strength To Love</u>, p. 161.

32. <u>Ibid</u>., p. 57.

33. Dulles, pp. 83-96.

34. King, <u>Strength To Love</u>, p. 158; Rauschenbusch, <u>A Theology for the Social Gospel</u>, pp. 73-76.

35. <u>Ibid</u>., p. 40.

171

36. _Ibid._, p. 42.

37. Lois Diane Wasserman, _Martin Luther King, Jr.:_
    The Molding of Nonviolence as a Philosophy and
    Strategy 1955-1963 (Unpublished Doctoral Disser-
    tation: Boston University, 1972), pp. 13-30.

38. Smith and Zepp, pp. 71-97.

39. _BU Coll._, I (7); XIV (55); XIV (58); XIV (7); IV
    (10A); XIV (70) provide confirmation for this
    claim.

40. _BU Coll._, XIV (7).

41. King, _Stride Toward Freedom_, p. 79.

42. _BU COll._, IV (10A).

43. King, _Stride Toward Freedom_, pp. 80-81; Reinhold
    Niebuhr, _Does Civilization Need Religion?   A_
    Study in the Social Resources and Limitations of
    Religion in Modern Life (New York: The Mac-
    millan Company, 1928), pp. 9-10, 31.

44. Reinhold Niebuhr, _Moral Man and Immoral Society_
    (New York, London: Charles Scribner's Sons,
    1932).

45. _Ibid._, pp. 252-256.

46. Martin Luther King, Jr., _Why We Can't Wait_ (New
    York: The New American Library, 1964), p. 37.

47. King, _Stride Toward Freedom_, pp. 80-81; Reinhold
    Niebuhr, _The Nature and Destiny of Man_, 2 vols.
    (New York: Charles Scribner's Sons, 1941,
    1964), I, pp. 178-240 for Niebuhr's doctrine of
    the human being as sinner.

48. King, _Stride Toward Freedom_, p. 80.

49. Niebuhr, _Moral Man and Immoral Society_, pp. 241-
    252.

50. _Ibid._, pp. 171-175.

51. King, "Nonviolence and Social Change," _The_
    Trumpet of Conscience, pp. 51-64.

52. A good example of the traditional pacifist position is Robert Barclay, Barclay's Apology in Modern English, ed. Dean Freiday (no publishing data, 1967), p. 435.

53. Niebuhr made this point in Moral Man and Immoral Society, p. 175.

54. Niebuhr, The Nature and Destiny of Man, II, pp. 184-212.

55. See Chapter II, pp. 84-87.

56. King, Where Do We Go From Here, p. 73; "If every Negro in the United States turns to violence, I will choose to be that one lone voice preaching that this is the wrong way."

57. Reinhold Niebuhr, An Interpretation of Christian Ethics (New York and London: Harper & Brothers Publishers, 1935), pp. 223-237; "A Note on Pluralism," Religion in America, ed. John Cogley (Cleveland and New York: the World Publishing Company, 1958), pp. 42-50.

58. King Stride Toward Freedom, p. 80.

59. Niebuhr, An Interpretation of Christian Ethics, pp. 184-198; See also Dennis P. McCann, Christian Realism and Liberation theology Maryknoll, NY: Charles Scribner & Sons, 1944), p. xi.

61. Herbert Marcuse, Eros and Civilization (New York: Vintage Books, 1955).

62. Ibid., p. 215.

63. Ibid., p. 216.

64. Compare Niebuhr's treatment of the question of violence and revolution in Moral Man and Immoral Society, pp. 169-198 with Marcuse's treatment of the same question in Herbert Marcuse, "Ethics and Revolution," Ethics and Society, ed. Richard T. DeGeorge (Garden City, NY: Doubleday & Company, Inc., 1966), pp. 133-147.

65. King, Strength To Love, pp. 87-89.

173

66. King, *Stride Toward Freedom*, p. 82; *BU Coll.*, XIV (55), (58).

67. This difference between Niebuhr and King is, of course, the fundamental point at issue in almost all philosophical, theological, and political controversies about what human beings can and should do. To side with either Niebuhr or King, however, is not yet to settle the issue of violence.

68. John C. Bennett, "Reinhold Niebuhr's Social Ethics," *Reinhold Niebuhr: His Religious, Social and Political Thought*, eds. Charles W. Kegley and Robert W. Bretall (New York: The Macmillan Company, 1961), pp. 74-77; see also Niebuhr's reply in *Ibid.*, pp. 433-434.

69. King's caution was a trait that brought him into conflict with his younger and more adventuresome supporters. This difference seems to be more one of temperament and experience than of ideology as Lewis has suggested. Lewis, pp. 277-287.

70. Coretta Scott King, *My Life*, p. 55.

71. Cf. supra, Chapter I, p. 47.

72. King, *Stride Toward Freedom*, p. 82.

73. This shift in theological emphasis from past to present and future, from doctrinal orthodoxy to ortho-praxis, is at the heart of the various modes of liberation and political theologies and finds its basic mandate in the words of the Second Vatican Council: "At all times the Church carries the responsibility of reading the signs of the times and of interpreting them in the light of the Gospel, if it is to carry out its task." "Pastoral Constitution on the Church in the Modern World," Austin Flannery, O.P. (ed.) *Vatican Council II* (Collegeville, Minnesota: The Liturgical Press, 1975), 4, p. 905. The importance of this task for ethical reflection is explored in Franz Böckle (ed.), *Understanding the Signs of the Times, Concilium*, 25 (New York, Glen Rock, N.J.: Paulist Press, 1967).

74. King, <u>Stride Toward Freedom</u>, p. 83.

75. It is interesting that most theologians who advocate a specifically unique content for Christian ethics also adopt some form of nonviolence as the dominant aspect of that unique content. For example, Yoder, <u>The Politics of Jesus</u>, Ellul, <u>Violence</u>; for a theoretical discussion of the issue, Charles E. Curran and Richard A. McCormick (eds.), <u>Readings in Moral Theology No. 2: The Distinctiveness of Christian Ethics</u> (New Jersey: Paulist Press, 1980).

76. See note 40 in this chapter.

77. <u>BU Coll.</u>, XIV (30); it may or may not be relevant to the point being made here about the nature of Gandhi's influence on King that Gandhi's name was spelled incorrectly in King's notes.

78. <u>BU Coll.</u>, XIV (75).

79. Gandhi was an important influence on King. It is the nature of his influence that I am concerned to clarify.

80. The letter was from a Miss Juliette Morgan; it appeared in the <u>Montgomery Advertiser</u> (December 12, 1955), p. 4.

81. The two were clearly not separated in King's understanding, but it was only gradually that he came to see it would not be sufficient to attack only the segregation laws.

82. The parable of the sheep and the goats in Mt. 25:31-46 would illustrate and confirm this view.

83. The debate over method continues in black theology, not over the ultimate goal, but over intermediate goals; concretely over whether liberation must be fully achieved before reconciliation with the white oppressor is possible, or whether reconciliation must go hand in hand with liberation. The second view would be closer to King. See James H. Cone, "Epilogue: An Interpretation of the Debate Among Black

Theologians," Black Theology: A Documentary History, 1966-1979, pp. 612-614.

84. Obviously Gandhi's example proves nothing about the possibilities of nonviolent resistance in other circumstance and times than his own. That is why I have said his example was a confirmation of a faith.

85. Gandhi, An Autobiography, pp. xii-xiv, 70, 137; Ashe, pp. 86-89; Bondurant, p. 12.

86. Such disciplines were completely foreign to King.

87. Smith and Zepp, pp. 78-79.

88. Ashe, p. 217.

89. Lewis, pp. 212-214.

90. Gandhi, An Autobiography, pp. xiii-xiv.

91. June J. Yungblut, in Nonviolence After Gandhi, p. 52. It may be that King learned much about Gandhi from Dr. Chalmers while at Boston University. But the transcript of the courses he took there does not include any under that professor.

92. King, Stride Toward Freedom, p. 45.

93. BU Coll., I (38), (15), (29), VII (55), XIV (7); even with such help King's movement was not long on practical techniques. In a memo to Governor Adlai Stevenson dated 4/25/60, Harris Wofford, Jr., wrote as follows: "Several years ago I participated in a two-day institute on Non-Violence and Social Change which King arranged in Montgomery to commemorate the second anniversary of the bus boycott. The approach was primarily that of holding evangelistic meetings with long sermons on Gandhian action. King is better than this, but I gather he is still having to spin most of the education being given his followers out of his head. CORE is more workmanlike in teaching the techniques of nonviolent action." BU Coll., VII (55).

94. Glen Smiley, Bayard Rustin, and others from the Fellowship of Reconciliation, CORE, and the

Society of Friends carried a major role. <u>BU</u>
<u>Coll.</u>, VIII (22), X (58). There is also a
letter from Rustin to King commenting on his
manuscript for <u>Stride Toward Freedom</u> in which he
tells King that it gives the general impression
that everything in Montgomery depended upon him,
and that it is important to avoid such an
impression even if it were fact. The reader
might note the use of the subjunctive in the
last clause. <u>BU Coll.</u>, IV (10A).

95. <u>BU Coll.</u>, IV (10A).

96. Coretta Scott King, <u>My Life</u>, pp. 178-179.

97. Gandhi, <u>An Autobiography</u>, pp. 328-330. See also
G. N. Dhawan, <u>The Political Philosophy of
Mahatma Gandhi</u> (Bombay: The Popular Book Depot,
1946), pp. 82-84, for the great importance
Gandhi placed on voluntary poverty.

98. James H. Cone, <u>Black Theology and Black Power</u>
(New York: The Seabury Press, 1969), pp. 32-33.

99. Vincent Harding, <u>Beyond Chaos: Black History
and the Search for the New Land</u>, Black Paper
No. 2 (Institute of the Black World, August
1970), p. 20.

100. Carmichael and Hamilton, p. 44.

101. Walton, pp. 10-35 provides a brief but useful
outline of the various theories and methods
employed by black Americans in their efforts at
liberation before the time of King. August
Meier, <u>Negro Thought in America 1880-1915</u> (Ann
Arbor: University of Michigan Press, 1970)
provides a fine intellectual history for the
period he covered. Lerone Bennett, Jr.'s <u>Before
the Mayflower: A History of the Negro in
America 1619-1966</u> (Chicago: Johnson Publishing
Company, Inc., 3rd ed., 1966) is a readable and
thorough general history. The volume edited by
Wilmore and Cone covers the contemporary period
since King.

102. The point, of course, is not that a given
individual might not achieve great wealth, or
high status, but that the minority group as a
whole would not.

103. This will be recognized only as black novelists win a wider acceptance and reach a wider public.

104. A good comprehensive study of these factors in one volume, relative to the time of King, is to be found in _Daedalus_ (Fall 1965).

105. The experience can also be read rather differently and seen as a question of physical survival as, for example, Samuel F. Yette, _The Choice: The Issue of Black Survival in America_ (New York: Berkley Publishing Corporation, 1971). Even so, even if Yette's interpretation is sound, there is still the question of whether one will forfeit one's humanity in the interest of survival. The use of nuclear weapons would pose the same sort of question to people. See Francis X. Winters, "The Bow or the Cloud?: American Bishops Challenge the Arms Race," _America_ 145, 2 (July 25, 1981), pp. 26-30; National Conference of Catholic Bishops, _The Challenge of Peace: God's Promise and Our Response_, in _Origins_ 13, 1 (May 19, 1983), pp. 1-32.

106. This returns us to the distinction between conscientious and pragmatic nonviolence and emphasizes the significance of that distinction. See Introduction, pp. 2-3.

107. King, _Why We Can't Wait_, pp. 81-82.

108. I refer the reader back to the ideas of Maurice Friedman in Chapter I, pp. 53-54.

109. _BU Coll._, XIV (7); see also Coretta Scott King, _My Life_, pp. 60-61.

110. C. Eric Lincoln, _The Black Muslims in America_ (Boston: Beacon Press, 19610, pp. 67-80.

111. King, _Where Do We Go From Here_, pp. 127-129.

112. See, for example, Washington, _The Politics of God_, pp. 153-227, for a full development of the theme. Also Cone, "Epilogue," _Black Theology_, pp. 620-622.

113. King, _Where Do We Go From Here_, pp. 53-56.

114. See the testimony of Coretta Scott King, _My Life_, p. 95 and pp. 292-293.

115. Henry H. Mitchell, _Black Preaching_ (Philadelphia and New York: J. B. Lippincott Company, 1970), pp. 65-94; James H. Cone, "Black Spirituals: A Theological Interpretation," _Theology Today_ 28, 1 (April 1972), pp. 54-69, the _The Spirituals and the Blues_ (New York: Seabury Press, 1972).

116. Cone, _Black Theology and Black Power_, pp. 94-115.

117. Mitchell, pp. 42-50.

118. This paragraph unfolds what King meant when he wrote: "The end of life is not to be happy nor to achieve pleasure and avoid pain, but to do the will of God, come what may." _Strength To Love_, p. 162.

119. Karl Rahner, _Dangers dans le catholicisme d'au-jourd'hui_; cited in Louis Monden, S.J., _Sin, Liberty and Law_ (New York: Sheed and Ward, 1965), p. 117.

120. King, _Stride Toward Freedom_, pp. 83-88.

CHAPTER V

THE PRINCIPLES OF A MAN

The central symbol of the Christian faith, the cross, or more accurately, the crucified and risen Christ, which Paul recognized was a scandal to the Jews and madness to the Gentiles,(1) has generated certain attitudes and values which are considered to have placed a distinctive mark upon Christian life and practice. Virtues such as meekness, self-denial, self-sacrifice, passive non-resistance in the face of evil, forgiveness of enemies, and other-worldly hope are often regarded as representing the highest achievement of the Christian spirit. Though the Christian Church has listed among its roster of heroes and heroines a few warrior saints, the figure of the gentle St. Francis of Assisi would seem to be far more typical of its ideal for the human. At the same time the ambiguous nature of this ideal and these virtues, especially in the face of grave injustice, has raised serious questions and dilemmas among Christian people themselves. The issue under discussion in this study, violence or nonviolence, is but one such question. The perennial need to reconcile justice and love, self-assertion and self-sacrifice, freedom and authority, truth and goodness, points to the nature and source of the dilemma. How is it possible to have both justice and love, freedom and authority in our human relationships?(2)

H. Richard Niebuhr, in his classic work, Christ and Culture, has typified the possible theoretical answers to the dilemma as they have emerged historically.(3) His book remains a valuable source for understanding the nature of the problem and how the problem is affected by changing historical circumstances. But even a successful theoretical resolution of the dilemma would not indicate how the dilemma is to be resolved in practice. For there can be little doubt, I should think, that historically certain of the sayings of Jesus and the teachings of the Church have been interpreted and used in ways that fostered submissive attitudes toward and passive acceptance of tragically unjust conditions. Among the sharpest criticisms of this tendency is Karl Marx's attack on the social principles of Christianity, an attack which is worth quoting at some length.

The social principles of Christianity justified the slavery of antiquity, glorified the serfdom of the Middle Ages, and equally know, when necessary, how to defend the oppression of the proletariat...

The social principles of Christianity preach the necessity of a ruling and an oppressed class, and all they have for the latter is the pious wish the former will be charitable...

The social principles of Christianity declare all vile acts of the oppressors against the oppressed to be either the just punishment of original sin and other sins or trials that the Lord in his infinite wisdom imposes on those redeemed.

The social principles of Christianity preach cowardice, self-contempt, abasement, submission, humility, in a word all the qualities of the canaille...

The social principles of Christianity are cringing, but the proletariat is revolutionary.

So much for the social principles of Christianity.(4)

Regardless of the accuracy of Marx's criticism, it was a criticism often repeated in the nineteenth century and culminated in Nietzsche's proclamation of the death of God. More recently it has been recognized that Christian symbols and doctrines have at times been turned into an ideology designed to legitimate the oppression of blacks, women and people of low economic status. If at times the Christian gospel has had a liberating impact upon human social development, at other times it has had a regressive or conservative impact, an impact which hindered human beings from exercising their proper freedom and responsibility for human well-being.(5) The bondage may be sexual, involving affirmations of male headship and wifely submission and insisting upon only "natural" uses of one's sexuality while refusing to admit women to a full share of the authority and responsibility of ministry. The bondage may be economic, insisting on the rights of private property and family inheritance, while hallowing the virtues of poverty. The bondage may be political, insisting on certain "natural" qualifications or attributes as essential for voting and holding political office, or it may be social, defending the need for law and

182

order to keep human sinfulness under control. In
such cases Christian faith is often seen to be on the
side not of liberation but of bondage.

Nonviolence is very often taken to mean more of
the same. It is regarded as one more device to keep
people submissive, weak and orderly. It is looked
upon as a morality devised by the rulers to be
practiced by the oppressed, a code defended by the
haves to be lived by the have-nots. It is but one
more form of resignation to the thralldom of human
existence. Martin Luther King came, finally, to
recognize this dangerous interpretation and attributed it to the separation of love and power, a
separation we noted earlier. In his last book he
addressed himself to the problem.

> One of the greatest problems of history is
> that the concepts of love and power are
> usually contrasted as polar opposites.
> Love is identified with a resignation of
> power and power with a denial of love. It
> was this misinterpretation that caused
> Nietzsche...to reject the Christian concept
> of love. It was this same misinterpreta-
> tion which induced Christian theologians to
> reject Nietzsche's philosophy of the "will
> to power" in the name of the Christian idea
> of love.(6)

The first basic principle of militant nonviolence is designed to meet these kinds of objections
and criticisms. The principle is simply stated:
nonviolence is not a morality or a practice for
cowards and weaklings. Nonviolence is not chosen
because a person is afraid of violence and its
consequences. It is not chosen because one does not
wish to pay the high price violence might exact. Nor
is it chosen because one lacks the means of violence.
The choice of nonviolence, if it is to be authentic,
does not represent an "I cannot" in regard to participation in a violent struggle, and even less an "I
dare not." Rather the choice of nonviolence represents an "I can but I will not." Authentic nonviolence is understood to be the way of the strong, the
courageous, requiring every bit as much preparation,
discipline, sacrifice and courage as would be required for participation in war or revolutionary
uprisings, and then some. It understands that the
personal price one pays for the nonviolent resolution

of conflict is every bit as high as that paid in the violent elimination of conflict.(7)

Martin Luther King, following Thoreau and Gandhi, made it a cardinal point that a human being's fundamental moral obligation was to resist evil. Non-resistance to evil, or, more accurately, passive acquiescence in the face of evil,(8) was cowardice, and cowardice was looked upon as the essential perversion of the human spirit. The one merit Gandhi ever conceded to war was that it at least summoned people to courage, and defensive war was at least a form of resistance to unacceptable conditions.(9) Hence the first principle of nonviolence strongly insists that nonviolence must be militant, that it must resist evil both inwardly and outwardly, that it must embody personal strength and not be a consequence of weakness. Given the choice between non-resistance to evil and violent resistance to it, the latter choice is the morally preferable one.(10)

As a way of sharpening a moral issue, this is an intriguing claim. It certainly distances the demand for nonviolence from sentimentalized good will or psychological squeamishness. Even less does it applaud the pseudo-innocence that sees no evil or pretends that evil is not nearly as terrible as pessimists would have us believe.(11) To be nonviolent in the Kingian and Gandhian sense, requires that one could and would, for example, resort to violent means to protect an innocent life if that were the only way to resist evil.(12) The choice of nonviolence is exactly that, a choice, not as to whether or not one will resist evil, but of the way one will do so. It is a choice of a means, not of an end, except in so far as it is understood to be a method of conflict revolution which makes possible the achievement of a yet wider range of ends.(13)

Seen in this perspective, there seems to be implicit in militant nonviolence a notion of moral development. The human person proceeds from the defensive struggle with his or her own personal fears and weaknesses to active participation in resisting the forces that limit or degrade the humanity of one's self and others. The choice of violence as a means of resistance and self-affirmation must be seen to have a positive psychological and moral quality, as Rollo May has pointed out in reference to personality growth.(14) But it is not yet a complete victory over the forces of evil that assault the human person. There remains too much egocentrism, too much attachment to the security and absolute importance of the self over against others. The higher moral courage and the next stage of moral character development are found in the choice of nonviolence.(15) Consequently, as a moral imperative, nonviolence is relative to the personal development of the individual, but is also a moral demand to accept and foster such development.

King suggested that in nonviolent resistance a person's mind and emotions are active even if one's physical strength is not.(16) But that does not give a fully accurate picture of the actual practice. Nonviolence resistance involves an opposition of powers; on the one side stands the human ability to make and keep covenants, to keep promises, to stand together and act in concert. In doing so people affirm a common humanity. Against this human power stand the impersonal forces of biological and technological necessity. Bypassing any metaphysical considerations, nonviolence represents the power that unifies and binds together; it is a humanizing power that makes community possible. Violence, on the other hand, represents the force that divides and controls; it is a dehumanizing force because it reifies persons and excommunicates them from community. The power of nonviolence as the moral ability of people to make and keep promises means to put a common cause, a truth, a pledge before one's own material well-being. As Hannah Arendt has shown, it is not power and nonviolence that are opposites; power and violence are the genuine opposites.(17) As she has also shown, in any conflict between power and violence, violence will always win as along as its instruments are adequate to its purpose.(18)

As a mutual commitment of a people, the choice of nonviolence marks the stage of their life, as well as in the life of the individual, that follows upon life under the guidance and rule of an externally imposed law. Such mutual commitment exceeds the strict demands of retributive justice, goes beyond the lex talionis,(19) and makes a place for both forgiveness and freely chosen responsibility. The capacity and the willingness to deal with evil and conflict in this way indicate a distinct advance in human morality both individually and socially. It is an advance not only in the degree of courage it demands, but also in the quality of courage it represents. Since the nonviolent option finds its personal center outside the whims and demands of ego, it is much more than a stoic apathy or adamant self-reliance, such as the objective egoism of an Ayn Rand.(20) At the same time it makes an insistent demand that a people be true to themselves and to their word. In Christian religious terms it is what is properly meant by trust in God. Gandhi explained it by the imperative to follow one's own inner voice. From his perspective King suggested that until a person has found something worth dying for, he or she has not found anything worth living for.(21) Unfortunately neither man paid sufficient attention to the graced quality of such courage(22) and the consequent impossibility of ever institutionalizing nonviolence.

Like other moral virtues, however, the courage that nonviolence displays is not always easy to distinguish from the vices that are its extremes, cowardice, passive acquiescence, the desire to avoid conflict at any price on one side, stubbornness and fanaticism on the other. The scorn of many social critics for the bourgeois class and their hostility toward bourgeois morality are directed mainly toward this fear of conflict and the desire to be comfortable.(23) The inability of the bourgeois to dream great dreams and ambition noble deeds is revealed in their timidity in the face of violence and conflict, by their willingness to make unholy compromises or concede a point of principle in the face of violent threats. This cowardice also shows itself in what may be called the mercenary impulse, the impulse to hire others to fight one's own battles. This impulse has such concrete manifestations as hiring additional police to suppress domestic unrest or in spending money for a so-called all volunteer army,(24) rather than personally accepting the obligations of citizenship. While many people see such practices as sensible and less conflictual approaches to social problems, they represent what Gandhi called the nonviolence of the weak. Such nonviolence he took to be counterfeit, a cloak for passivity and cowardice, a form of apathy and indifference.(25)

Because of the possibility of confusing nonviolent resistance with cowardice or passivity in the face of evil, the other principles of militant nonviolence are needed to guard against the danger.

They also help to distinguish nonviolent courage from simple subbornness and unreasoning fanaticism.(26)

A second fundamental principle of militant nonviolence has to do with the end being sought by nonviolent means. That end is not the destruction of or victory over one's opponents, but victory over the source of conflict and, accordingly, reconciliation with one's opponents.(27) In ultimate terms the end is, in King's own language, the creation of the beloved community. In more intermediate stages it is the resolution of the present conflict or point at issue in such a way that co-operative life can be begun or resumed on a basis of mutual agreement and with an awareness of new possibilities.

Several things are worth noting in regard to this principle. First, nonviolence cannot be simply equated with the techniques of nonviolence. Boycotts, marches, sit-ins, strikes, all such activities are means which, to be rational and moral, must be appropriate to both the concrete situation and to the nonviolent vision. Gene Sharp has pointed out in The Dynamics of Nonviolent Action that such techniques may be used equally for a good cause or an evil cause. They are as readily available to people seeking to impose segregation as to people seeking to overcome segregation.(28) The difference is precisely in the end that is being sought, reconciliation with, as opposed to victory over, one's opponent, or the winning over or redemption of an enemy rather than the oppression or elimination of the enemy.

Second, it is clear that reconciliation with an enemy is not possible if the enemy is killed and is rendered highly improbable if the enemy is severely mutilated. Nor is it possible to respect the human dignity of an enemy if he or she is dominated or controlled by threats of violence. From the nonviolent perspective there is also the matter of the nonviolent resister's own self-development, of the agent's own freedom and integrity as a person. If, as King held, we develop ourselves humanly in and through our actions, then our actions are extremely important. To resort to the tactics and methods of one's opponent is already to concede the victory to the enemy and abandon the nonviolent end of reconciliation. This is clearly illustrated in one of King's favorite sayings: "Let no man pull you so low as to make you hate him."(29) The development of the human personality, growth in freedom and rationality for both the nonviolent resister and the opponent, are tied to reconciliation rather than to victory. To be sure, the freedom at stake is not initially political or economic or social freedom, but moral freedom, the freedom to be human, which is the foundation stone for the genuine use of all particular freedoms, and without which freedom becomes license.(30)

Third, given that the end is reconciliation rather than victory and that moral freedom is the necessary basis for all freedom, serious questions arise about the place of law and the enforcement of law in human society. These are questions about which King was less than clear in both theory and practice, as will be indicated in a later chapter. Here it will be sufficient to note that because reconciliation is the end freedom must be understood to be both logically and temporally prior to law and order in human life.(31) One effect of such an understanding is the radical relativization of all political, social and economic orders. Because order is the creation and servant of human freedom, as well as being its necessary safeguard, there is not and cannot be one right order, one correct and unchanging system. There is no place, then, for dogmatism or inflexibility in regard to any concrete way of ordering social existence.(32) Or to put that more positively, while compromise is not tolerable about matters of fact and principle, it is quite in order about matters of policy and program. To insist that the end of nonviolent action is reconciliation, therefore, is to take human freedom and responsibility with absolute seriousness.

A fourth point to notice about reconciliation as an end of nonviolent resistance is that the end need not be hopelessly idealistic or even a-political. It is based not on a surrender of one's own interests in favor of the interests of others, but on a common recognition of mutual interests. If this point were more clearly understood, the political relevance of nonviolent resistance and tactics required for its exercise would also appear in a clearer light. Perhaps the sharpest difference between exponents of nonviolence and violence is to be found here. Exponents of violence generally do not recognize or believe that mutual interests do in fact exist between enemies. Such mutual interest must be created by the use or threat of violence. Nonviolent resisters, on the other hand, are convinced that mutual interests do exist and need only to be brought to light. They are willing to pay a high price to effect this recognition. What often hurts or renders ineffective nonviolent protests is the lack of clarity on what specific interests are being appealed to or a utopian desire to realize a complete harmony of all interests at once.

The third principle of militant nonviolence is the insistence that the human struggle for justice and right is a struggle against the impersonal forces of evil and not against other human beings. In the language of St. Paul, our struggle is not with flesh and blood but with the principalities and powers.(33) This claim is clearly a corollary of the second principle and once again suggests a reason for repudiating violence. In the simplest terms, it is possible to kill a liar by violent means but it is not possible to so kill a lie. It is possible to imprison the thief, but it is not possible to lock up injustice. On a more complicated level, one can speak about structures of injustice and systems of oppression. It is these systems and structures of evil that human beings are to struggle against, not the people who shape and are shaped by them.

The distinction between the impersonal forces of evil and the persons who do evil is first of all an analytic one. As such it is both possible and clear, as well as being analytically useful. As a directive for attitudes it is also both clear and practical, as in the ancient Christian injunction to hate the sin and love the sinner. It is possible, albeit at times difficult, to hate murder and love the murderer, to hate alcoholism and love the alcoholic. But whether the distinction is also real and useful when applied to the domain of action is debatable since evil, like good, is always incarnate. Lies do not exist except as people tell them, write them, think them. Injustice does not exist except as people do deeds that deny to others what is their due.(34) To act against the lie or the injustice is also to act against the person who embodies the lie or the injustice. Even institutions or structures or systems, while undoubtedly having a kind of objectivity and independence which makes them susceptible to objective analysis, are altogether dependent upon the people who give them reality. The fact that they are not dependent for their existence and function upon this or that particular person is what makes traditional arguments about the moral legitimacy of tyrannicide inapplicable today to questions of liberation, and not the principle that our struggle is against impersonal forces of evil. For example, the immediate reason why the assassination of Lyndon Johnson would not have been an appropriate way to resist the Vietnam war, on the assumption that that war was morally evil, is that it would not have been an effective means to the end. It is only where the leadership of a movement or a group is wholly charismatic--King himself is illustrative of this--that the death of a person may also mean the death of impersonal forces.

While the third principle, then, is not very helpful in clarifying the domain of practical action, it can be quite helpful in shaping practical attitudes which have serious implications for action. The attitude immediately in question in the struggle to resist and eliminate social evil may be described as one that seeks to help rather than hurt, or as an attitude to which revenge is foreign and forgiveness commonplace. It is an attitude whose primary concern is not to destroy or punish the oppressor but to liberate and make whole the oppressed. It is an attitude easily counterfeited and hard to come by. Two examples will serve to clarify what is at stake here.

The first is the example of Dietrich Bonhoeffer and the men around him who plotted the assassination of Hitler. Their main concern was never with the destruction of Hitler, but rather with the restoration of sanity, justice and peace to Germany and the world. So central and clear was this concern that they refused any attempt at the violent act until it was clear that the positive, constructive goal was within reach.(35) The second illustration is drawn from the checkered history of revolutions which in so many cases have a way of devouring their own offspring.(36) Whenever the revolutionary concern has been focused on revenge, on throwing over the hated oppressor, be the oppressor or tyrant, a class, another nation, on destroying to avenge past wrongs, the liberation process has proved abortive. Where the concern has been positive, emphasizing the founding of freedom or the reconstruction of a new social order, the liberation process has realized at

190

least a partial fulfillment. In Christian faith the same dynamic of liberation is present. It is not enough for freedom to have one's sins forgiven, to wipe out the past, to merely destroy what has held one in bondage. A new principle of life is required, a new power to be, a function fulfilled in Christian existence by the sending of the Holy Spirit and the foundation of the Church.

This common dynamic of all human liberation does not deny that there is a time to cast down as well as a time to build up. But the third principle of nonviolence, in insisting that the human struggle for justice and freedom is not directed against other human beings, serves as a healthy pointer to the essentially constructive task required for the establishment of justice and freedom. It also serves as a strong restraint on the vengeful potentialities within all people engaged in the struggle against oppression. The principle shapes an attitude far more than it guides concrete acts, but in doing so it provides a context and a direction for specific decisions.

The fourth principle of militant nonviolence advocates a willingness to accept suffering upon oneself rather than inflict suffering on others.(37) This principle fulfills several functions. It is first of all a practical check on the fanaticism that often poses as moral courage. It is a limit upon the Holy War or Crusade mentality which is blind to its own sins and injustice.(38) As a sign and test of personal sincerity, the willingness to accept rather than inflict suffering is also a useful restraint upon self-righteousness and selfishness, if not altogether a certain one.

Secondly, this principle involves an appeal to the conscience of the opponent rather than to self-interest or personal welfare. The conviction behind this appeal is that human beings react to pain and will change their behavior to be rid of pain. This conviction is common to violence and nonviolence. Unlike violence, however, which counts upon a person's instinctive reaction to physical pain, nonviolence, by absorbing suffering on one's self, appeals to the freedom and fairness of the opponent. The nonviolent resister who suffers willingly challenges the conscience of the one inflicting the suffering;

191

he or she is invited to repent and change the hurtful behavior to avoid the moral wound.

There are several obvious difficulties with this principle. What happens if one's opponent enjoys inflicting suffering on others? There are sadistic people in the world who are only deepened in their sick tendencies by the willingness of others to suffer. Such willingness can only appear to the sadist as masochism. One cannot seriously speak of an appeal to conscience in such cases. Or again, it might be the case that the opponent does not enjoy inflicting pain, but the pain involved in changing one's attitudes and behaviors may well appear more intimidating and frightening than that involved in seeing the continued suffering of others. Indeed, it is just such a dynamic that is ostensibly operative in war, in capital punishment and other violent acts. The fears that were visible in some ethnic groups who opposed the civil rights movement, sometimes with great and surprising violence, may have been misguided and unnecessary fears, but they were nonetheless real. The possible loss of a home, a job, a cherished school or neighborhood, of traditional habits and securities, can generate powerful fears which are unlikely to be overcome simply by an appeal to conscience. On the contrary, faced with such prospects, many consciences are stimulated to rise up and proclaim an obligation to fight back in defense of what is rightly theirs. Since the point of nonviolence is to provide alternatives to violence and not to see who can endure the most suffering, appeals made to conscience through self-suffering have treacherous possibilities.

A third difficulty with the principle of self-suffering is that it assumes that there is a happy resolution to every conflict. While that may be the case in theory, it is not always clear in practice what such a resolution could be. Self-suffering in such cases invites not a change in behavior but an accumulation and intensification of guilt feelings. The principle also implies that evil is a result of ignorance or sickness, for both of which there are remedies, but not of deliberate and willfull choice.(39) The disillusionment and cynicism that can result from a naive belief that self-suffering will overcome all opposition from one's opponents are fertile grounds for the outbreak of new violence, as well as affording strong inclinations toward self-

192

righteousness and false innocence.(40) The principle
of self-suffering, therefore, needs to be treated
with great care and further discussion of it will be
deferred to a later chapter.

The fifth principle of militant nonviolence, and
the pivotal one, requires that the nonviolent resister not only renounce all physical violence but
also all internal violence of spirit.(41) Hence this
principle is directed at the attitude and the inner
spiritual state of the person engaging in nonviolent
resistance. It is at this inner level that the most
difficult struggle takes place and the question of
the human-ness of nonviolence arises. Before engaging in the temporal struggle for justice and peace,
before entering into the worldly conflict, a certain
degree of interior struggle and self-conquest is seen
to be mandatory.(42) In the most basic terms the
nonviolent resister really must love the opponent and
not just pretend to do so or give mere lip-service to
the idea.

In this context the refusal to inflict physical
harm on others and the willingness to accept self-
suffering on one's self are but the minimal signs and
necessary conditions of genuine love for one's enemy.
By themselves they are not sufficient conditions;
they are no guarantee of sincere and purified motivation. They are, however, seen as basic and necessary
dimensions of authentic love for the other. It is
for this reason that King and Gandhi concede that the
use of nonviolent techniques without a nonviolent
spirit is but another form of violence.(43) Even
such a pragmatic advocate of nonviolence as Gene
Sharp suggests that this "proper" motivation is
likely to increase the effectiveness of nonviolent
resistance,(44) an observation which surely cries out
for some explanation.

The emphasis on the interior attitude and
motivation of the nonviolent resister changes the
nature of nonviolence from being simply an alternative means to violence to being what King called a
way of life or to what I prefer to call a spirituality. It makes of nonviolence a way of living and
acting that is designed to open the human person to
the concrete substance of truth and justice in any
situation, or in specifically religious terms, it is
a way of finding God's Will for the individual in the
concrete circumstances of his of her life. King

covered this whole interior, attitudinal dimension of nonviolence by saying that the fundamental motivation that directs a person to nonviolent resistance is love or agape.(45) A more accurate way of putting the matter would be to say that the dominant, operative value in the nonviolent resister's moral horizon is agapeic love, both as the fundamental orientation of his or her total self, and as the specific value the person seeks to serve and realize in concrete actions.

The analysis of this value which King offered was one he borrowed from Paul Tillich and first used in writing his doctoral dissertation, despite the fact that he disagreed with aspects of Tillich's understanding of love.(46) He repeated the same analysis in several places,(47) usually omitting the first form of love described by Tillich, libido, which King took to mean the instinctive basis for spontaneous attraction between people. He regarded this as no more than something comparable to the attraction exercised by magnetism or gravity and so undeserving of moral attention.(48) Aside from the question of whether he misunderstood Tillich, his ignoring of libido was a mistake. Libido, no less and no more than the other forms of love, is involuntary. It cannot be willed into existence. It has the character of being a given of existence; if welcome a gift, if unwelcome a burden. Whether such attraction is present or absent is, therefore, not a matter for moral evaluation and judgment. But its presence or absence does make a difference to what kinds of moral actions can be reasonably expected of human beings and can be truthful expressions of love at any given time.

Philia, the love of friendship, which is based upon mutuality of interests and shared likings, King also regarded as of no great significance for nonviolence.(49) A closer analysis, however, might suggest that it is important for binding together in unity a group of nonviolent resisters, and for the mutual support and strength in the on-going struggle for justice that friendship provides.(50) In the long run we do not create the beloved community, nor do we even think it worth trying to create, in the midst of people we do not like. Without the love of friendship, the love of concrete, living human beings, the struggle against injustice becomes abstract, impersonal and inhuman.

Eros, the third form of love, the passionate longing to possess and be possessed by one's beloved, was also not the form of love at the heart of militant nonviolence. Consequently it, too, received little attention from King. The obvious demonic possibilities of eros which are evident in jealousy, possessiveness, chauvinism, and in the close relationship between human sexuality and violence and between patriotism and militarism, make eros a likely source of violence if uncontrolled. On the other hand, it is only human beings moved by eros who care and care passionately for their fellow human beings, who hunger and thirst after justice and are moved to engage in the struggle for what they desire. To eliminate or stifle eros in the struggle against injustice in the interests of nonviolence would be to remove the militancy and put an end to the struggle. The absence of the erotic drive for unity does not signal the presence of a disinterested, selfless and nonviolent love so much as it signals the presence of disinterest, indifference, and the deadly sin of sloth.(51) Like marriage and prayer, the struggle against injustice needs more rather than less release of the erotic drive.(52)

The form of love that King saw as central to nonviolence, and indeed to his whole world view, is agape,(53) which, therefore, needs a closer examination. The entire nonviolent position King defended depends upon the possibility and experiential reality of this form of love. It is understood to be the one force which can move the human person beyond cowardice and self-defensive violence to genuine other-caring. In itself agape is held to be the power of reconciliation which is the aim of nonviolence and in its discriminatory ability it makes real the distinction between the impersonal forces of evil and the people who do evil things. Agapeic love reverses the ordinary understanding of people who do evil as free, responsible agents deserving of punishment. Rather it recognizes the power of evil to enslave people and so can see that people who do evil acts are not themselves evil but enslaved and in need of liberation.(54) Evildoers are therefore rightly met with compassion, not with hatred and vengeance. Further, while agapeic love is not the only power that can bear suffering without collapse, - hatred also can - it alone can bear suffering without bitterness and resentment, without falling prey to the deadly sins of anger and envy. If the sixth principle of non-

195

violence, that the universe is on the side of justice,(55) is to be anything more than a pious wish,
agapeic love must be an experienced reality.

Theologically, agape is understood first to be
God's love for human beings as revealed in Jesus
Christ.(56) It is operative in human beings in so
far as God has poured out His Holy Spirit into their
hearts, enabling them to love one another as He loves
them. Agape is, therefore, a transforming, enabling
power in the life of an individual, and it is this
facet of it which meets the psychological questions
and objections about the possibility of human nature
to be nonviolent. This is not to claim that agapeic
love renders a human being perfect or elevates him or
her above nature. An important point made by Rollo
May in regard to the development of human capacities
remains true, that such development is always two-
sided.(57) As one's capacity for joy increases, so
also does the capacity for sorrow. As one's capacity
to love increases so also does one's capacity to
hate. The same can be said for the capacity to
experience pleasure and pain, to act violently or
nonviolently. This two-sided character of human
growth does not contradict anything in the nonviolent
vision. But it does suggest a reason for the ascetic
discipline of a Gandhi, as well as indicating why
nonviolent action, without the inner commitment and
careful discipline, can so easily and quickly turn
into violence.

As a transforming power in persons, agape is
said to enable human beings to love one another as
God has loved them in Christ. And so it is from the
paradigmatic story(58) of Jesus of Nazareth that the
chief characteristics of agapeic love are drawn. The
first characteristic is that agape is free, a gift,
or in theological idiom, a grace. Like the other
forms of love, agape is not a willed or self-adopted
attitude. It rather bears the character of something
that happens to a person, of something that breaks
into one's life and consciousness from the outside,
as it were, and elicits a response. That response,
effected by grace, is multi-form: gratitude, joy,
praise, freedom, but one of its aspects is love for
others, agape at work in the human person.

Borrowing from Reinhold Niebuhr, Rollo May has
warned against the danger of not recognizing the
graced quality of agapeic love:

196

love for one's enemies is a matter of grace. It is, in Reinhold Niebuhr's phrase, "a possible impossibility," never to be realized in a real sense except by an act of grace. It would require grace for me to love Hitler - a grace for which I have no inclination to apply at the present moment. When the element of grace is omitted, the commandment of loving one's enemies becomes moralistic: it is advocated as a state an individual can achieve by working on his own character, a result of moral effort. Then we have something very different: an oversimplified, hypocritical form of ethical pretense. This leads to those moral calisthenics that are based upon a blocking-off of one's awareness to reality and that prevent the actually valuable actions one could make for social betterment. The innocent person in religion, the one who lacks the "wisdom of serpents," can do considerable harm without knowing it.(59)

This graced character of agapeic love suggests some important things about militant nonviolence. It is simply not intelligible as something a person ought to do. Nonviolence is intelligible as something a person finds he or she is called to be. This again highlights the importance of paying attention to one's own personal and social experience where the vehicles or occasions of grace are to be found. For strictly speaking, one does not apply for grace; one opens one's heart and mind to what is freely offered in the interest of finding the truth of one's existence,(60) a truth the nonviolent vision understands to be found rather than created by the self.(61)

Another implication of the graced character of agapeic love for nonviolence is that it first of all calls forth an attitude or formal orientation of the self, but it does not supply the content of what one's actions should be. Even if one were to find the grace to love a Hitler, the question would still remain as to what actions would best embody and give expression to that love. That question cannot be answered by any pre-formed set of rules or laws, which is a negative way of expressing the essentially creative character of agape.(62)

197

The second characteristic of agapeic love is
that it is, as King expressed it, "purely spontaneous, unmotivated, groundless.... It is not set in
motion by any quality or function of its object."(63)
This formulation of the matter, however, can be
misleading, especially if it suggests, as it may
readily do, that agapeic love is irrational or
independent of reason.(64) In its primary meaning of
God's love for His creation, it is quite true that
agape is not set in motion by any quality or function
of creatures. God does not find something attractive
in His creation which causes or moves Him to love.
To that extent agapeic love can be described as
spontaneous, unmotivated, groundless. For God does
not love in response to the goodness of creatures.
Instead He creates that goodness by loving His
creatures into being.

But human beings do not and cannot love in this
way. We do not initiate goodness; we respond to it.
An unmotivated love, a love that is without some
ground in reality, a love that is not intent upon
some good, is simply humanly inconceivable. Human
beings always have reasons for their loves, however
bizarre they may be. By the same token to describe
agape as a disinterested love is also misleading and
opposes agape to eros in a false way. Even in His
loving creation of the universe God was not disinterested; He wanted something. Most generally He wanted
the well-being of His creation,(65) and the biblical
witness testifies that the divine wanting was passionate and powerful. The characteristic of agape
that is under discussion here, therefore, is better
described as an other-directed love. It is a love
that is called forth not by a need or a desire of the
self for the self, but by a need or a desire for the
other. Agapeic love is a love of the other in his or
her own interest, not in despite of one's own interest but in present disregard of it. More simply
agapeic love affirms and rejoices in the being of the
other.(66) Unlike God, humans do not will the other
into being and goodness, but they can accept, affirm
and rejoice in that being. The obvious problem such
love presents to human beings is the same problem
such love presents to God - the other may be indifferent to or even hostile to receiving such love.
Since force or violence are of no use in resolving
this problem, the nonviolent vision again rejects
violence, but in doing so it often ignores the
chastising quality of divine love. That is a quality

which has its familial counterpart in the parental discipline of children. What the social or political counterpart of this aspect of agapeic love might be remains a question.(67)

The third and most distinctive characteristic of agape is that it is a forgiving, redeeming love, a characteristic that is often misinterpreted to mean a sloppy sentimentalized tolerance which takes no offense. Read in this way agapeic love is stripped of its substance and strength. Dorothy Day's characterization of the forgiving, redeeming love of God as a harsh and dreadful love(68) is much closer to the reality. For the immediate implication of this love is that there are things to be forgiven and conditions from which others need to be redeemed. Agapeic love is initially and inescapably confrontational. It begins by proclaiming the sinfulness of the other and insisting upon the need for repentance. It is the intrinsic link between truth and love that demands nonviolence be militant and challenging, that insists that sin be called sin and the sinner called to account to acknowledge his or her sinfulness and to change one's ways. There is nothing soft or sentimental about such love. It is the same intrinsic link between truth and love that demands the militancy be nonviolent, that insists that forgiveness and reconciliation rather than revenge and vindication be the result of repentance.

In a religious context of the human relationship to the divine, the right and ability of God to summon human beings to repentance is not seriously problematic. But, when human beings who are themselves sinful and in need of repentance engage to exercise this function for other human beings, charges of self-righteousness, moralistic preaching, and intolerance are inevitably to be expected. Above all the authority of the prophetic voice will be silenced violently. It is this all too likely prospect that makes the final principle of nonviolence essential.

Strictly speaking, the sixth principle of militant nonviolence is not a principle at all, so much as it is a hope - that the universe is on the side of justice or that we have cosmic companionship in our struggle against injustice.(69) Is this merely a groundless hope, a product of wishful thinking, or an ideological tool to convince nonviolent resisters to accept injury and even death

without retaliation? Doubtless it can be so interpreted and has been so explained.(70) But it was
certainly not what King understood or intended. At
root this hope involves the recognition that a truly
human existence must come to grips with the facts of
human finitude, sinfulness and mortality, as well as
with one's own personal responsibility for the
authentic human quality of one's life. In the face
of these facts it becomes clear that the meaning of
an authentic human existence cannot lie in the
perfect accomplishment of human tasks, or in the
successful resolution of human conflicts, or still
less in the length of one's earthly existence.
Unless life is without any authentic human meaning,
in which case the violence-nonviolence issue is
absurd, the meaning must be elsewhere, in the quality
of one's personal effort to act humanly, to live and
to die courageously, freely and rationally.

This conception of where life's meaning is to be
found is a highly individualistic conception in that
it involves a profound awareness of personal mission
and personal accountability. At the same time it is
a social or universalistic conception in that it
involves an equally profound awareness of the claims
being human makes upon oneself. Such claims are made
not by one's own idiosyncratic needs and desires nor
by one's own family, tribe, nation or church, but by
one's humanity. That everyone is called or graced to
this depth of personal responsibility seems highly
doubtful, which again argues that the commitment to
nonviolence is a product of one's spirituality, a
personal response to the call of God's Spirit, and
not a general ethical imperative binding on human
beings in virtue simply of being human, or even in
virtue of being a Christian.

The six principles of militant nonviolence are
not without problems, as has been indicated above.
Three problem areas in particular seem especially
worthy of notice: the relationship of means and ends
in the nonviolent vision; the place, function and
authority of law in human social relationships; and
finally the meaning and purpose of suffering in human
life. It is to a more critical analysis of these
questions that we now turn.

200

NOTES: CHAPTER V

1. 1 Cor. 1:23-24.

2. Donald Evans, "Does Religious Faith Conflict
    with Moral Freedom?", Religion and Morality,
    eds. Gene Outka and John P. Reider, Jr. (Garden
    City, N.Y.: Anchor Books, 1973), pp. 348-388,
    esp. pp. 348-350, provides a good discussion of
    the general problem. The literature on the
    specific problem is too voluminous to cite here
    but some representative works are Jurgen Molt-
    mann, The Crucified God, (New York, Evanston,
    San Francisco, London: Harper & Row, 1974);
    Paul Lehmann, The Transfiguration of Politics,
    (New York, Evanston, San Francisco, London:
    Harper & Row, 1975); David Hollenbach, S.J.,
    Claims in Conflict, (New York, Ramsey, Toronto:
    Paulist Press, 1979); Richard J. Cassidy,
    Jesus, Politics, and Society, (Maryknoll, N.Y.:
    Orbis Books, 1978).

3. H. Richard Niebuhr, Christ and Culture, (New
    York: Harper & Row, 1951). Also of great
    importance are Ernst Troelstch, The Social
    Teaching of The Christian Churches, 2 vols. (New
    York, Evanston: Harper & Row, 1960); and the
    social teachings of Pope Leo XIII to be found in
    Etienne Gilson (ed), The Church Speaks to the
    Modern World, (Garden City, N.Y.: Image Books,
    1954), which gives one consistent, if outdated,
    answer to the problem.

4. Karl Marx, "The Communism of the Paper Rhein-
    ischer Beobachter," in Lewis S. Feuer (ed.),
    Marx and Engels: Basic Writings on Politics and
    Philosophy, (Garden City, N.Y.: Anchor Books,
    1959), pp. 268-269.

5. Gregory Baum, Religion and Alienation (New York,
    Paramus, Toronto: Paulist Press, 1975); Cone, A
    Black Theology of Liberation, pp. 116-120; Mary
    Daly, Beyond God the Father (Boston, Beacon
    Press, 1973), pp. 98-131; Segundo, The Libera-
    tion of Theology, pp. 97-124, are representative
    works.

6. King, Where Do We Go From Here?, p. 43.

7. This understanding is articulated clearly in Daniel Berrigan, S.J., <u>They Call Us Dead Men</u> (New York: The Macmillan Company, 1966), p. 114; <u>No Bars to Manhood</u> (Garden City, N.Y.: Doubleday & Co., 1970), pp. 57-58; and James W. Douglas, <u>The Non-Violent Cross</u> (London: The Macmillan Company, 1969), pp. 48-78.

8. Even Paul did not urge doing nothing. His injunction was to "Resist evil and conquer it with good.", Rms. 12:21.

9. <u>Gandhi on Non-Violence</u>, p. 38; "War is an unmitigated evil. But it certainly does one good thing. It drives away fear and brings bravery to the surface."

10. <u>Ibid.</u>, p. 36; "He who cannot protect himself or his nearest and dearest or their honor by non-violently facing death, may and ought to do so by violently dealing with the oppressor. He who can do neither of the two is a burden." Also Kind, <u>Stride Toward Freedom</u>, pp. 83-84.

11. May, <u>Power and Innocence</u>, pp. 199-217.

12. King, <u>Stride Toward Freedom</u>, p. 38; "This is why Gandhi often said that if cowardice is the only alternative to violence, it is better to fight. He made this statement conscious of the fact there is always another alternative...".

13. Bondurant, pp. 230-233.

14. May, <u>Power and Innocence</u>, p. 137.

15. Lawrence Kohlberg, "Stages of Moral Development as a Basis for Moral Education." C. M. Beck, B. S. Crittendon, and E. V. Sullivan (eds), <u>Moral Education: Interdisciplinary Approaches</u> (New York: Newman Press, 1971); and "Moral Development and the New Social Studies," <u>Social Education: Journal of the National Council for the Social Studies</u> (May, 1973), p. 140, for explicit reference to King.

16. King, <u>Stride Toward Freedom</u>, p. 84.

17. Arendt, <u>On Violence</u>, p. 56.

18. Ibid., pp. 53-55.

19. Dt. 19:1-21; it is worth noting that the lex talionis itself is already a curb on the use of violence; it limits it.

20. Ayn Rand, For The New Intellectuals: The Philosophy of Ayn Rand (New York: New American Library, 1961); The Virtue of Selfishness: A New Concept of Egoism (New York: New American Library, 1964); she also spelled out her brand of individualism in her novels, most notably Atlas Shrugged (New York: Random House, 1957) and The Fountainhead (Indianapolis: Bobbs-Merrill, 1968).

21. Gandhi on Non-Violence, p. 34; King, Strength To Love, pp. 95-105.

22. May, Power and Innocence, p. 256.

23. Fairlie, pp. 114-117.

24. Richard A. Gabriel, "About-Face on the Draft," America (February 9, 1980), pp. 95-97.

25. Gandhi on Non-Violence, pp. 72-75.

26. Winston Churchill had this mistaken view of Gandhi. Ashe, p. 296.

27. King, Stride Toward Freedom, p. 84.

28. Sharp, p. 633.

29. King, Stride Toward Freedom, p. 87, where he attributes the saying to Booker T. Washington.

30. Leo XIII, Libertas Praestantissimum in Gilson (ed), pp. 57-61, gives a clear explanation of the meaning of moral freedom.

31. Lehman, The Transfiguration of Politics, pp. 240-249.

32. Paupert, The Politics of the Gospel, pp. 127-135.

33. What exactly Paul meant by principalities and powers is disputed by scholars and it is not to

the point to enter the dispute here. Our concern is with what King took Paul to mean. For an analysis which reflects King's position see Patrick Kerans, Sinful Social Structures (New York: Paulist Press, 1974), pp. 57-72.

34. I can find no clear definition of justice in King's writings nor can I infer a theory of justice from them so I have limited myself to the classic definition of justice, suum cuique; see Joseph Pieper, Justice, trans Lawrence E. Lynch (New York: Pantheon Books, 1955).

35. Larry L. Rasmussen, Dietrich Bonhoeffer: Reality and Resistance (Nashville: Abingdon Press, 1972), pp. 187-196; "The goal of the conspiracy was not only the end of the war and of Nazism but the replacement of the Nazi state with a just state.", p. 175.

36. Crane Brinton, The Anatomy of Revolution, rev. ed. (New York: Vintage Books, 1960).

37. King, Stride Toward Freedom, p. 85.

38. See James P. Hanigan, "War and Peace: Christian Choices," Today's Parish (Nov/Dec 1983), pp. 21-24.

39. Gandhi on Non-Violence, p. 49; "Crime is a disease like any other malady and is a product of the prevalent social system. Therefore (in a non-violent India) all crime including murder will be treated as a disease."

40. May, Power and Innocence, pp. 205-211.

41. King, Stride Toward Freedom, p. 85.

42. Gandhi on Non-Violence, p. 44; "non-violence is impossible without self-purification."

43. This claim provides a clue to what the moral evil in violence is perceived to be - the determination to have things my own way in complete disregard of others.

44. Sharp, p. 634; he attributes this greater effectiveness to the dynamics of nonviolent action, but argues that it is only a likelihood,

which depends more on the subjective disposi-
tions of one's opponents than on anything
intrinsic to nonviolent action.

45. King, _Stride Toward Freedom_, p. 86.

46. See above, Chapter II, p. 93.

47. See Chapter II, n. 134.

48. King, _A Comparison_, p. 158.

49. King, _Stride Toward Freedom_, p. 86.

50. Parker, J. Palmer, _The Company of Strangers_ (New
York: Crossroads,   1981),   pp. 28-29   has   an
interesting   example   of   the   importance   of
friendly support in the struggle for justice.

51. Fairlie, pp. 113-130; 197-207.

52. For   an   interesting   discussion   of   the   erotic
drive and its relationship to prayer see Marilyn
May Mallory, _Christian Mysticism: Transcending
Techniques_ (Amsterdam: Van Gorcum Assen, 1977),
pp. 158-182.

53. King, _Stride Toward Freedom_, p. 88.

54. James   T.   Burtchaell,   _Philemon's Problem_ (Chicago: ACTA, 1973), pp. 67-71, 78-83, has some
excellent illustrations of this changed point of
view.

55. King, _Stride Toward Freedom_, p. 88.

56. Rudolf Schnackenburg, _The Moral Teaching of the
New Testament_ (New   York: Herder   and   Herder,
1965), pp. 90-105, 217-225, 316-329.

57. Rollo May, _Love and Will_ (New York: W. W. Norton, Inc., 1969), pp. 100-105.

58. For the notion of a paradigmatic story see John
Shea, _Stories of God_ (Chicago: The Thomas More
Press, 1978), pp. 7-10.

59. May, _Power and Innocence_, pp. 156-157.

60. Gandhi on Non-Violence, p. 25; "If love or non-violence be not the law of our being, the whole of my argument falls to pieces."

61. Stanley Hauerwas, Vision and Virtue (Notre Dame: Fides/Claretian, 1974), pp. 93-126.

62. King, Stride Toward Freedom, p. 87.

63. Ibid., p. 86.

64. This seems to me to be the fundamental mistake of all varities of situation ethics; e.g. Joseph Fletcher, Situation Ethics (Philadelphia: The Westminster Press, 1966), pp. 46-50; see Hauerwas, pp. 11-126 for a direct refutation of situation ethics on this very point.

65. I borrow this expression from James M. Gustafson, The Contributions of Theology to Medical Ethics (Milwaukee: Marquette University Theology Department, 1975), p. 17.

66. I borrow this notion from Hauerwas, pp. 187-194.

67. Traditionally one such political counterpart of the chastising quality of agapeic love was the power of the sword given to the state, a power that was both the result of and the remedy for sin.

68. See Introduction, n. 1.

69. King, Stride Toward Freedom, p. 88.

70. For example by Joseph Washington, The Politics of God, pp. 160-161.

CHAPTER VI

THE MATTER OF MEANS

The fundamental criticisms that can be directed against traditional pacifist nonviolence, and at its later-day counterpart, militant nonviolence, have not changed nor become more profound over all the years they have been voiced. But, while the basic criticisms themselves have not changed, what has altered considerably is that the interest in and arguments about pacifism and nonviolence have switched their major emphasis from war to revolution, or from self-defense to liberation. Where formerly it was a question of determining the effective and legitimate means of restraining an unjust aggressor,(1) the contemporary discussion centers more on specifying effective and legitimate means for overthrowing an unjust oppressor.(2) This change in historical concerns does not affect the formal philosophical and ethical issues involved in such discussions, but it does make the determination of the substantive general principles and their application a more subtle and difficult business. It has also called into question the relevance and meaning of some of the traditional just war principles, in much the same way that the advent of nuclear weapons has.(3) One important factor, for example, is the difference in the psychological and social condition between the defender of his or her homeland against an unjust aggressor and the oppressed victim of racism or colonialism or economic imperialism.(4) The Frenchman defending his homeland against the Panzer divisions pouring across his northern border was faced with an entirely different set of questions, resources and possibilities than the South African black man who is forced to live and work under conditions which deny his worth and dignity as a human being. In the former case the injustice is vividly clear and the use of violence has a clearly rational purpose, to restore rights by destroying those who seek to rob them. In the latter case, while the injustice may be felt vividly, the rational purpose of violence and the enemy inflicting the injustice are not at all clear. One may well wish to strike out in protest, but at whom and to what purpose remain very real questions.

These differences in the psychological and
social conditions suggest that the problem of liberation is a quite different one than the problem of
defense and offers the likelihood that different
means are required for their solution.(5) For if
different ends are in view, it would seem that
different means need to be used. What offers reasonable hope of success in one situation might be highly
inappropriate in another.(6) This variety of situation and purpose, then, highlights the two lines of
criticism traditionally directed at the nonviolent
claim.

The first, more practically oriented criticism
speaks to the question of the responsibility to use
effective means in achieving the end. It finds a
distinct lack of or even rejection of responsibility
in the absolute insistence on nonviolent means.(7)
The second, more theoretically oriented criticism
speaks to the question of the relationship of the
means to the end. It finds a theoretical confusion
to be present in the way nonviolence understands this
relationship.(8) The two lines of criticism meet in
any practical application of nonviolent teaching
since the charge of irresponsibility rests ultimately
upon the philosophical understanding of the ends as
imparting the obligatory quality to the means. The
theoretical argument, therefore, has a primacy in
logic. But it also has primacy in historical experience, a fact which is reflected in the open rejection
of all political and social responsibility by traditional pacifist sects and exponents of nonviolence.

The moral dilemma posed by the obligation to
resist evil without resorting to violent means has
long been the central problem of the pacifist position in Christian thought. A variety of ways have
been articulated to resolve the dilemma, but the
dilemma persists. The two obligations can be contradictory. It was just such a contradiction that faced
Martin Luther King, Jr. as he prepared to address his
audience at the opening rally of the Montgomery bus
boycott. In his own mind, as he has told us, the
problem struck him like this:

> In the midst of this, however, I found a
> new and sobering dilemma: How could I make
> a speech that would be militant enough to
> keep my people aroused to positive action
> and yet moderate enough to keep this fervor

within controllable and Christian bounds...
What could I say to keep them courageous
and prepared for positive action and yet
devoid of hate and resentment. Could the
militant and the moderate be combined in a
single speech?

I decided that I had to face the challenge
head on, and attempt to combine two
irreconcilables.(9)

Eventually, of course, what matters is not whether
the two irreconcilables can be united in a speech,
but whether it can be done in fact and in action.

In traditional Christian pacifism the exclusion
of violent means to resist evil as a legitimate moral
choice was based on one of two grounds. In a negative formulation there is the prohibition in the
decalog against killing. Understood as a direct
expression of the divine will, "Thou shalt not kill"
quite simply defines one limit of permissible human
activity.(10) To faithfully obey the divine will is
above all else the human task and responsibility.
The commandment puts an end to any further discussion. The responsibility for the consequences of
such a decision must be left to God or to the
evil-doer. In a more positive approach the New
Testament injunctions to love one's neighbor, to turn
the other cheek, to overcome evil with good, to
forgive without limit, and other similar sayings, are
taken to be absolutely incompatible with the employment of violent means.(11) To shoot a human being
with calculated deliberation, and at the same time
lovingly, presents any human being with an intrinsic
impossibility. On either ground, then, the use of
violent means is flatly forbidden to the person who
accepts the authority of the scriptures antecedent to
any further discussion.

The general implications of such a position
follow readily enough. The moral task of the believer is to live in the world but not be of the world.
The Christian's service to and responsibility for the
world, such as it is, consists precisely in the
judgment upon the world which is constituted by his
faithful witness to God's Will and by his or her
efforts to live at peace with all other people as far
as that depends on the Christian believer. The time
and the energies of the Christian are to be devoted

exclusively to the things of God; the worldly affairs of human beings are not the business or the responsibility of the Christian.

When one explores the practical implications of this position, serious moral difficulties begin to arise. In its starkest form, traditional pacifism is an ethic of conscience that has no objective grounding in reality; that is to say, it simply ignores consequences and sees no significance in the content of human action. Only obedience to God's will has moral significance. It give no consideration to the relationship between means and ends so that the means and the end become identical, obedience to God's Will. That God's Will seems to be curiously apart from and indifferent to the problems and concerns of human living indicates one reason for calling such a position irresponsible. It simply does not help and ends up leaving responsibility to others.(12)

This inadequacy in such a defense of pacifism has been traditionally recognized. Thinkers have known that whatever assessment one makes of the scriptural data and the early teaching and practice of Christians in regard to questions of war and violence,(13) the dilemma must be faced. Origen, for one instance, in his famous controversy with Celsus, invoked the obedience to the empire and the prayers for the Emperor which characterized Christian practice as signs of good citizenship, but frankly affirmed that the Christian had no political or social responsibility beyond that.(14) Augustine, on the other hand, while denying the Christian had a right to self-defense, insisted on the obligation in love for the defense of others and so was led to work out a theory of just war.(15) Since the time of the Constantinian turn the pacifist position has defended itself on more restricted, less universal grounds. The obligation not to participate in war, not to use the instruments of violence to shed blood, became an obligation correlative to a special vocation, as it was for Ambrose and many monks.(16) When the same obligation emerged as a central tenet of heretical sects in the Middle Ages and later among many Protestant sectarians, it always involved a radical rejection of the value of human pursuits and hence of all political and social responsibility for the human enterprise.(17) In its more positive aspect, pacifism was seen as a special, elite call to witness to the truth in the face of the evil of the world.

The elitist character of this vocation to pacific witness is reflected in the interesting conclusion of Robert Barclay's Apology in which he attempted to set forth the Quaker teaching about war and resistance to evil. The conclusion is interesting because it reflects in its own way the conviction common to both King and Gandhi that violent resistance to evil is morally preferable to cowardly submission. Wrote Barclay:

> ...today's Christians are still an admixture of the old and the new. They have not achieved a patient suffering spirit which would equip them for this form of Christianity. Therefore, they cannot leave themselves undefended until they attain that degree of perfection. But it is always unlawful for those whom Christ has already brought to that state to defend themselves with arms. They, of all people, should have complete trust in the Lord.(18)

Pacifism, as a form of witness, makes a significant impact under conditions of persecution and intolerance. But once tolerated and accepted in a given society, its refusal of social and political responsibility for that society takes on a parasitic flavor. Modern pacifism has certainly come to recognize an obligation of service to and responsibility for society. This is reflected in the very wording of the choice given to conscienteous objectors to war in the United States - the choice of alternate service. If the obligation to resist evil nonviolently is to be joined with the obligation of service to and responsibility for society, one way is to stress the importance of doing the works of peace and social development which will make violence less likely. This positive emphasis(19) in much of contemporary nonviolence is a distinct easing of the dilemma, but it does not totally resolve it. What is unique about the nonviolence espoused by King and Gandhi as they faced the dilemma inherent in nonviolence is that not only do they not reject political and social responsibility, but they propose nonviolence as a demand of and method for exercising such responsibility. Thus, while they may have been wrong in the claims they made for nonviolence, they did not embrace nonviolence as simply a witness of conscience or as a correlative of a certain vocational responsibility. Both would agree with Augustine that "it is a wickedness to abandon society."(20)

The theoretical criticism of nonviolence upon which the charge of irresponsibility is ultimately based finds a confusion of means and ends behind it. As a doctrine nonviolence asks human beings for a commitment to a means rather than to an end. This commitment so absolutizes a method that the means to the end becomes an end in and of itself. Yet by the very nature of a means we are speaking about an instrumental value. Any means has worth or value, can claim our ethical interest and loyalty, require our action, only because it can achieve or produce something else that claims our loyalty and demands our action in its own right. But the judgment as to whether or not a particular means is in fact effective and essential in achieving a determinate end is a situational and empirical judgment. It requires the accumulation of data from concrete experience. To make this judgment into any other kind of judgment, namely an a priori judgment, as nonviolence inevitably must, is to be false to the matter under consideration.

Additionally, when it comes to social and political matters, the judgment about the effective means to an end is, and can only be, either a technical or a prudential judgment.(21) To absolutize a means in the way that King did with nonviolence is to say that it is a necessary and sufficient means to a determinate end, and that, therefore, the ethical authority that it bears with it and which demands our allegiance is derived from its relationship of necessity to an obligatory end. In order to establish the truth of such a claim, two things would need demonstration. First it would have to be shown that militant nonviolence is in fact a necessary means to some determinate and obligatory end. For example, if the desegregation of the Montgomery city buses is an obligatory end, it would have to be shown that militant nonviolence is a necessary means to that end. Secondly, it would have to be shown that the end is itself an absolute moral imperative. Unfortunately, neither of those two things can be demonstrated at anything more than a highly abstract level, namely that justice should be done and in achieving justice one should not perpetrate greater injustice. But to say that the desegregation of the Montgomery city buses was an absolute moral

212

imperative demanding everyone's action and that militant nonviolence was the necessary form such action must take is simply not an a priori demonstrable proposition.

The actual experience of King and others during the bus boycott in Montgomery was fraught with these theoretical difficulties. The original demands of the MIA were, to be sure, quite modest. The demands were three: courteous treatment of black passengers by all bus drivers; passengers to sit on a first-come, first-served basis, with the blacks to start seating from the rear to the front and the whites proceeding from front to rear; some black bus drivers were to be employed for predominantly black routes.(22) Such demands were the minimum that the MIA leadership felt it could and would accept, and the maximum it dared, for the moment, to make. If we take such demands to be the end, they may well be regarded as both reasonable and due, but hardly as claims that command everyone's action (agreement and support are a different story). Secondly, it is clear that the means King employed in Montgomery did not succeed in achieving this end, that the boycott was, at best, ancillary and supportive, but hardly either necessary or sufficient.(23) The actual end was achieved in the courts, mandated by the affirmation of the United States Supreme Court of a prior decision by a district court, and the final end went far beyond the demands and hopes of the MIA leaders. Thirdly, if the means were taken to be the boycott of the Montgomery city bus line with all the additional efforts that went to support the boycott as a practical and peaceful act, it must be said that the means were not succeeding and were very close to failure, as King himself admitted.(24) "God Almighty has spoken from Washington, D.C.," one joyful bystander was reported to have said upon hearing the Supreme Court decision,(25) but that was not the same as saying the sore and weary feet of Montgomery's black citizens were the cause of the court's decision. Fourthly, the successful achievement of ending segregation on the buses was not accompanied by the redeeming good will and mutual reconcilation of black and white citizens in Montgomery which was stressed as the end to be achieved by nonviolent resistance.(26) The success of the black community was a result of the coercive power of the state to enforce its will upon recalcitrant citizens through the instrumentality of law. It was not true in

Montgomery, and it was never true in any of King's campaigns, that militant nonviolence was the necessary and sufficient means for attaining the end of peaceful desegregation, a thing which would have to be true if militant nonviolence is to be regarded as an absolute moral demand.

For the reasons presented in the preceding paragraph I suggest that militant nonviolence, as King practiced and understood it, cannot be fairly dealt with in such a framework of means to an end. For the same reasons I have called it a spirituality rather than, strictly speaking, a philosophy or ethical theory. For it does, beyond any doubt, call for a commitment to a method or a means, a commitment to a process of personal self-discipline. It is not a way of explaining reality, or God, or truth, or justice, but a way of responding to reality which is comprehended only as mystery, only as concretely unknown or unfinished. The key insight of nonviolence is that in moral affairs no one knows the end, indeed the end cannot be known for the good and sufficient reason that no one has yet arrived at the end. Therefore, no end, be it abstract or concrete, can have any kind of ethical authority over the present. To lend the end such authority is to falsify reality, to substitute willfulness for responsibility, desire for truth. It is to be an ideologue. What King's nonviolent claim does is to set on its head the question of the relationship between the means and the end. The end cannot possibly justify the means, but the means can, in time, lead to an end of value, for the end will be no more than the realization and completeness of the means.

King himself expressed this view of the relationship between the means and the end in his rejection of Communism. "Constructive ends can never give absolute moral justification to destructive means, because in the final analysis the end is pre-existent in the means."(27) But he did not pursue the point at any further length. The perspective under discussion was not, of course, unique to King. Gandhi had used a simile to illustrate the same view of the matter. "There is as close a link between the means and the end as between the seed and the tree." Jacques Maritain, a thinker of completely different background and depth than either King or Gandhi, has written of the means as "in a sense the

214

end in the process of becoming."(28) In this perspective the end is not identified with the means nor is it confused with the means. One can tell the difference between the seed and the tree. While the end does not justify the means it does provide a measure of intelligibility to the means and so it affords some guidance in the choice of a means that is suitable and adapted to the end. There is, indeed, an intimate, intrinsic link between the means and the end, as situational or utilitarian ethics suggests, but in regard to human action it is not the case that to will the end is to will the means.(29) Nonviolence insists that one must first will the means and only in doing so does one truly will the end.

This understanding of the means-end relationship can be further clarified by suggesting that it gives the primacy of value and authority to the process rather than the product. While the future may direct the present, it should not dictate to it, so ethical responsibility must be exercised in regard to the means far more than in the achievement of ends. Or in a different formulation, human actions stand in need of authorization, which has to be found in the present, or in the past, and not justification which comes from the future. If one were to apply the Christian faith's rejection of all human efforts at self-justification to the present issue, it would become clear that God's free offer of justification through faith in Christ places human responsibility in the present and authorizes now a way of life. For control and responsibility are possible for historical human beings only in the present, only over the process, only during their actual practice. In a remarkably insightful little essay, On Caring, Milton Mayeroff has explored and unfolded some of the implications of what it means to care for anyone or anything, or, in the terms of this discussion, what it means to take responsibility. His ideas have direct relevance to the point under discussion so it is worth quoting him at some length.

> The process rather than the product is primary in caring, for it is only in the present that I can attend to the other...Control is possible only in the present...To speak of the primacy of the process is not to deny the important role which anticipated goals and general aims

> play; they contribute to direction and
> meaning in the present...But if the present
> (the process) is not taken seriously for
> its own sake, and is basically subordinated
> to the future (the product) by being
> treated either as a necessary end or as a
> mere means to something lying beyond, then
> caring becomes impossible. The father
> impatient for his child to grow up and
> become "something" that he is not now does
> not really take the child seriously and
> makes caring impossible.(30)

This emphasis on the ethical primacy of the process,
the present, the means, is directed at the human
effort to know what is the good or right thing to do
in a given situation. As an answer to that question,
it is quite similar to an answer that is as old as
Aristotle,(31) that to know what is good, observe
what good people do, for it takes a good person to
know what is good. Of course, that response is
circular as far as logic is concerned yet is true
nonetheless. The more that we experience the competition of values and the historical relativity of
values, the more we become aware that the basic human
condition is an unanswered question and an unfinished
task. We perceive that the problems of personal and
social relationships are essentially moral, not
technical problems to be settled once and for all.
For "we are born into a social world that forces us
to be free, to be autonomous; for now the moral
imperative is to actually fashion ourselves by
choosing among the numerous alternatives our social
world presents to us,"(32) even while that world
affords us no substantive guidance. It is we who
must decide, but on what basis are we to do so?
Marx's famous question about who is to educate the
educators remains as formidable and as relevant as
when he first asked it(33) and requires a dialectical
answer as much as ever.(34) To know what is good we
must be good ourselves; yet to become good we must do
the good; but to do the good we must know the good.
It is, seemingly, a hopeless position.

Ethical theory is the persistent effort to break
out of this ethical circle. In the history of
western thought on the subject various solutions have
been proposed which have generated a series of
dichotomies which appear, at least intellectually, to
be at odds. Emphasis may be placed upon one side or

the other of the following polarities: the motive or intention of the agent in contrast to the intrinsic nature of the act itself; the context or situation of the act as opposed to unchanging principles; the demands of love in contrast to the demands of law; the role of conscience over against the role of consequences.(35) All of these apparent dichotomies are reflected in King's concern for social justice and for a method to eliminate social evil. A consideration of how they affected that concern will help to show why he accepted militant nonviolence as a way through the theoretical morass and how it settled the question of means and ends for him.

King was concerned with two basic matters in Montgomery. One was his responsibility toward the attitudes and deeds of the black community. His second concern was his responsibility toward the attitudes and deeds of the white people of Montgomery. He wanted to foster and sustain good will on both sides, but he also wanted action that would effect real change. His choice of militant nonviolence seemed to him to represent what he was looking for. The motivation he proposed, the attitudes he emphasized in his speeches to the MIA audience were love, the refusal to hate or be haughty, openness, truthfulness, a blunt appeal to conscience.(36) At the same time he was adamant in his demand for action and for an end to the passive acceptance of injustice. What was most significant in this combination, however, was the relationship it established toward the white citizens of Montgomery. For it provided an opportunity for the only responsible measure of control available to him and his people for the attitudes and actions of the white citizens.

The Montgomery boycott was, without any question, an exercise of power on the part of the black community, and it forced upon the minds and emotions of the white community some unwelcome and unsought for news. It confronted them with the need to choose a new course of action. They had to do something; the boycott could not simply be ignored. Therein lay the power of militant nonviolence. At the same time no specific attitudes or courses of action were dictated or coerced by the boycott. It merely posed an invitation to change, an opportunity to recognize the truth and do justice. In short it afforded the white community the chance to know what was good and to do it. Ironically enough, the intervention of the Supreme Court decision precluded the victory of militant nonviolence and returned the situation to one of coercion and the limitation of choice. The good deed got done without the good being recognized and chosen.

In a somewhat comparable way militant nonviolence was an effort to reconcile the demands of principle and situation by creating a new situation in which the principle would become clear in its practical implications and be possible to implement. The demands of the MIA were both modest and negotiable, but unmistakably clear. It is unlikely that the MIA leadership would have settled for less than their original demands, but they left room for alternate solutions and mutual agreement. Neither the situation of injustice nor the principle of injustice alone determined or justified a specific course of action. The situation created by the nonviolent boycott made possible a mutual determination of what specific demands of justice could be implemented here and now. King also thought that nonviolence overcame the love-law polarity by the determination to put love first and to invite law to respond as a need of love.

Finally, the insistence upon making clear the truth of the black citizens' reality in Montgomery in one specific aspect of their lives pointed to the reconciliation of the good and the true, or of the useful and the true. The impossibility of building anything stable and lasting on a lie was revealed in a concrete way. The basic condition for determining what measures would be useful was shown to be the truthful manifestation of the actual condition of those for whom the good was intended. All this King thought militant nonviolence was able to do without pre-empting anyone's freedom of choice and without inflicting physical injury on persons or property.

What King thought he had found in militant nonviolence was a method for bringing to light in actual situations the concrete content of general ethical principles and imperatives. In doing this he demonstrated in a visible way that motive and deed cannot be held radically apart in human beings, that the manifestation of bad practice will also manifest bad will which needs conversion, and that bad will sooner or later will always result in bad practice.

218

He also made clear that it is not the situation which dictates or determines what is the appropriate moral action, nor can abstract principles simply be imposed upon actual situations without coercion and resentment, a thing which to a considerable degree happened finally in Montgomery. Rather it is possible for human beings to act to create new situations in which the specific demands of justice become clear and practical. The distinction between love and law was shown to have little practical merit. The necessary gift of love of one social being to another is law, and law that is not such a gift is only another form of coercion, supported only by the threat to use the instruments of violence. It also appeared in the Montgomery boycott that the determination of the practical good for people is a function of the truth, that the first good work available to people is to being to light the truth about themselves and their condition.

The significance of nonviolence as a means, therefore, can be summarized in four propositions. First, because of the human condition of being both historically limited and self-determining creatures, human beings do not and cannot assume responsibility for or control over the final outcome of the human enterprise. Human responsibility for and control over human life and deeds is a present one; it is over what we are now, do now, create now. The ideals we have, the dreams and hopes we fashion are directive and suggestive, but they have no right to claim to be authoritative or determinative of human action. Second, the human commitment to the accepted abstractions of religious or ethical wisdom, to justice, to peace, to goodness, to love and truth, is precisely a commitment to a means, to a process and not a commitment to some ideal society or some imaginable set of human relationships. Because we do not and cannot know antecedently what the concrete determinations of abstract ideals and principles are or should be, we can only care for and commit ourselves to the process by which such determinations can be made in specific situations. Third, militant nonviolence, at least as it is evidenced in King's practice of it, was exactly such a commitment to a process of means. It involved a submission to a discipline which enabled one to determine what was concretely true and good for oneself and one's fellow human beings in a particular situation. To forego or to reject this process would also be to close out any possibility of coming to know what is true and good. To that extent nonviolence can be described as the only means. Fourth, not only is militant nonviolence in accord with the gospel message, which was of fundamental importance to King, but it manifests the same sort of commitment called for by the gospel, as well as that demanded by democracy. Indeed, everything worthy in human life calls for the same commitment to a process or a means, not in the hope that the process will produce something that will in turn justify or give value to the commitment, but in the knowledge and conviction that one has, in making the commitment, already grasped the substance of what is worthy. This last proposition requires a more extended elaboration and will serve as a final elucidation of the matter of means.

It has been mentioned earlier in the book how often King spoke of Christianity, democracy, and the philosophy of nonviolence in a univocal fashion. At the root of his rhetoric there was, I suggest, an unformulated and unexpressed insight of singular importance. That insight was simply that in each of the three terms King perceived that what was being called for was an open-ended commitment to a process, a commitment that was rather disciplined and specific. In his early wrestlings with nonviolence and in his writings and rhetoric King often confused method and substance. The employment of the power lodged in militant nonviolence naturally requires certain strategic methods and tactical forms. These forms - for example, a boycott, marches on city hall, sit-ins at commercial establishments, prayer vigils in public buildings and so forth - are not to be confused with the substance of militant nonviolence. The tactical form that is chosen in a particular situation obviously needs to be judged by criteria of practicality and effectiveness to achieve specific ends. King was certainly vulnerable to negative criticism at times in this regard.(37) Nonviolent demonstrations may also be, perhaps most often are, nothing more than one specific tactic among others for achieving certain political goals. Unlike Gandhi, King invited people to join his demonstrations and allowed people to be regular members of his organization who accepted nonviolence as nothing more than such a tactic. In doing this he was basically at odds with Gandhi,(38) believing that actual participation in a nonviolent protest could bring people to see the deeper truth in nonviolence as a way of life. He thought that the actual submission to the nonviolent discipline could be a means for achieving the deeper insight.(39)

It can be demonstrated that this conviction of King's about the efficacy of participation in a particular act of nonviolence to bring a person to a permanent commitment to it as a way of life was only a hope, and a hope often frustrated.(40) But that does not mean that his hope was foolish or groundless. King himself remained convinced to the end that such a hope, however many times it was disappointed, remained our only hope.(41) The reason for his hope is to be found in a more carful analysis of what ends and means concretely are in human life. For King, an end was not, as it so often is in ethical and political discussion, an intended reality, a plan, a dream, a purpose, what one hoped or wanted to happen. The end was rather the concrete, objective result of an action and included all the consequences of an act, not just the consciously intended ones. Understood in this way the end is precisely what human beings cannot control. The pretension that they can so control the end is no more than utopian foolishness of ideological blindness. But it does not follow from this that human beings are without responsibility for or control over their life and destiny. They can and should take responsibility for the means, and for three reasons.

The first reason has to do with the nature of the human person and the human enterprise. Since the human being is by nature a becoming reality, the human enterprise is open-ended, unfinished. There is no known point of fulfillment or completion along the way. If human beings set their minds and hearts upon caring for anything other than the becoming process itself, they are caring for an illusion, for something unreal and non-existent, or for something dead and gone. Caring for the becoming process, while altogether concrete and situational, is by no means an unstructured and arbitrary thing. This is not because the process of history is not unstructured and arbitrary - it often is - but because the human agents in the process are charged with the creation of a structured and purposeful process in the light of past experience and future hopes. But not knowing the final, concrete outcome of the process prevents construction of a purposeful process according to some fixed blueprints. Therefore construction must proceed in a largely negative fashion - recognizing, opposing, and struggling to eliminate the destructive and incoherent elements that appear in the process, while at the same time holding firmly and inalterably to the truths one does know and the level of justice one has achieved. It is for this reason that King explained the basic responsibility of social practice to be opposition to injustice and untruth whenever they appear. Human beings cannot do more than that without violating their own humanity. Nor does this involve a compromise with evil. It is not a matter of trading off a truth one knows or a good one has achieved for some other truth or good. On such matters as truth and goodness there is no compromise, which means there is a deeply conservative aspect to militant nonviolence.

A second reason for taking responsibility for the means rather than the end looks at the human agent of the process. In the becoming process itself, in human history, the primary element that is becoming is the human being. The human person is becoming human, becoming truthful, just, loving, good, or perhaps the opposite. In King's terms, he or she is becoming like Jesus, growing into the ethical divinity that marked King's Christ. There is no magic formula that insures the success of such becoming, no guaranteed method for achieving it.(42) Once again the directional signals of human becoming are largely negative. It is possible to say what will inhibit, distort or prevent human growth, to point to some things that will insure the failure of the human enterprise. But only personal attention to and care for the actual process of growth can be recommended as the way or the means to growth. Human becoming is not a function of human wishing or hoping or intending but of doing, and that is as important for social as for personal growth. Only free action can achieve freedom, only truthful search can find truth, only just dealing can realize justice. Hence it is essential to care for the means of human becoming rather than for the anticipated ends of the process.

The third reason for placing emphasis on the process rather than on the end product is that the human desire and demand for the realization of ethical ideals find fulfillment not in some end, but in the actual process itself. The commitment to the process or means is not done in the hope that it will lead to something else that will terminate the commitment. Rather it is done in the conviction that one has already, in making the commitment, begun to realize the substance of the ethical ideal. That is, perhaps, capable of being interpreted as another form of virtue is its own reward, but it is not meant in any moralistic or pietistic sense. What is involved here is a perception of where and how ethical and human values are realized in our lives.(43) Very early in the civil rights movement the watchword or the slogan become "freedom now." The freedom referred to was often spoken and thought of as a goal to be achieved or as a condition that would one day come to pass. But at a more profound level it was slowly perceived that freedom was already becoming a reality, that to have begun to act against the injustice that limited and distorted human life and growth was itself to have begun to experience and realize the freedom that was being sought. The repeated reference to the new psychological outlook of black Americans as one of the major achievements of the civil rights demonstrations was not done for the lack of something better to mention.(44)

It was not Martin Luther King, Jr. alone among black leaders who realized this. James Farmer, for one example, in his reflection upon ten years of the civil rights movement, wrote that "the civil rights movement, we now know, is not simply a means to achieve the state of abstract equality; it is also a form of self-expression and self-determination for America's Negroes and their brothers in spirit."(45) Later in the book he offered an even more penetrating reflection.

> But freedom is not an end: it is a begin-
> ning and a process. We feel furth r from
> the end now than we did before a decade's
> progress was wrought. We have settled down
> for a long haul. Things are not so clear
> as they once seemed, but the complexity is
> splendid; perhaps that is freedom too.(46)

The confusion over means and ends, therefore, that has often been attributed to militant nonviolence, while often justified in relation to King's rhetoric, does not appear to be well-founded criticism in regard to the practice itself. It is necessary, to be sure, to recognize and allow for a certain amount of semantic confusion in all discussions of means and ends, as well as taking note of the very real competition among various hopes, demands and desires. It is, for example, quite clear that what King meant by freedom and looked forward to as integration was not at all what the White Citizens Council of Montgomery called freedom or feared as integration. Yet that does not mean that one is dealing simply with different verbal definitions or conflicting desires and interests. A few final reflections upon the human value that is freedom will indicate clearly that there is no confusion of means and end in militant nonviolence and will further clarify what King meant by calling it the method for eliminating social evil.

The human value of freedom is not an end in the sense that it is a substantive reality or a goal of human activity.(47) It is not a product to be possessed but a process in which one participates. It is a context or a condition of human life and action rather than its content or substantive purpose. As such it is a necessary condition for the realization of goodness, truth and beauty, but it is not a sufficient condition. For instance, in the scientific search for knowledge and truth freedom of inquiry is essential, but of itself it is not a guarantee that knowledge and truth will be found. Likewise in political society the freedoms of speech, press and assembly are necessary conditions for the existence of a free and democratic people, but they are no guarantee that truth, justice and good taste will prevail among such people. Or again, in the religious world, freedom to believe in accord with one's own conscience is an essential condition of authentic faith, but such freedom is in itself no guarantee that one will believe what is true or find salvation. The commitment of the scholar, the citizen, the believer is in each case a commitment to a process, a method, a means. The violation of the process, the suppression of the appropriate freedom automatically insures that the end will not be realized.(48) Adherence and loyalty to the process on the part of scholars, citizens, believers is their only hope of realizing the end they seek. It is in this precise sense that militant nonviolence is to be considered as a means, and the only means available to human beings, to achieve justice and eliminate social evil.

This perception of the means-end relationship in nonviolence moves the method of nonviolent resistance beyond the level of mere political strategy and tactics, though it does not remove the necessity for such strategy and tactics. If one were to make a comparison between the commitment of a people to a constitutional democracy and the commitment to nonviolence, certain similarities would prove enlightening in understanding the meaning and the limitations of militant nonviolence.

Both commitments in question are clearly commitments to processes, not to ends. The people who govern themselves within a constitutional framework are simply committed to a method of organizing and distributing power and authority, to a way of determining the due limits upon the power that is entrusted to offices and individuals, and to a method for adjudicating conflicts of interest and power. One may regard a constitution as establishing a framework within which life will be lived or as laying down the basic rules of the game. The game still remains to be played and there is no way of guaranteeing the successful outcome of the game other than to adhere to the rules of the game. In a similar way, the commitment to militant nonviolence is a commitment, at a more concrete level of political and human experience, to a means of making the specific demands of justice evident and compelling. It establishes a second framework or a second set of rules within the prior and larger constitutional framework. It is not a general framework for activity, as a constitution or a religious faith is, but a more concrete determination of the rules for activity within the larger framework. Indeed, as King specified and practiced militant nonviolence, it was really nothing more than the actual participation of citizens in the democratic process within the framework provided by the Constitution of the United States.

Since King found the Constitution to be fully consonant with the higher moral law, it made no difference in practice to which one he appealed. This was not the case with Gandhi, since he was in a position in which he totally rejected any claim of British authority in India to establish the framework for human activity.(49) For that reason he found himself in a different situation and had to appeal directly to a higher moral law, or to truth as he called it. Nonetheless, such an appeal provided the larger framework within which nonviolence functioned and only the fact that the British acknowledged this larger framework, at least to some degree, made nonviolent resistance practical and effective. In the absence of a shared larger framework of activity within which militant nonviolence can function, it ceases to be practical or effective. There is nothing left but the use of violence for self-defense or the acceptance of martyrdom. But it is important to note that violence in itself cannot build or even restore the needed larger framework. The threat of it may, however, move people to attempt to establish it.

It is also worth noting in regard to King and Gandhi that the latter was faced primarily with a problem of political liberation. Despite the rhetoric of the black power movement and the many analogies made between the situation of black people in the United States and the neo-colonial condition of people in Latin America and Africa,(50) King was not faced with a problem of political liberation. He had to address himself to problems of psychological, social and economic liberation in the context of the United States. Only in the southern states could his task be conceived of as one of political liberation. It was not accidental, as we shall see, that the success of militant nonviolence for both King and Gandhi took place mainly on the psychological and political levels, but had little impact in solving problems of economic and social justice.

A second important similarity between the commitment to constitutional democracy and the commitment to militant nonviolence is that neither one requires or depends upon either prior truths or future results for the justification of the commitment. That is simply a way of saying that neither commitment is justified by any end nor dependent upon a previously shared faith. The commitment is authorized - made right - by the very act of commitment itself.(51) Despite the claims of the Declaration of Independence that we hold certain truths to be self-evident,(52) the authority of the United States Constitution does not derive from nor depend upon any such self-evident truths, nor is any acceptance of such truths necessary to hold the democratic fabric together. While both King and Gandhi thought that nonviolence made no sense without belief in God,(53)

226

the commitment to it does not in fact require such a belief as something that grounds or justifies such a commitment, though it may well be necessary to motivate one to make such a commitment. For Gandhi, the essential condition incumbent upon his search for Truth - or God - was nonviolence. The very meaning of nonviolence was this search for Truth. For King, obedience to the God he knew in Christ was the meaning of nonviolence. Or nonviolence was the essential condition for discerning and responding to the work of God in human history. When seen as essential conditions for making and keeping human life authentically human these commitments can have no other justification. What such commitments do not settle and what stands in need of justification are the various actions that flow from the initial commitment. That is why even a genuine commitment to nonviolence cannot eschew every use of violence in every circumstance.(54)

The major difficulty in affirming that militant nonviolence is nothing more nor less than a framework for the actual participation of citizens in the democratic process is that it often involved the violation of law, or what King called civil disobedience. That is a type of action which is not allowed for within the constitutional framework of a democracy. It would appear, therefore, that militant nonviolence is something more or something other than what it has, to this point, been explained to be. The following chapter, then, will consider the matter of disobedience to law in King's word and deeds, and will take up the questions of authority and power and coercion in their relationship to love and moral persuasion. The campaigns King conducted in Birmingham and Selma, Alabama will provide some concrete references for the discussion.

1. Some typical and useful discussions of the just war are Paul Ramsey, War and the Christian Conscience (Durham, NC: Duke University Press, 19610; John Courtney Murray, S.J., We Hold These Truths (Garden City, NY: Image Books, 1964), pp. 238-261; Richard A. Wasserstrom (ed.), War and Morality (Belmont, California: Wadsworth Publishing Company, 1970); Thomas A. Shannon (ed), War or Peace? The Search for New Answers (Maryknoll, NY: Orbis Books, 1980).

2. The change is reflected in various works all concerned with the problem of liberation. A few typical works are Frantz Fanon, The Wretched of the Earth and Black Skin White Masks; Herbert Marcuse, "Ethics and Revolution" in Ethics and Society, ed. Richard T. DeGeorge (New York: Doubleday & Co., 1966; Dennis P. McCann, Christian Realism and Liberation Theology (Maryknoll, NY: Orbis Books, 1981).

3. The single best formulation of the just war theory that I know of is to be found in Joseph C. McKenna, S.J., "Ethics and War: A Catholic View," The American Political Science Review, LIV, 3 (September 1960), pp. 647-658; the challenge to the theory posed by nuclear weapons is treated by James Douglas, The Non-Violent Cross (London: The Macmillan Company, 1969), pp. 155-178. See also Francis X. Winters, "The Bow or the Cloud? American Bishops Challenge the Arms Race," America 145, no. 2 (July 25, 1981), pp. 26-30.

4. Fanon, The Wretched of the Earth, pp. 73-106, "We have seen that it is the intuition of the colonized masses that their liberation must, and can only, be achieved by force" p. 73.

5. Arendt, On Revolution, pp. 31-70, has a clear exposition of what the problem of liberation entails and why it is a different problem than mere self-defense.

6. Marcuse, "Ethics and Revolution," Ethics and Society, pp. 140-143.

7. Niebuhr, <u>Moral Man and Immoral Society</u>, pp. 171-175.

8. Washington, <u>The Politics of God</u>, pp. 131-150; Cone, <u>Black Theology and Black Power</u>, pp. 138-152.

9. King, <u>Stride Toward Freedom</u>, pp. 45-46.

10. An extended discussion of the imperative against the use of violence which starts from this commandment is Jean Lasserre, <u>War and the Gospel</u>, trans. Oliver Coburn (Scottsdale, PA: Herald Press, 1962).

11. This approach is developed in G. H. MacGregor, <u>The New Testament Basis of Pacifism</u> (Nyack, NY: Fellowship Publications, 1960).

12. Harvey Cox, <u>The Secular City</u> (New York: The Macmillan Company, 1965), pp. 105-123.

13. For two conflicting assessments of this early tradition see Roland H. Bainton, <u>Christian Attitudes Toward War and Peace</u> (New York: Abingdon Press, 1960), pp. 66-84; Edward A. Ryan, S.J., "The Rejection of Military Service by the Early Christians," <u>Theological Studies</u> 13 (March, 1952), pp. 1-32.

14. Umphrey Lee, <u>The Historic Church and Modern Pacifism</u> (New York, Nashville: Abingdon-Cokesbury Press, 1943), pp. 64-65.

15. <u>Ibid.</u>, p. 78.

16. <u>Ibid.</u>, pp. 100-118; also see the story in 2 Sm 7:1-16 for the biblical roots of this idea.

17. Ronald Knox, <u>Enthusiasm</u> (New York: Oxford University Press, 1961) documents this tendency throughout the book.

18. Barclay, p. 435.

19. Examples of this emphasis on doing the work of peace can be found in <u>Peace in Vietnam</u> (New York: Hill and Wang, 1966) which was a report prepared for The American Friends Service Committee; "The Pastoral Constitution on The

Church in The Modern World" <u>The Documents of Vatican II</u>, ed. Walter M. Abbot, S.J. (New York: Guild Press, America Press, Association Press, 1966), #77, p. 270, #82, p. 296, #84, p. 298; the encyclical letter of Pope Paul VI, <u>Populorum Progressio</u> in Joseph Gremillion (ed.), <u>The Gospel of Peace and Justice</u> (Maryknoll, N.Y.: Orbis Books, 1975), pp. 387-415; "...peace is something that is built up day after day, in the pursuit of an order intended by God, which implies a more perfect form of justice among men.", #76, p. 410.

20. Lee, p. 79.

21. See Passmore, pp. 11-18 and J.A.K. Thomson (ed.), <u>The Ethics of Aristotle, The Nicomochean Ethics Translated</u> (Baltimore: Penguin Books, 1955), pp. 176-177; Dino Bigongiari (ed.), <u>The Political Ideas of St. Thomas Aquinas</u> (New York and London: Hafner Publishing Company, 1966), p. xxviii and <u>Summa Theologica</u>, II, II, Q.47, A.12.

22. King, <u>Stride Toward Freedom</u>, p. 49.

23. Lewis, pp. 78-79; King himself recognized the need for mass action to be supplemented by legal initiatives; <u>Stride Toward Freedom</u>, pp. 174-179.

24. King, <u>Stride Toward Freedom</u>, pp. 138-139.

25. <u>Ibid</u>., p. 140.

26. <u>Ibid</u>., pp. 158-164.

27. <u>Ibid</u>., p. 74.

28. Both quotations are cited from P. Regamey, O.P., <u>Non-violence and The Christian Conscience</u> (London: Darton, Longmann and Todd, 1966), p. 200.

29. Fletcher, p. 133.

30. Milton Mayeroff, <u>On Caring</u> (New York: Harper & Row, 1971), pp. 31-32.

31. Thomson, p. 23.

32. Stanley Hauerwas, "Toward an Ethics of Charac-
    ter," _Theological Studies_ 33, no. 4 (December
    1972), p. 698.

33. Karl Marx, "Theses on Feuerbach" in Feuer (ed.),
    p. 244.

34. The problem mentioned in the text was at the
    heart of the Black Power insight and is equally
    applicable in both liberation and feminist
    theology. In a racist society, racism will be
    taught and propagated, and where are we to find
    anyone not infected by it? The only answer is
    in the victims of racism; it is black people
    themselves who will have to be the educators in
    their saying no to the prevailing teaching. See
    Carmichael and Hamilton, p. 81, and Cone, _Black
    Theology and Black Power_, pp. 36-37.

35. One useful work that brings these polarities
    into the open may be cited here among numerous
    possibilities: Richard A. McCormick, S.J. and
    Paul Ramsey (eds.), _Doing Evil to Achieve Good_
    (Chicago: Loyola University Press, 1978).

36. King, _Stride Toward Freedom_, p. 48.

37. The campaign in Albany, Georgia was a disaster
    in this regard, as King himself acknowledged in
    Why We Can't Wait, pp. 43-44.

38. Yungblut, in _Nonviolence After Gandhi_, p. 53.

39. King, _Stride Toward Freedom_, p. 83, _The Trumpet
    of Conscience_, pp. 57-58, also Ashe, p. 227,
    358.

40. King, _Where Do We Go From Here?_, p. 63.

41. King, "A Testament of Hope," _Playboy_, p. 175,
    236; "I am profoundly secure in my knowledge
    that God loves us. He has not worked out a
    design for our failure. Man has the capacity to
    do right as well as wrong, and his history is a
    path upward, not downward." Since the hope was
    founded on God's love and purpose, the only
    practical expression of that hope for King was
    obedience to God or nonviolence.

42. King, Where Do We Go From Here?, pp. 32-33; "Like life, racial understanding is not something that we find but something that we must create. What we find when we enter these mortal plains is existence; but existence is the raw material out of which all life must be created. A productive and happy life is not something that you find; it is something that you make."

43. I am indebted here and in the analysis that follows to Hannah Arendt, The Human Condition (Chicago and London: University of Chicago Press, 1958), pp. 79-247 and to Germain Grisez and Russell Shaw, Beyond The New Morality - The Responsibilities of Freedom (Notre Dame, London: University of Notre Dame Press, 1974), pp. 1-30.

44. King, Where Do We Go From Here?, p. 18; "This was the victory which had to precede all other gains."

45. Farmer, pp., 181-182.

46. Ibid., p. 197.

47. I draw here in part upon Martin Buber, Between Man and Man, trans. Ronald Gregor Smith (New York: The Macmillan Company, 1965), pp. 90-95.

48. Gandhi was even more committed to this conviction than was King as shown by his rejection of a successful course of action when it involved violence. Ashe, p. 230, wrote of Gandhi's behavior in 1922: "Here and here alone in the human record is a revolutionary who could have launched his revolution, could very likely have carried it through, yet refused because it would be the wrong sort of revolution. Rather than lead his people along the old paths of bloodshed and terror and cheated hope, Mahatma Gandhi, the Great Soul, was willing to fail."

49. Ibid., p. 205.

50. King, Where Do We Go From Here?, pp. 71-72 addresses himself realistically to some of these comparisons.

51. Arendt, On Revolution, pp. 179-180, 203-206.

52. Murray, <u>We Hold These Truths</u>, pp. 39-54, points out the important function of commonly held truths, but that function is not to authorize.

53. King, <u>Stride Toward Freedom</u>, p. 88, thinks that one must at least believe in some kind of creative force in the universe working for good.

54. I affirm this as a matter of simple fact, despite the various redefinitions of violence people engage in to avoid any casuistry applied to the moral and immoral uses of violence. From among many possible illustrations I cite only one. <u>Gandhi on Non-Violence</u>, p. 70; "I am not able to accept in its entirety the doctrine of non-killing of animals. I have no feeling in me to save the life of these animals who devour or cause hurt to man. I consider it wrong to help in the increase of their progeny...To do away with monkeys where they have become a menace to the well-being of man is pardonable." The following chapter will illustrate King's lack of "pure nonviolence."

CHAPTER VII

THE MATTER OF LAW

In the often turbulent history of Western
Civilization there has been no more difficult or more
controversial question than that of the relationship
between the individual person and the social body to
which he or she belongs. The mere fact that more
than one individual inhabits the world creates the
necessity for some way of structuring and ordering
human relationships, some way of assessing rights and
obligations and of balancing competing claims and
interests, some principles or framework in accord
with which human life may be carried on as something
other than a war of all against all.(1) Political
theorists of the most divergent views have generally
agreed upon the basic task of their enterprise.
Their concern, in broad outline, is to discover an
authoritative basis for political power(2) and a form
of its exercise that would prove to be both just and
effective. An alternate way of expressing the same
concern is to define their task as safeguarding and
promoting the common good while preserving at the
same time the rights and freedom of the individual.
More than a few political theorists achieved the
fundamental insight that the common good and individual freedom are not, in principle, contrary to one
another, but the form of political and social organization that could in fact harmonize the two remains
elusive. One formal instrumentality developed to
make social living possible in the modern world has
been the instrument of law. Whatever the source,
ultimate nature and justification of law may be, it
has become the formal means of ordering social life.
It is an instrument for establishing relationships,
assigning rights and obligations, and resolving
conflicts. It is law which defines what a given
order will be for a determinate number of people and
it is law which orders their activities and relationships within the given order. However arbitrary or
however rational it may be, law orders people in some
way and has become an essential element of civilization.

For the purposes of our discussion about the
relationship of law to nonviolence there are two
things about law which need to be noted here. Law
itself is a victory over violence. It is a way of

ordering human relationships and resolving human conflicts which affords human beings an alternative to the constant recourse to personal strength or the instruments of violence to achieve their purposes or resolve their differences.(3)   Yet, somewhat ironically perhaps, while law itself is not violence nor intrinsically coercive, its effectiveness ultimately rests upon the coercive power of the society it organizes and orders.   The last resort of the State to preserve order and to quell disorder is to the use of force or violence.(4)   In the world as it is conceivable to us, laws without some kind of coercive sanction are unintelligible.(5)

Secondly, while law has the function of defining and preserving a social order, it does not bear within itself as a formal notion any determination of what a given order ought to be.   The formal means of ordering society does not have a self-evident content, but requires a more substantial principle for this specification, a principle of justice.(6) Therefore law is clearly not order nor is it justice. It has rather an instrumental relationship to both order and justice which are its ends.   What deserves especial notice is that the discovery of allegiance to law as a means of making human life more civil is the discovery of allegiance to a process or a means. Since the rule of law becomes the means by which a society regulates and orders its affairs, it is clear that the commitment to the rule of law is not a commitment to some ideal of order or justice.   This formal similarity between law and militant nonviolence, as explained in the previous chapter, provokes the question of the relationship between them.   It also highlights the problem of disobedience to law, or civil disobedience,(7) which seemed to have been a major element in Martin Luther King's practice of militant nonviolence.

The problems that law creates for militant nonviolence are several.   There is, first of all, the problem of the coercive power of the state which undergirds the enforcement of law and which would seem to conflict with the nonviolent rejection of the use of violence or coercion to achieve one's purposes.   Second, there is the matter of civil disobedience itself and the threat or actual result of lawlessness which it represents, and the violation of process which it inevitably is.   Third, there is the question of how anyone decides which laws rightly

236

claim obedience and which do not, that is, how one distinguishes between just and unjust laws. We will examine here each of these questions in turn, using King's activities in Birmingham and Selma, Alabama as the chief, but not exclusive, source of illumination.

The problem of the government's use of sanctions and even of the instrument of violence to uphold the law was not one to which King devoted much consideration nor one which troubled him to any marked degree. Some of his compatriots, more sensitive to or more schooled in a refined Gandhian tradition of nonviolence, felt the problem much more acutely than he did. On the face of it, for example, there would appear to be something contradictory about a fifty mile, four day, nonviolent march from Selma to the state capitol at Montgomery which was made possible only by the deployment of 1800 armed federal troops and several fully armed helicopters.(8) This apparent contradiction was noted for its tactical inadequacy in the bitter recriminations made by younger black leaders in the Selma march who were eager to force the hand of both state and federal officials.(9) It has also been noted by more detached observers for its philosophical incompatibility with the ideal of nonviolence. Marquis Sibley has remarked upon it and was of the opinion that King himself was aware of the problem. He quoted the noted nonviolent figure. A.J. Muste who had spoken to King about the matter and who offered his own interpretation of King's explanation. "According to those who don't believe in the ethic of nonviolence, it is necessary to use federal troops and the National Guard to 'preserve order.' I am simply saying that, given their premises, the employment of troops is a duty."(10) Sibley's laconic comment was that he found such an explanation unsatisfactory.

This same kind of incompatibility showed itself frequently in King's experience even before the Selma march. On June 27, 1958, King addressed the General Conference of the Society of Friends. His remarks brought a response from one of the members of the conference, Mr. J. Frederick Dewhurst. Dewhurst asked if the use of law courts and federal troops to integrate schools was not an effort at coercion and violence, and if it did not bring bitterness, and were not both of these contrary to King's own principles.(11) In responding to the question King afforded no clear answer other than that it was necessary to uphold the law of the land. A clearer statement of his position, though no less incompatible, can be found in his address to the National Bar Association the following year. After conceding that it belonged to religion and education to try to alter the errors of the mind and heart, and after criticizing President Eisenhower for his lack of moral leadership during the integration crisis in Little Rock, Arkansas, King added the following comment: "But meanwhile it is an immoral act to compel a man to accept injustice until another man's heart is straight."(12) Earlier in an article, entitled "Our Struggle," which he wrote for Liberation magazine, King had given a quite similar reply to a similar question. He insisted that law is an important factor in bringing about social change, but that under certain conditions the effort to adhere to new legal decisions did create tensions and provoke violence. This he recognized. But his critics, he claimed, had no answer for how to deal with or absorb this violence other than to beg for a retreat into the past lest things get out of hand and lead to violence. This King refused to do. "It is," he wrote, "hardly a moral act to encourage others patiently to accept injustice which he himself does not endure."(13)

The events surrounding school integration in Little Rock had also forced King to deal with the same issue. At the time of the first major crisis in 1957 King had gone on record with a letter of praise to President Eisenhower for sending in federal troops to protect black children. "You have shown to the nation and the world that the United States is a nation dedicated to law and order rather than mob rule. In an hour so charged with the tragic possibility of world conflict, America can ill afford to be guilty of sins against her own way of life."(14) He had suggested to the President that, however regrettable the presence of the troops might be, they must remain until black children could attend school freely without any threat of physical or psychological violence. And in a succinct sentence to cheer the hearts of all champions of law and order, King had added: "But the law of this land must be enforced or the result will be anarchy."(15) Near the end of 1959 King again was forced to concern himself with the issue in a letter replying to a question about the jail sentence given to two white men for bombing the Little Rock Board of Education.

238

Now he had to deal with punishment after the fact and with the coercive ability of the State to incarcerate people. His attitude toward law and violence are fairly revealed in his letter so that it is worth quoting at length.

It seems to me that the court system with its juries and judges is the best answer society has worked out to deal with an offender. This does not mean that the system is perfect for ultimately judgment is left in the hands of God. But society must have some system by which it controls and regulates behavior. Those individuals who trespass the laws of society are arrested to demonstrate to others that no one is to go beyond certain fixed boundaries. Now I must stress the fact that when an individual is arrested for a criminal act he is not being paid back for what he has done, but he is being placed in a position to be improved. Ultimately punishment must be for the improvement of the criminal rather than an act of retribution. This is the view of modern criminology and I wholeheartedly agree with it.

Now I certainly agree with you that these men are not whole-heartedly responsible for their acts. They are the victims of the system...I also agree with you that justice must be tempered with mercy. But even after conceding these points I think it would have been a mistake to allow these men to go scotch [sic] free. Such an act would only have given other violent forces in the community an excuse and even a justification to follow through on acts of terror.(16)

Given such an attitude, it is clear that King himself did not perceive law enforcement or the threat or use of governmental coercion, in principle, to be in conflict with his understanding of nonviolence. He was certainly no anarchist and he did not regard law as intrinsically coercive. He looked upon law as a teacher and the enforcement was part of the means for changing the minds and hearts of people, but only one instrument of such change and an incomplete one. Religion and formal education had their

place in the solution of the problem as well.(17)
Yet he rated law enforcement highly. "Today compli-
ance with the Constitution is still the best 'in-
struction' in our constitutional duties. Negroes
voting will do more to change the habits and opinions
of those who oppose such voting than any amount of
talk."(18) What law does, then, is to control the
external effects of people's internal feelings, even
as it instructs them in proper behavior. It is left
to religion and education to instruct and change the
internal feelings themselves.

One may well judge this position to be neither
altogether consistent nor fully compatible with a
truly nonviolent stance. Nevertheless it was King's
position on the matter. In a letter to Thurgood
Marshall in 1958 King indicated some understanding of
how he viewed the relationship between law and
militant nonviolence. "You continue winning the
legal victories for us," he wrote, "and we will
work...to implement those victories on the local
level through nonviolent means. It seems to me that
this dynamic legal approach supplemented by mass
non-violent implementation is the most powerful and
constructive avenue open to the Negro at this
hour."(19) To paraphrase, nonviolence was not about
establishing rights but exercising them. While King
was in India in 1959 he furthered clarified the
relationship between law and nonviolence. Law, he
felt, could bring about desegregation, but only the
techniques of nonviolent resistance could achieve the
positive reality of social integration. The merit of
nonviolence, as he then saw it, was that it could
restrain racial bitterness on the part of whites and
help blacks avoid the victory complex - "a real
danger in the United States because of favorable
court verdicts on the segregation issue."(20)

It is also of some interest and importance that
King began his public career with a call for law and
order. In his testimony before the National Democratic Platform and Resolutions Committee in 1956
King defined the problem of civil rights as a break-
down of law and order for black people in the South.
"The state of affairs in the South has come to such a
point that the only agency to which we can turn for
protection is the federal government."(21) He
pledged to the committee that the black community
would respond within the framework of legal democracy. In 1959, again while in India, he repeated the

same theme and again pledged that "the American Negro has faith that he can get justice within the framework of the American democratic set-up."(22)

From the above evidence, and one could adduce a great deal more to the same effect,(23) one must conclude that King saw no conflict between the rule of law and his practice of militant nonviolence. They were simply compatible and complimentary approaches to regulating and changing human behavior and relationships. The two had different functions, but not contradictory or competing ones. Law, as we have been using the term here, meant to King concretely the Constitution of the United States, a document which to his mind was fully in accord with his understanding of Christianity. Indeed, it was his belief that the "new Negro" was being stirred up to move against injustice because of the Constitution and the Christian Church.(24) There was, in King's perspective, no thought of respect for law as such. His perceptions and allegiances were altogether concrete. Consequently he proves to be of little help in determining the theoretical justification of, and the limits upon, the use of governmental coercion. As Hanes Walton has pointed out,(25) whatever King's political philosophy was, it assumed public shape as a political theology, a view of human social life that rested upon faith, and which tried to extend divinely revealed law, as King interpreted it, to all peoples and situations. Either one shared that faith or one didn't. But in a highly pluralistic society such a view is not very helpful, for it doesn't advance reasons which could commend themselves to all citizens.

The second problem which the rule of law poses for militant nonviolence is the practice of civil disobedience, a tactic in the nonviolent arsenal which King talked about far more than he practiced. In so far as law itself defines a process for regulating and changing social relationships, disobedience to law inescapably involves a disruption or violation of the process and poses a threat to the peace and order of society. Is there ever, or can there ever be, given this inevitability, such a thing as either a right or an obligation to disobey the law, to violate the process?

For King, working from a position of Christian faith, the answer was very quickly an affirmative.

241

He claimed such a right, however, not only on the ground of his faith, but also on the ground of historical precedent.

> We feel that there are moral laws in the universe just as valid and basic as man-made laws, and whenever a man-made law is in conflict with what we consider the law of God, or the moral law of the universe, then we feel we have a moral obligation to protest. And this is an American tradition all the way from the Boston Tea Party, on down. We have praised individuals in America who stood up with creative initiative to revolt against an unjust system. So that is all we are doing.(26)

Two years later he repeated his position in somewhat more ethically-oriented terms, giving credit to Thoreau for the inspiration. "I became convinced then that non-cooperation with evil is as much a moral obligation as is cooperation with good...evil must be resisted and no moral man can patiently adjust to injustice."(27) King's language and thought here are bold and positive, but the confusion of issues and meaning is large. He claims an obligation in conscience to protest injustice and unjust laws, but he failed to specify what protest means or entails. Certainly protest and disobedience are not always the same thing. Additionally, he spoke of revolt against an unjust system. But it is by no means evident that every act of civil disobedience implies a revolt against a system, and most assuredly protest and revolution are not the same thing.(28)

What precisely is to be understood by the term civil disobedience is a matter of some debate and difficulty.(29) As a matter of definition there can be no question of a legal right or a legal obligation to disobey law, civil or otherwise,(30) though one certainly may have a legal right to protest against a law. From the standpoint of monotheistic faith, there can be no question that there is an obligation to disobey any law that expressly contradicts God's Will. That is to say, there is a clear obligation to refuse to do what the law mandates when God's Will mandates the opposite. The obligation to disobey is less clear when the law allows what God's Will does not allow.(31) In theory King was quite clear about the priorities of human loyalty. "I [am] an apostle of Jesus Christ by the will of God." Our responsibility is to live as Christians in an unchristian world. "That is what I had to do. That is what every Christian has to do." The human person's ultimate allegiance is owed to God and "if any earthly institution conflicts with God's will it is your Christian duty to take a stand against it."(32) While this again may be something of an over-statement, and while the means for determining when such a conflict does, in fact, exist remain unclear, the obligation of civil disobedience as a moral demand is clear enough in principle. What is not clear, either in fact or in principle, is why civil disobedience must be nonviolent and to what lengths it may or may not go.

In so far as theoretical positions may be inferred from King's writing, it would seem that the obligation of nonviolence attached to the practice of civil disobedience is not based primarily on respect for law itself, but rather on the hope of reconciliation and mutual agreement that must follow upon the act of civil disobedience. "If we respect those who oppose us, they may achieve a new understanding of the human relations involved."(33) Nonviolence, as a moral requisite of civil disobedience, serves as a necessary, built-in control upon the disorder and discord that civil disobedience would other wise cause, so that neither the actors nor their adversaries find themselves engaged in violent attempts at mutual self-destruction.(34) Nonviolence, as one moral limit on civil disobedience, therefore, becomes the substitute against chaos for the law that is being disobeyed. It is the alternate form for keeping social relationships orderly and peaceful in a situation in which it is felt the ordinary form, law, has to be set aside.

In practice King was more sensitive to the charge of lawlessness or disrespect for law that the practice of civil disobedience provoked than he was in his rhetoric. He was also less sweeping in his claims and more specific about the purpose of this kind of nonviolent resistance. In addressing a mass meeting of the MIA on the day of his conviction for violating Montgomery's anti-boycott laws, King made the following points. He was not bitter about his arrest or conviction nor was he losing hope in the efficacy of nonviolence. He felt confident that his

243

conviction would be reversed on appeal and that there was still a basis for hope in the democratic creed. "If we have the courage in America to transform democracy from thin paper to thick action, we will find that we are involved in the greatest form of government that the mind has ever conceived. So we're not to lose faith in democracy. We feel that democracy gives us this right to protest."(35) In brief, his conviction will be shown to have been illegal, protest is a legal right, King was actually protesting not disobeying, and militant nonviolence is nothing more nor less than the translation of democracy from theory to practice.

This same kind of explanation of his activities was offered repeatedly by King. On the National Broadcasting Company television program, Face The Nation, King affirmed that, in breaking local laws that violated the federal Constitution, he and his followers were really seeking to dignify the law, to affirm its real, positive meaning. The fundamental law of the land said that separate but equal facilities were unequal. To violate laws that supported separate facilities was to honor the basic law of the land.(36) This was also the whole defense of his actions in Birmingham and Selma. He appealed against local law to the more fundamental law of the Constitution and the decisions of the Supreme Court, and pointed to the legal victories that had been won as vindication of his actions. In actual practice, at least until the events at Selma, King always had the built-in control of honoring and never disobeying federal court decisions.

The first breach in this dyke came over the now controversial incident of the march from Selma to Montgomery. In the face of a federal injunction, King led his followers over the Edmund Pettis Bridge and up to the waiting state troopers who barred his way. His wife has reported that King had agonized over the decision to disobey the injunction "because it was against his principles to flaunt federal law,"(37) but that he finally decided to go ahead rather than butcher his conscience. It has become sufficiently clear from the available data that this episode was not one of King's finer moments, and it won him no admiration or support from either the principled advocates of nonviolence or from the tacticians of it.(38) On this occasion mighty Homer nodded. If any defense can be offered for King's decision - none can be offered for his equivocation - it can only be that he was not fond of seeing people beaten up and bloodied, and in the face of certain violence he made a prudential decision that it was not worth enduring the violence at this moment. Depending on one's viewpoint, the incident shows King's pragmatism or his cowardice and lack of principle. But it certainly reinforces the interpretation of nonviolence in relation to law that is being offered here. The judgment on his pragmatism or cowardice seems best left to a wisdom higher than humans possess.

The hardest problem law posed for militant nonviolence was how to determine the difference between a just law and an unjust law. Granted the importance of the rule of law, granted the moral obligation to disobey unjust law, how did one determine which laws were just and which were not? Even if he used federal law as a guideline for what was just and unjust, did not King set himself up at times as his own Supreme Court? How did he tell the just law from the unjust one? King was forced to address himself to this question on more than one occasion and he did so without making any original or startling contribution to its resolution. In a television interview in 1960 he offered a few thoughts on the subject. He proffered the dubious generalization that segregation generated a feeling of inferiority in those who were segregated and so this was a violation of the equal protection clause of the fourteenth amendment to the U.S. Constitution. He pointed to the equally doubtful general principle that, if the law of a nation conflicted with the higher moral law, or if local law conflicted with federal law, resistance or disobedience was in order.(39) But he offered no norms to indicate how one would know or judge these things.

Later in the same year King appeared on a televised debate with the nationally syndicated, conservative columnist, James Kilpatrick. The question debated was whether or not the sit-ins at commercial establishments refusing to serve black patrons were justified.(40) During the debate King was pushed to articulate his position more fully and more deeply. He repeated the familiar point that the sit-in strikers were showing the highest respect for law in as much as they wanted to see all laws just and in line with the moral law of the universe.

Their willingness to suffer in order to bring local customs and laws in line with the moral law and the federal Constitution showed this respect. Under questioning and challenge King insisted that an unjust law was no law at all and that one told the difference on the basis of conscience. As for ways to test the correctness of one's conscience, King suggested three: the insights of history that come from saints and prophets; the best evidence of today's intellectual disciplines; all that we find in the religious insights of the ages. As a summary statement of his position he added that "I think we will all agree that any law that degrades human personality is an unjust law, and one's conscience should reveal that to him."(41) When asked whether everyone has the right to decide for him or herself what is just and unjust, King put two limitations on such a right; that the person do it on the basis of conscience and in a nonviolent, peaceful, loving way.

King's most extensive discussion of how to determine an unjust law appeared in his famous <u>Letter From Birmingham Jail</u>.(42) A classic though it undoubtedly is, the letter itself is more of an apologia than a clear, systematic treatment of a question. In order to put King's ideas in as clear a context as possible, a few precisions are in order at this point.

There are two ways in which law may malfunction in society. A law may be improperly applied or misused with the consequence that a legal injustice occurs. Or the law itself may be objected to on moral grounds, as being itself unjust. An example of the first type of malfunction would be the use of laws directed against disorderly public conduct that disturbs the public peace to inforce racial segregation. The injustice involved in such a practice is not intrinsic to the law itself but in the application and misuse of the law. The result of such misuse of the law is a legal injustice - of course, if done deliberately, there is also a moral injustice - for which there is a legal remedy.(43) The malfunction of the law occurs because what was theoretically required by the law was not carried out in practice. The charge of injustice is an objection not to the law itself, but to the way in which the law was administered. And the appeal for justice is not an appeal to some higher law or norm, but to the actual law itself.

For an example of the second way in which law can malfunction we may turn to the classic case of Socrates. Socrates himself - or Plato - seemed to accept the laws under which he was tried and convicted as valid, constitutionally correct laws. Nor did he find any injustice in their application. If such was, in fact, the case, then there was no legal injustice done. To object to his execution as unjust would be, therefore, to object to the laws themselves as unjust. That is to say, the objection would have to be made on moral rather than legal grounds. The appeal for justice would require an appeal to some norm or law that transcended the actual law of Athens. These two types of malfunction both result in injustice and both may provoke disobedience to unjust law, but the challenge inherent in each case is quite different.(44)

King was aware of this difference. In determining how to tell whether a law is just or unjust, he offered the following guidelines in his famous letter. "A just law is a man-made law that squares with the moral law or the law of God."(45) To give more specific content to that general principle, he added that any law that upgrades human personality is just, any law that degrades human personality is unjust. A law that urges upon a person a false sense of inferiority or superiority would be degrading and therefore unjust. In addition, a law that separates people arbitrarily or which relegates them to the status of things to be used by others would be degrading. A second norm for the justice of law is its universal applicability. A law made by a majority which applies to and binds a minority, but does not equally bind the majority who made it would be unjust. A law made by the majority but which binds all citizens alike would be just.(46) A third norm for discriminating between just and unjust law is whether or not a minority had a role in devising or enacting the law. If the minority were excluded from participation in framing and passing the law, whether by force, subterfuge or law itself, the resulting law is unjust. These three norms all speak to the intrinsic justice of the law itself. Lastly, King considered the just law which is misused. "Sometimes a law is just on its face and unjust in its application." Indeed, King was sitting in the Birmingham

247

jail for just that reason. "For instance, I have been arrested on a charge of parading without a permit. Now, there is nothing wrong in having an ordinance which requires a permit for a parade. But such an ordinance becomes unjust when it is used to maintain segregation and to deny citizens the First-amendment privilege of peaceful assembly and protest."(47)

In this last instance, King was obviously talking about a legal injustice. It was not the ordinance that was unjust, and strictly speaking it did not become unjust in its misuse. It was the administration of the law that was unjust. Civil disobedience in this case, and in almost every case in which King himself was involved, was not against the law itself, but against its misuse. It deserves to be noticed that protest or disobedience against misuse of law is itself an act of reverence not only for the rule of law in general but also for the specific law being misused. Although King talked in more dramatic fashion and used examples that were of genuine revolutionary import,(48) his own practice of civil disobedience was confined to protest against the law's misuse, a type of reform activity rather than the revolutionary overthrow of a system.

It was simply not true, therefore, as Lionel Lakos, one of King's severest critics, has charged,(49) that King's concept of civil disobedience was that any person could flout any law he or she conscientiously could not obey. King was careful, if not terribly precise and profound, in hedging what conscientious disobedience meant. As an additional safeguard and limit on such disobedience, he insisted that it had to be done in an open or public manner, lovingly, and with a willingness to accept the penalty for violating the law. But the real point for King was not really the justice or injustice of law, but the difference between what he called the enforceable and the unenforceable. Law could, at best, define and control the enforceable limits of human behavior, and so guard against the disturbance of public peace and order. The customs and habits of people, their sense of values and their common sense attitudes, these were the more binding and positive forces of a society.(50) Militant nonviolence, as King practiced it, was an effort to speak to the customs and values of a people, to illuminate and challenge them, even while acting within the framework of the law. That this kind of activity also needs some ordering and regulating was exactly the insight and the purpose of the nonviolent requirements.

Unlike his inspiration, Thoreau, whose civil disobedience was basically a private act done to safeguard the integrity of his own conscience, King saw civil disobedience as an instrument of social change, as an instrument of power and persuasion aimed at the integrity of society's conscience. As he defined its limits, it was a type of activity not only compatible with the Christian command to love one's neighbor, but was the actual content and meaning of that command in certain circumstances. Unfortunately his own thinking on the relationships involved was not always clear or consistent. With the passage of time he gave up speaking about love as a powerful tool of social change and granted power a more independent status.(51) But he continued to look upon civil disobedience as a powerful weapon in the nonviolent arsenal, and one in accord with Christian morality, though justice rather than love moved to the forefront of concern.(52) Despite the rhetorical confusion in many of King's pronouncements, a careful reflection will bring some accuracy and order to the relationships of love, power, justice and authority.

Power according to King, is "the ability to achieve purpose."(53) Defined in this way power is clearly an ethically neutral reality, in divine as well as in human life. As we have seen, in his understanding of the divine being, King effected only a contingent unity between God's goodness and God's power. God's love was seen as a self-imposed limitation on His own power. It was precisely in this loving self-limitation that God's goodness was both reflected and effected. That is a conception which is inherently contradictory.(54) But in any case, power, to be morally good in its exercise, stands in need of both authorization and justification. Love was understood to be of a different nature than power. It was redeeming good will for human beings. As the supreme value, it served as the authorization for all human activity, while being self-authorizing. What love needs in its concrete expression in particular acts is justification. Although King spoke of love as being itself powerful, it is very hard to understand what this could mean, and it is beyond doubt that such rhetoric clouds clear thinking. But it would appear that in his own mind there was a sharp difference between the persuasion at which loved aimed and which was the way it worked, and coercion which, at least at times, he seemed to think was the way power worked. This sharp difference lies at the very heart of militant nonviolence and is ultimately the reason why King accepted it as the only method of social change in keeping with love. But once again there is no clear or systematic explanation of this difference and many people have seen in militant nonviolence, particularly when expressed through massive civil disobedience, a very overt form of coercion that is not only psychological but often physical.(55)   To conclude this chapter, then, an effort will be made to assess the charges of lawlessness and coercion in regard to militant nonviolence.

From a purely pragmatic viewpoint King was convinced that the ability to achieve purpose, power, was not to be acquired through violent means. "There is more power in socially organized masses on the march than there is in guns in the hands of a few desperate men."(56)   If we start with this perception, one thing that emerges about power is that it is "an instrumental value, something that is sought not in its own right, but to obtain something else."(57)   Consequently, part of the ethical justification of any exercise of power will be based upon the end or purpose it seeks to achieve. Yet power also has the nature of being an end in itself in as much as it is a necessary condition for acting at all and for even thinking in terms of goals and ends.(58) Power is as essential to human acting as is air and food and water.   Also from King's initial perception, it appears that power is "the human ability not just to act but to act in concert.   Power is never the property of an individual; it belongs to a group and remains in existence only as long as the group remains together."(59)   Power, then, is a necessary condition for social human beings to act at all, and from an ethical and theological standpoint an "appreciation of power as a basic good, which can be perverted but need not be, is fundamental."(60)   It is a basic, ontic or pre-moral good in as much as it is essential to human life.(61)   Human beings have a right to it.   Power, then, is something that may be used badly, in both moral and pragmatic ways, but it need not be.   King's hesitation in the face of the slogan, Black Power, showed his ambivalence and lack of clarity in regard to power, but the emergence of the slogan forced him to clarify the distinction of love and power and to accept the basic necessity and goodness of power.

As a necessary condition of social action, power needs no further justification. While it is true that power can quickly take on the guise of an ultimate value simply because it is necessary for the pursuit of other ends,(62) it still requires no more justification than food or fresh air. What power does need is authorization,(63) a direction in which to act, a charter, as it were, for its exercise, in accord with which particular exercises of power can be judged to be moral or immoral, in accord with the original authorization or contrary to or beyond it. For King this authorization came from God's Will, or the moral law of the universe, or from love, all of which stand at the beginning of action rather than at the end. Love, seen as the authority for power, means much more than the motivation out of which one acts or the attitude one takes toward action. As the charter or authority for one's actions and consequently as the norm in accord with which one's particular actions are morally justified, love refers explicitly to <u>agape</u>, to the forgiving and redeeming good will of God, to a given and not to an ideal to be realized. The place that love occupies indicates how deeply and fundamentally religious King's conception of nonviolence was, and clearly marks it off from a purely pragmatic nonviolence that can only seek justification from the results it achieves. Love, as the authority of power, is perceived to be powerful and so can easily be confused with power, simply because the hallmark of all authority that is recognized as such is unquestioning obedience. Authority recognized as such focuses people in a common direction and enables them to act in concert.

This abstract analysis can be clarified and confirmed if we consider to what extent King himself can be said to have had power. Properly speaking King had no power. Power is the property of a group, not an individual. What King had was a kind of charismatic authority that was rooted in certain qualities of his personality but also in the convergence of certain beliefs, values and hopes of parts of the black and white communities of the United States at a particular point in history. His authority drew these people to act in concert and they were powerful as long as they stayed together and acted together, as long as they remained "socially organized masses on the march." The few desperate men with guns or bombs in their hands had them because they lacked power. Nor can the instruments of violence create power; they can, however, certainly destroy it, either by terrorizing people so that they are too afraid to act together or by killing the charismatic authority that brought them together.

On the political level, and as a translation of the moral order into practical, social life, the Constitution of the United States was the charter or authority for King's actions, most especially for acts of protest and civil disobedience. Within the framework of social life established by the Constitution, the human right to power can only be insured by guaranteeing the basic human rights of free speech, press, assembly, worship and so forth. That is to say, what can be legally assured is not the ability to act, not the moral right to act, but only the opportunity or space to act, the legal right to act. Within the same constitutional framework specific laws also authorize action, but such laws draw their authority not from themselves but from the Constitution, and so again they may provide a legal right to act but not necessarily a moral right. As King's critic Lionel Lokos rightly pointed out, "King realized - and made a legion of mayors and sheriffs realize - that virtually any law can be rendered null and void if enough people chose to disobey it."(64) True as that is, the mayors and sheriffs should hardly have needed King to remind them of that. For the real point is not that law can in this way be rendered null and void, but that a law that is so widely disobeyed is a law that has been perceived to be without authority, and so no law at all. It is without right. In such a situation the legislative authority has no choice but to abrogate or change the law or to resort to the means of violence to preserve order. The great displays of violence both in Birmingham and Selma were exactly such a resort by Alabama state and local officials in the absence of authority. Such displays merely served to confirm what King had claimed from the first, that lawful order had broken down completely in the South and order was being preserved through terror and violence. The judgment of the Courts and the majority

252

of his fellow citizens, and certainly of history, was that he was quite right.

Lokos has also called King's tactics in Birmingham and Selma a form of political blackmail and an imposition of his will and purpose upon the black and white moderates, upon parents and federal officials.(65) Since King left Birmingham and Selma proclaiming victory, it could well be taken that he had his way against the will and purpose of all those who opposed him and who he had failed to freely persuade and win over to his viewpoint. In order to speak to this charge of coercion and blackmail, and to clarify how persuasion differs from coercion, some definitions are in order.

The common dictionary definition of coerce is "to restrain or dominate by nullifying individual choice, to compel an act or choice, to enforce by force or threat;" on the other hand, to persuade is "to move by argument, entreaty, or expostulation to a belief, position or course of action, to plead with."(66) King, although a great sermonizer and a man of many words, certainly used more than words in Birmingham and Selma. If to go beyond words is in every case to turn to coercion and abandon persuasion, then militant nonviolence has to be acknowledged to be a form of coercion, because its genius is as a form of action. But at least this much must be said. The freedoms offered by the Bill of Rights extend beyond the freedoms of speech and press, the freedom to use words. Human freedom above all else means the right and the ability to act, and to act not only on one's own private concerns and business, but to act together with others in the public world. Human freedom properly includes the right and ability to be noticed and acknowledged.(67)

If power, understood as the ability of people to act in concert, and action itself, are in every case coercive, then the charge of coercion becomes meaningless.(68) If, on the other hand, it is possible to exercise power in non-coercive ways, if action, with the very real demands it imposes on both the agents and the recipients of action, is not essentially coercive, then it becomes critically important to know the difference. With the refinements and advances in understanding the processes of communication and motivation, the lines between persuasion, manipulation and coercion grow very hard to draw.

253

Yet human freedom demands that there be some lines drawn, both moral and legal. Not all such limits can be set by law. In a democratic society law provides the space in which public action is possible. Within that space a measure of moral control is also required, or what King called obedience to the unenforceable. The discipline of nonviolent resistance as practiced by King was designed to provide the needed moral control. King expected to guard against coercion, not merely by the emphasis on love and humility as basic attitudes of the actors, but also by leaving open to others the choice of how they would respond. There was nothing about his demands or activities in Birmingham or Selma that dictated or forced a specific course of action upon others. He acknowledged quite openly that he and his followers did what they did in order to change the present situation, to create tension, to make negotiation a desirable option.(69) He was willing to negotiate even before he acted, but the action itself was of singular importance. For the action was not an instrument of coercion but was already the first step in achieving the freedom he was seeking.

A final criticism directed by Lokos at King's activities in Birmingham was that "there is not a particle of evidence that all of King's demonstrations and foot-soldiers-all of King's crisis-ridden confrontations accomplished anything in Birmingham that could not have been accomplished if he had never set foot in the city at all."(70) Such a charge is correct if human freedom and responsibility are understood in abstract and ideal terms. But the evidence that King and his followers made a major difference is abundant, if one understands the significance of action to be precisely the concrete exercise of responsible freedom, a freedom which leads to new possibilities for action and so increased freedom and responsibility. Charles W. Walker caught this notion in his assessment of the nonviolent action in the South.

> The major contribution of nonviolence in the Southern struggle was to enable black people to act in new ways no longer immobilized by their fears of the white man nor of themselves. A great new flowering of energies resulted, and made possible more wide-ranging efforts to change American life.(71)

Charles Hamilton grasped the same point in his suggestion that "the considerable amount of direct action that has characterized the decade of the 1960's is very much a consequence of broadening the base of political participation," and was by no means a rejection of the rule of law or of legal action.(72) To be free not only must human beings have the opportunity and the ability to act; they must act. What ultimately marked off action that is persuasive from action that is coercive in King's own mind and what he offered as the final safeguard against willful and lawless activity was the norm of suffering. Who suffers and who is inflicting the suffering become the central questions. We turn then to the place and function of suffering in militant nonviolence.

1. This, of course, is Hobbes' expression in Leviathan, Oakeshott (ed.), p. 100, but it is well to keep in mind Marx's insistence on class warfare, an insistence which has permeated all liberation movements in the contemporary setting and which has made the positive virtues of conflict rather than harmony the central focus of modern concern.

2. Arendt, On Revolution, pp. 156-164, 182-205 discusses the unnecessary quest for an absolute to authorize political power.

3. For the notion of personal strength as distinct from power, and of violence as an instrumental reality, which is an extension of personal strength, see Arendt, On Violence, pp. 44-46.

4. R.M. McIver, The Modern State (Oxford University Press, 1964), pp. 5-13, 221-230, 250-263.

5. Since this point may be readily disputed, an additional word seems in order. I am not concerned here with whether in an ideal world there would not be law of some kind. I am merely claiming that in an ideal world where people both freely know the good and freely did it, there would be no need for any possible laws to have sanctions attached to them, and that such a world is unintelligible to us, albeit not unimaginable. More simply put, we can only dream of such a world; we do not know how to achieve it.

6. Robert T. Hall, The Morality of Civil Disobedience (New York, Evanston, San Francisco, London: Harper & Row, 1971), pp. xi-xv.

7. Ibid., pp. 13-17, discusses the difficulties of defining civil disobedience without prejudicing its ethical character.

8. Bishop, p. 394.

9. Lewis, pp. 276-282.

10. Sibley, in Nonviolence After Gandhi, p. 22.

11. BU Coll., XIV (58).

12. Ibid., I (11A), p. 8 of the manuscript of the speech.

13. Ibid., V (177), p. 4 of the manuscript copy of the article. The "he" in the quotation refers specifically to the novelist William Faulkner who had publicly urged such a retreat.

14. Ibid., IV(40); the letter was dated 11/5/57.

15. Ibid.

16. Ibid., IV(3); the letter is dated 11/18/59; William MIller, Martin Luther King, Jr: His Life, Times and Martydom, p. 97, has summarized King's attitude in this matter extremely well. "He had few qualms about the use of armed restraint to enforce justice if it could not be secured directly by the moral appeal of nonviolence itself. In this, his idealism was tempered by a Niebuhrian pragmatism not seen in a Tolstoy or a Gandhi. No one knew better than he the potential of the oppressed for violence, but he saw too that it had best be held back as a tragic last resort, for mob violence, black or white, spelled chaos."

17. BU Coll., V(177).

18. Ibid.

19. Ibid., IV(19); the letter was dated 2/6/58. Thurgood Marshall, later to be a Justice of the United States Supreme Court, was at the time chief legal counsel for the NAACP.

20. Ibid., I(5); the comments appeared in The Times of India February 13, 1959).

21. BU Coll. I(11A); the testimony was given August 11, 1956.

22. Ibid., I(5); the quote appeared in American Reporter New Delhi (February 13, 1959).

23. BU Coll., I(30); I(50); V(177); VI(152); III(10); XIV(7); also see the interview with

King in <u>U.S. News and World Report</u> (March 21, 1960).

24. King, <u>Stride Toward Freedom</u>, p. 167; <u>BU Coll.</u> V(177).

25. Walton, pp. 114-116.

26. <u>BU Coll.</u> I(17); the quotation is from the transcript of the NBC television program <u>Meet the Press</u> (April 17, 1960). Given the nature of television programs King may be excused for failing to note that the Boston Tea Party was not a nonviolent action by anybody's definition.

27. <u>BU Coll.</u>, XIV(7); from the manuscript copy of an article, "A Legacy of Creative Protest," written by King for <u>The Massachusetts Review</u>, IV, I (Autumn 1962), p. 43.

28. Hall, pp. 17-23.

29. In addition to the pertinent works already cited, see Thomas A. Shannon, <u>Render Unto God: A Theology of Selective Obedience</u> (New York: Paulis Press, 1974) and the excellent bibliography, pp. 173-180, and Hugo Adam Bedau (ed.), <u>Civil Disobedience, Theory and Practice</u> Indianapolis, New York: Pegasus, 1969).

30. Hall, p. 18.

31. The classic example in Acts 5:22-33 is an instance of the first situation. Those people who find themselves opposed to the present abortion laws in the United States as too permissive are in the second situation. This difference was not clarified by King.

32. <u>BU Coll.</u>, I(11), from the manuscript of a sermon given on November 4, 1956, at the Dexter Avenue Baptist Church. See also King, <u>Strength To Love</u>, pp. 157-158.

33. <u>BU Coll.</u>, V(177); from the article, "Our Struggle," p. 2.

34. <u>Ibid.</u>, I(11A); from the manuscript of an article intended for <u>The Progressive</u> (April 4, 1960).

35. _Ibid._, X(40); the speech was given on March 22, 1956.

36. _Ibid._, I(17).

37. Coretta Scott King, _My Life_, p. 262.

38. Lewis, pp. 276-282 has a good account of the incident and the criticisms. The best discussion of the events in Selma can be found in David J. Garrow, _Protest at Selma: Martin Luther King, Jr., and the Voting Rights Act of 1965_ (New Haven: Yale University Press, 1978).

39. _BU Coll._, I(17); I have called the generalization and the principle doubtful because segregation did not generate a feeling of inferiority in all who suffered it, and because it is more than theoretically possible that a local law could be just while the conflicting federal law was unjust.

40. _Ibid._, IV(28); Manuscript of the NBC television program _The Nation's Future_ (November 26, 1960).

41. _Ibid._; the failure here to distinguish between a legal right and a moral right, between protest and disobedience, and between the sources of moral insight and the norms of moral judgment is obvious, and it again makes clear that King is engaged in exhortation rather than explanation. The one important norm for morality is how law objectively relates to the dignity of the human person.

42. King, _Why We Can't Wait_, pp. 76-95.

43. Hall, pp. 2-10.

44. _Ibid._, pp. 10-12.

45. King, _Why We Can't Wait_, p. 82.

46. It is worth noting the somewhat problematic nature of this second norm. The segregation laws King was protesting were made by a majority and bound everyone equally. White people could get in as much trouble violating them as black people, though obviously they burdened black people to a much more extensive degree.

259

47. King, <u>Why We Can't Wait</u>, p. 83.

48. <u>Ibid.</u>, pp. 84-85.

49. Lokos, pp. 460-461.

50. <u>BU Coll.</u>, I(50).

51. King, <u>Where Do We Go From Here?</u>, pp. 42-43.

52. King, <u>The Trumpet of Conscience</u>, pp. 53-54.

53. King, <u>Where Do We Go From Here?</u>, p. 42.

54. If God has the ability to limit his own power, that itself is power, the ability to achieve purpose, even if one wishes to call it love. If one tries to think this through, it is clearly incoherent.

55. King himself sounds like this at times. See King, <u>Why We Can't Wait</u>, p. 37. and <u>The Trumpet of Conscience</u>, p. 15.

56. <u>BU Coll.</u>, I(58); from the manuscript of an article intended for <u>The Southern Patriot</u>, XVIII, (January, 1960), p. 3.

57. Barrington Moore, Jr., <u>Political Power and Social Theory</u> (New York: Harper & Row, 1965), p. 14.

58. Arendt, <u>On Violence</u>, p. 51.

59. <u>Ibid.</u>, p. 44.

60. Rahner, "The Theology of Power," <u>Theological Investigations</u>, IV, p. 401.

61. For a clear explanation of the difference between ontic and moral good and evil see Louis Janssens, "Ontic and Moral Evil," <u>Louvain Studies</u> 4 (1972), pp. 115-156.

62. Moore, p. 15; in this regard power is much like the value of life which is not an ultimate value but can appear readily to be so because it is the basic precondition for experiencing all other values. See Richard A. McCormick, "To Save or Let Die; The Dilemma of Modern Medi-

cine," <u>Contemporary Issues in Bioethics</u>, eds. Tom L. Beauchamp and LeRoy Walters (Belmont, California: Wadsworth Publishing Company, 1978), pp. 334-337.

63. Arendt, <u>On Violence</u>, p. 52.

64. Lokos, p. 461.

65. <u>Ibid.</u>, p. 154, 461.

66. The definitions are taken from <u>Webster's Seventh New Collegiate Dictionary</u>, pp. 160 and 631.

67. Arendt, <u>On Revolution</u>, pp. 123-130. Of course, human freedom also properly includes the right to privacy, the right not to be noticed. But not all acts carry either right at the discretion of the actor. It is not always easy to distinguish between private and public acts, or personal and social acts, but in assessing rights it is essential. Much of the confusion over the abortion issue is located in this failure, as well as debates over the kinds of public disclosures appropriate to public officials. To give but one example, one's sexual behavior is a private or personal act and deserves privacy. Becoming pregnant is a public or social act, one which rightly merits public attention.

68. Segundo, <u>The Liberation of Theology</u>, pp. 156-162, fails to see that action needs authorization as well as justification, and so treats all action as coercive.

69. King, <u>Why We Can't Wait</u>, p. 79.

70. Lokos, p. 152.

71. Charles C. Walker, in <u>Nonviolence After Gandhi</u>, p. 81.

72. Charles V. Hamilton, "Direct Action, Racial Protest, and Public Policy," <u>Law and Disorder: The Legitimation of Direct Action as and Instrument of Social Policy</u>, compiled by Samuel L. Shuman. The Franklin Memorial Lectures Vol. XIX (Detroit: Wayne State University, 1971), p. 128. James Farmer, p. 196, made the same point:

"There is no freedom without political self-expression."

CHAPTER VIII

THE MATTER OF SUFFERING

In the experience of classical Christian pacifism the theoretical criticism of ethical irresponsibility was often accompanied by the far more
troublesome practice of persecution. In the face of
overt hostility and persecution the moral viability
of the pacifist position is considerably strengthened. For, in the context of suffering for one's
beliefs, it becomes more visibly a witness for truth
and a protest against injustice. It loses any guise
of being self-serving indifference or a comfortable
escape from worldly responsibility. The suffering
that pacifists patiently endure becomes itself the
mark of their sincerity and credibility to the world.
It was such a stance of suffering that won for the
pacifist position a great deal of respect and provided it with a measure of justification. The end of
the persecution of pacifists sects created the same
kind of dilemma for pacifists that confronted the
early Christian Church when it was first tolerated
and then established as the religion of the Roman
Empire. Some share of responsibility for the order,
protection and well-being of society had to be
assumed. And so the forms and meaning of suffering
in human life also had to be reassessed.(1)

Despite the fact that suffering was regarded as
a sign of authentic Christian witness and a mark of
seriousness and sincerity, it was not considered to
be of value for its own sake. In traditional pacifist witness it was something to be expected in a
violent and sinful world but not something to be
sought after. In militant nonviolence, however, the
claims made for suffering are more extensive and the
meaning of suffering more intrinsic to the nonviolent
vocation. Suffering is looked upon as

> a powerful social force when you willingly
> accept that violence on yourself so that
> self-suffering stands at the center of the
> nonviolent movement and the individuals
> involved are able to suffer in a creative
> manner, feeling that unearned suffering is
> redemptive and that suffering may serve to
> transform the social situation.(2)

The Christian roots of this idea are obviously to be found most directly in the redemptive suffering and death of Jesus of Nazareth and in the resultant faith which sees in the cross and resurrection the key to the meaning of life. But the significance which militant nonviolence attached to suffering was wider and more profound than a simple imitation of Jesus or the desire to be a martyr as the highest embodiment of love, although, as a personal motivation, the former motive was of no small moment for King himself.(3)

The earliest explanation King offered to account for the redeeming power of suffering that was willingly accepted looked to the ambiguous power of suffering to reflect sincerity and seriousness of purpose. This reflection of one's moral dedication was thought to result in one's adversaries being touched in conscience and shamed by their own attitudes and actions, with the consequence that they would be won over to a new way of perceiving and dealing with the conflict situation. The power invoked in this perception of the matter appears to be a form of psychological manipulation in which one tries to play upon the shame and guilt feelings of one's adversaries. A letter King addressed to some freedom riders being held in the Rock Hill, South Carolina county jail is a typical instance of this view. "Every day that you remain behind bars sears the conscience of that immoral city. You are shaming them into decency."(4) This line of explanation was very prominent among some American followers of Gandhi(5) and was one King never quite surrendered.(6) But it had less and less importance for him as time went on and consciences were neither seared nor shamed.(7) Even from the very outset of his public career, King had been explicit that the power of suffering did not lie in the pity that one's weakness, pain or helplessness might evoke. Nonviolence was not a method for the otherwise weak and helpless, nor was the suffering he extolled the result of an inability to escape it. "If one uses this method because he is afraid or merely because he lacks the instruments of violence, he is not truly nonviolent."(8)

Although his understanding of the power of suffering underwent change, the basis on which the central importance of suffering rested did not. The basis was and remained the suffering Christ. In his university days King had looked upon the vicarious redemptive suffering of the suffering servant in the book of Isaiah as the most noble teaching of the Hebrew Scriptures, as well as the answer to the problem of evil.(9) He had the fanciful idea that it had been the suffering of Stephen, the first Christian martyr, that touched the conscience of the young Saul and enabled him to see Jesus as the supreme sufferer of humanity. The power of the cross, he judged, came from the impact upon conscience of the brutality of the crucifixion which led to a transforming awareness.(10) In the same way the suffering and self-limitation of Jesus awakened human beings to the nobler possibilities of their nature. The cross is salvific because it attacks the moral inadequacies of human beings and reveals to them their own higher possibilities.(11)

Once again in examining King's ideas on suffering we are dealing more with an attitude and a temperament than with a carefully thought-out and well-grounded idea. In his class notes from Boston University he discussed a view of the divine nature in which the divine power is finite while the divine goodness is infinite, and expressed his sympathy for such a view as the only adequate explanation for the existence of evil. He also thought his conception of the divine nature provided a metaphysical basis for the Christian idea of sacrificial love,(12) although I could find no clear explanation of how it does or why King thought it did. In all of King's early notes there is a certain romanticism about suffering. His reading of Christian history which appears to have been highly impressionistic reflects this romantic streak. The suffering of Christians during the period of the Roman Empire lent vim and vitality to the new social order that was coming into being. The martyr Wycliff was "the voice of the people crying for life and freedom."(13) These early ideas are reminiscent of King's public words at various times, and the romanticization of suffering never quite left him as the following later words show.

> We shall match your capacity to inflict suffering by our capacity to endure suffering. We will meet your physical force with soul force. Do to us what you will and we will still love you....throw us in jail and we will still love you. Bomb our homes and threaten our children, and, as difficult as

it is, we will still love you. Send your
hooded perpetrators of violence into our
communities at the midnight hour and drag
us out on some wayside road and leave us
half-dead as you beat us, and we will still
love you. Send your propaganda agents
around the country, and make it appear that
we are not fit, culturally and otherwise,
for integration, and we'll wear you down by
our capacity to suffer, and one day we will
win our freedom. We will not only win
freedom for ourselves; we will so appeal to
your heart and conscience that we will win
you in the process, and our victory will be
a double victory.(14)

This kind of dramatic rhetoric is quite moving,
and it comes easily to the lips as long as one is not
doing the suffering oneself. For all his verbal
exaltation of voluntary suffering King has been
accused of cowardice more than once.(15) In 1961, at
the height of the freedom rides through the deep
South, Robert Williams sent King a telegram containing the following challenge. "No sincere leader asks
his followers to make sacrifices that he himself will
not endure. You are a phony. Gandhi was always in
the forefront suffering with his people. If you are
a leader of this nonviolent movement, lead the way by
example."(16) Unfortunately King's caution and
connections lent him to this kind of charge. His
external sufferings were minimal for a man so much in
the public limelight, and with the growing conviction
in the civil rights movement that a jail sentence or
a beating was a badge of honor, King's credentials
were mediocre.(17)

The difficulties in regard to self-suffering
which beset any person in a position similar to
King's have their origin in the special status which
his role of symbolic leader bestowed upon him. These
difficulties were vividly apparent in his venture in
Chicago. Determined to have a ghetto-based residence
in order to share something of the life of the urban
slums, King took an apartment on South Hamlin Avenue,
only to discover on arrival four plasterers, two
painters, and two electricians busily transforming
his temporary residence to accord with municipal
housing standards.(18) Needless to say, this was not
the ordinary treatment given to most new tenants.
King and his family did experience something of the

stench, crowdedness and abrasiveness of the urban ghetto. It was especially noticeable in his children. But for the Kings there was always the way out. The children could be sent back to the comfortable and loving household in Atlanta, while King himself, busy with many tasks, devoted only three days a week to ghetto life.

King's decision to take a public stand against the Vietnam war again illustrated the difficulties that special status creates for anyone seeking to identify with and share the lot of the oppressed. While his outspoken opposition to the war lost him the confidence of and open access to the White House and influential government councils, and while it brought him into conflict with other civil rights leaders and drew upon his head the predictable charges of communist and traitor, it also won for him a new host of admirers and friends and a new basis of public support. There were no visible signs that King suffered greatly for his stand. Even the decrease in donations to the SCLC, while certainly a personal disappointment, did not cause physical pain or deprivation to King and his family as far as their personal style of living was concerned.(19)

This freedom to take up and to lay down the burden of suffering, to choose whom one's adversaries will be, or to control the extent of personal deprivation, is precisely the major objection that Joseph Washington has raised against the idea of the voluntary acceptance of suffering advocated by militant nonviolence. Washington's objection is essentially theological and is based upon his interpretation of the suffering servant theme in both the Hebrew and Christian scriptures. His challenge to King, and to others who share King's perspective, is both fundamental and profound. It will enable us to bring into sharp focus just how King understood the power in suffering and its meaning in human life.

Washington's argument begins by insisting that God does not ask for volunteers to be his suffering servants. As he has expressed it, "The real difference between being 'chosen' by God and choosing to be 'suffering servants' is the absence of choice; whites who choose to suffer, as do some Christians presently, have an escape hatch which neither Jews nor Negroes enjoy."(20) Therefore Washington's main objection to militant nonviolence rests upon this absence of choice which to his mind is the intrinsic mark of chosenness and which is evidenced in the fact that the truly chosen suffer whether they are willing to do so or not. The declaration of chosenness, he has written, is "a declaration of faith made by the interpreters who in historical perspective," have sought to grasp the meaning of the life of their people.(21) The fact of having been chosen is not something for ecclesiastical promulgation, but is rather to be found in the actual history of a people. The oppressed are recognized as God's chosen ones precisely because they are oppressed through no purpose or intent of their own.(22).

This central idea has led Washington to propose several serious objections against the practice of militant nonviolence. He has found it to be contrived, coercive and inhuman, all of which speaks against its claims to be in keeping with the Christian gospel. His objection to the kind of suffering that King and his followers endured, for example in their marches through the streets of Chicago,(23) was precisely that it was a suffering deliberately provoked and chosen for a purpose. "This is accomplished by advancing a situation to the point of violence and then claiming innocence, whereupon the resister becomes a sacrificial lamb. Yet a sacrificial lamb, in the classic sense, is innocent in a way that the resister is not."(24) In addition, Washington has argued that the cross of Christ was not contrived by Jesus or by God, that God did not force people to act in any particular way. The cross rather reveals that God's way is both a way that respects freedom of choice and a way of reconciliation. He, therefore, objected to nonviolent suffering because it preempted this freedom of choice.(25)

Washington has made several important points in his discussion. He is quite right in asserting that the suffering servant of God is not free to pick and choose suffering, to take it up and lay it down as whim or occasion suits. The servant's suffering is inflicted upon him or her by others as they will. The suffering servant cannot be understood, then, as either the voluntary ascetic or the guilt-ridden neurotic. Washington is also correct in his insistence that God's will and purpose are revealed in unmerited and involuntary suffering, that such suffering in some ways points the servant in the direction of God's plan. In making these points, however, he was not really at odds with King's own understanding of suffering. King, too, regarded unmerited suffering and oppression as opportunity and invitation. But for King suffering of any kind had to be seen as part of the process of life in a sinful world. "Ultimately, the question is not whether or not we will suffer, but whether or not we will have the inner calm to face the trials and tribulations of life."(26) In other words, the key insight for King was that not all suffering is of worth, nor did the mere fact that one was suffering give redemptive power to suffering, as Washington's argument seemed to suggest.(27) The suffering to be redemptive must be voluntarily accepted and willingly absorbed into oneself as an inescapable aspect of cooperating with God's redeeming activity.

The sharp difference between Washington and King on this point can be seen most readily in their different assessments of how one welcomes God's summons to suffer. Washington has written that "Negroes would not wish to be called - and would actively resist - being the 'chosen people' were they consciously to understand and accept the biblical meaning of being chosen by God: inflicted [sic], stricken, grieved, chastised, an offering poured out as intercession for the transgressors. But just as they have neither known nor accepted it, this is their history."(28) Whether or not Washington was factually correct in his judgment that black Americans would resist being God's chosen people, King was certainly of a different mind and had a different hope. It was a call he urged his people to accept and to embrace vigorously as their highest purpose and dignity. His closing statement at the first mass meeting in Montgomery struck this theme and he never retreated from it.

> If you will protest courageously and yet
> with dignity and Christian love, when the
> history books are written in future genera-
> tions, the historians will have to pause
> and say, "There lived a great people - a
> black people - who injected new meaning and
> dignity into the veins of civilization."
> This is our challenge and our overwhelming
> responsibility.(29)

What King consistently stressed, and what Washington appears either to have ignored or rejected,(30) was that the suffering servant suffers because of his or her service, because of fidelity to a personal calling and freely accepted responsibility; the servant is not of service simply by suffering. The suffering is a consequence of a steadfast loyalty to the work God has summoned the servant to do. The servant suffers because he or she must at whatever cost to self remain true to the mission that has been entrusted to him or her. In explaining why he refused to pay a fine and preferred to go to jail before the court of Judge Eugene Loe in Montgomery, King made it clear that he was not motivated by a desire for publicity or by a longing for martyrdom. That would have been a form of spiritual pride. "My action," said King, "is motivated by the impelling voice of conscience and a desire to follow truth and the will of God wherever they lead."(31) King realized that to follow this road, the road of truth, would involve suffering. Jesus had warned his disciples that following him they would encounter opposition and persecution and that warning was amply borne out in history. But it was imperative to go forward on the road and to face the opposition boldly in the faith that God would open the way.(32)

It must also be acknowledged, as Washington has insisted, that to be a black person in America had inevitably entailed suffering, indignity and oppression with no escape short of turning white. Not only was such a possibility not available, but even if it were, it would be a profoundly immoral denial of one's humanity, a denial as immoral as racism itself. What King had clearly grasped was the demand of the human conscience to oppose actively this denial of self, to affirm and insist upon who one was and was called to be without in turn denying any one else's humanity.(33) Only in such an affirmation could black Americans free themselves and make it possible for blacks and whites alike to see the truth and do the work of justice. He realized that such an affirmation would involve new, even additional suffering, not essentially different in kind, perhaps, from what was already the lot of black Americans, though possibly greater in degree. But the new suffering would be different in one essential point, and in this lay its redemptive power. For what King came to see in realizing that militant nonviolence was a life commitment was that only the voluntary acceptance of a suffering that resulted from affirming the truth and standing by that affirmation was redemptive. It was redemptive first for the one who suffered and secondly, and only contingently, for others. For others one could do no more than save and affirm the truth. It had to be left to them whether they would acknowledge and embrace the truth. In concrete terms, King grasped the truth that racism, prejudice, frustration and hatred - none of these could continue to stand against black people and destroy them, if they chose not to let them. Since they were already suffering from them in any case, they must acknowledge that fact, willingly take that suffering upon themselves and actively oppose them by their own self-affirmation. To submit to them in the interests of avoiding trouble - to hate, to despair, to turn bitter and violent - was once again to submit to and cooperate with white oppression and injustice. It was to suffer and yet also to forfeit all hope of redemption.

In this insight, I would suggest, King was at the very heart of the Christian vision and the movement he generated and invited others to join is disclosed as a profoundly religious one. It was a movement that set people free precisely by starting them on the road to freedom and which enunciated the only kind of commitment that would keep them free as they struggled to extend that freedom.(34) To the charge that voluntary self-suffering was manipulative and even inhuman King was not insensitive. It was precisely to avoid the possibility of that kind of coercion that self-suffering was placed at the very center of militant nonviolence. For the nonviolent commitment first does something to the hearts and minds of those who embrace it, generating in them a new self-understanding, a new self-respect, strength and courage.(35) Without this voluntary acceptance, without the inner struggle with self for the moral truth of one's own existence, the external tactics of nonviolence were empty or even coercive.(36) "It must be made palpably clear that resistance and nonviolence are not in themselves good....The tactics of nonviolence without the spirit of nonviolence may indeed become a new kind of violence."(37) To be God's suffering servant required, therefore, more than the mere fact of suffering. It required the interior struggle to accept willingly, if reluctantly, the cross that one has and will have, the struggle of Jesus at Gethsemane, that if the cup cannot pass, your will not mine be done. This is neither passive resignation to necessity nor ascetic self-discipline. William Miller is the biographer who has most accurately reflected this aspect of King's thought and located the dawning of it in his life.

> The real battle had been on the bombed porch of the parsonage - or, perhaps more basically, during the encounter with God, that preceded and prepared him for it. The real struggle, as Martin became increasingly convinced, was the interior one - that between hate and love, fear and courage. He had sought for the personal God of his theological beliefs and discovered the living reality within himself and among his companions in the movement. This growth was not instantaneous; anomolies and equivocations had to be worked through....(38)

Self-suffering, therefore, stands at the very center of militant nonviolence "because it reveals the human capacity to endure and overcome that which is inhuman. It negates the concept that survival is the first law of life. Suffering for a positive purpose says love of mankind is the first law of life."(39) Daniel Berrigan, another advocate of militant nonviolent resistance, has advanced the same point in a distinctive way in his reflections upon Jesus as the suffering servant. In the cross of Christ Berrigan has seen that "God has announced suffering and servanthood as pre-eminent forms of existence in the world. The two vocations are joined by logic and faith."(40) Voluntary acceptance of suffering manifests the human ability to be and to remain human in face of and in despite of the evil and violence that would deny and destroy the humanness of self and other selves. This power in suffering is ultimately rooted in the realities of truth and love whose ultimate origin is God. What is central, therefore, in King's perspective is the positive side of the vocation of the suffering servant, the service the servant performs. This service can be articulated in various ways; as the affirmation of human dignity and freedom, as the struggle to achieve justice, as the willingness to love in the face of hatred or to hope in the face of closed minds and fearful hearts. The resort to violence has to be seen as an act of despair of the humanness of others, as a forfeiture of one's own freedom and a submission to the realm of necessity.(41) It is, finally, to put more trust in the powers of the world than in the power of God which is made manifest in and through human weakness. Since the ability to suffer in this way is altogether dependent upon the gift of God's grace, it is questionable how relevant King's notion of suffering may be for those who do not share his faith.(42)

In addition to the importance of the interior struggle with oneself to which suffering points, there is also an external function of suffering in militant nonviolence which expresses the relationship of suffering to love. This external function sharply distinguishes King from all advocates of the Christian faith as something primarily interior, personal or "purely spiritual." Again William Miller has pointed this out most adequately in a comparison of King and Gandhi.

Gandhi had understood "Unmerited suffering" in terms of the law of karma, with its goal of salvation through an accumulation of merits. Implicit in King's vision is a related Christian idea of brotherly love... the really distinctive concept...was the belief that such love means taking upon oneself a burden of unmerited responsibility. Am I my brother's keeper? Martin King's response was an unequivocal yes.(43)

To be "my brother's keeper" may be a high, and at times even an impossible, ideal, but for King it was the deepest demand and truth of human life. His differences with Washington and other exponents of black power can be seen quite clearly at this point. Washington considered King's demand that neighbor-love be central to the struggle for freedom and justice to be both foolish and pre-mature. He dismissed it lightly. "Moreover" he wrote, "love concerns itself with the post-revolutionary period; it is the way of life in the millenium."(44) Albert Cleage, Jr., to offer but one other example, thought that it was ridiculous to talk about loving your enemy. "We believe in justice. We don't even think about love." Love, such as it is, was for inside the Black Nation and even there it was hard. Necessity and survival, not love, is what unites the Black Nation.(45)

273

For both practical and ethical reasons King rejected that line of interpretation and argument, even as a temporary necessity or strategy, and it is what most clearly divided him from the Black Power position.(46) The validity and persuasiveness of his practical reasons, however, were dependent upon the acceptance of his ethical vision. He continued, he said, to follow the nonviolent approach because it was "the most practically sound and morally excellent way for the Negro to achieve freedom."(47) Putting self-suffering at the heart of the liberation struggle had the merit and function of saving a person from ideology,(48) from expediency and willfullness. Self-suffering is to be understood as a functional and necessary condition of honoring the process and the present. So understood, it represents an explicit repudiation of situation ethics and utilitarianism. At its core King's position is a theological one and his differences with authors like Washington, Cleage or Cone are differences not in intention or hope or purpose, and not even over their reading of the contemporary situation and the depth of racism, but over what is true and required in Christian faith. King's espousal of nonviolence and voluntary suffering was rooted in his understanding of God and His Christ, and his basic willingness to let God's Will set the agenda for human action.

On the other hand, Black Power, as interpreted through the theology of an author like Cone with its explicit rejection of nonviolence, was based on one misunderstanding of King and on a conversion of theology to ideology. The misunderstanding lay in the unwarranted extension of militant nonviolence to the sphere of private and personal relationships.(49) As was pointed out in the previous chapter, King had few, if any, qualms about the use of federal troops to enforce law and restrain violence. Nor was his advocacy of nonviolence a demand that one should not defend his home against thieves or his wife against rape. He advanced nonviolence as a method to eliminate social evil and the only claims he made for it were that it was both a practical and moral way to achieve that end. He did not, unlike Gandhi, claim that it would put an end to private criminal activity.

The conversion of theology to ideology can be illustrated most clearly in the writings of James Cone. For one example, he has written as follows:

Black Theology is not prepared to accept
any doctrine of God, man, Christ or Scripture which contradicts the black demand for
freedom now. It believes that any idea
which exalts black dignity and creates a
restless drive for freedom must be affirmed. All ideas which are opposed to the
struggle for black self-determination or
are irrelevant to it, must be rejected as
the work of the Anti-Christ.(50)

In case his point was missed, Cone repeated the same
idea on the following page in explaining the ultimate
norm and authority of theological truth. "If [a]
doctrine is compatible with or enhances the drive for
black freedom, then it is the gospel of Jesus Christ.
If the doctrine is against or indifferent to the
essence of blackness as expressed in Black Power,
then it is the work of the Anti-Christ. It is as
simple as that."(51)

It was just this sort of inversion of truth and
consequences, of ends and means, of valid hopes and
wishful desires that King feared and which he found
so repulsive in Communism. He shared deeply with
Cone the conviction that the gospel of Jesus Christ
was on the side of black dignity and black liberation. But in proclaiming the truth and the promise
of human dignity and freedom equally for all of God's
children which was the gospel message, King saw the
danger and the falsehood in asserting that every
expression of what a person conceived to be his or
her right and dignity was, therefore, the way God
manifested himself and was to be taken as the touchstone of God's truth. It was this kind of ideological defense of self-interest that King had attempted
to challenge in Chicago, in Memphis and in his
opposition to the war in Viet Nam. Human beings do
not know what is ultimately for their good; only God
does. The method of militant nonviolence, with its
acceptance of self-suffering and unmerited responsibility, was King's answer to self-deception,
self-justification, and ideological blindness.
King's own theological insight and moral stature are
reflected in a passage of James Baldwin which King
himself quoted in one of his own books. It reveals
plainly the route King took to finding the good and
the true.

The really terrible thing, old buddy, is
that you must accept them. And I mean that
very seriously. You must accept them and
accept them with love. For these innocent
people have no other hope. They are, in
effect, still trapped in a history which
they do not understand; and until they
understand it, they cannot be released from
it. They have had to believe for many
years, and for innumerable reasons, that
black men are inferior to white men. Many
of them, indeed, know better, but, as you
will discover, people find it very difficult to act on what they know. To act is
to be committed, and to be committed is to
be in danger. In this case, the danger, in
the minds of most white Americans, is the
loss of their identity....But these men are
your brothers - your lost, younger brothers. And if the word integration means
anything, this is what it means: that we,
with love, shall force our brothers to see
themselves as they are, to cease fleeing
from reality and begin to change it....(52)

In addition to the theological and ethical
questions that can be asked about the meaning of
suffering in militant nonviolence, there also exist
certain psychological and practical questions relevant to self-suffering. James W. Vander Zanden has
pointed out some of the ambivalence and ambiguity in
the actual working out of King's program and especially in his insistence on loving one's enemies.(53)
Because of the considerable undercurrents of resentment toward white people and the whole southern
racial structure, Southern blacks harbored considerable latent aggressive impulses toward whites.
Having been socialized in a system that called for
the suppression of hostility and aggression toward
whites, and with a strong religious tradition of
Christianity stressing love and forgiveness and
tabooing hate, many blacks developed deep-seated
feelings of self-hatred and guilt. Vander Zanden saw
in militant nonviolence a solution to these conflicting currents of feeling. It was permissible to feel
hostility and to engage in aggressive activities
against the existing social order. Indeed, there was
even a moral obligation to do so. At the same time,
there remained the strong emphasis on such activity
being the work of Christian love. His conclusion

276

about the matter was this. "In essence King's message to Negroes has been that they can have their cake and eat it too, that they can 'hate,' but that really it is not animosity but 'love.' He has aided Negroes to redefine as moral and acceptable what otherwise would be defined as immoral and unacceptable."(54)

Such rationalizations or redefinitions, suggested Vander Zanden, are not always successful and often lead to deeply disturbing guilt feelings, which seek satisfaction in the need for punishment. This, he argued, accounted in part for the stress on suffering and the exaltation of the turn-the-other-cheek orientation of King's movement.(55) Suffering became a means for black people to enhance their own self-esteem, for it appeared to be uncommonly noble and heroic, as well as being better in the moral and spiritual sense. In addition to these psychological difficulties inherent in the emphasis on self-suffering, Vander Zanden also observed that there were dangers of moral self-righteousness, and of bitterness and frustration that followed so readily upon disappointed hopes. It was his prediction at the time of his article that, should King's movement fail, the attraction for the Black Muslim option would grow, a prediction that proved to be correct in the form of the response if not in the content.(56)

King was not oblivious or indifferent to these dangers. He was acutely aware of the importance of tangible success to ward off the evils of frustration and despair.(57) But in advocating militant nonviolence as the moral method for effecting social change, he was not proposing a mechanical formula assuring automatic success. He was attempting to solve a multitude of problems without himself having the authority and control to discipline every expression and use of his method. When he emphasized the philosophy of nonviolence, he meant much more than a few general ideas and a set of techniques according to which action would be directed. It was not a magic formula. He was preaching a faith that entailed an inner commitment and struggle without which nonviolent action could and did become an alternate form of aggressive hostility and violence. The emphasis on voluntary acceptance of suffering simply served as one practical touchstone for discerning the difference. As Vander Zanden's observations make clear, it was obviously not an entirely adequate touchstone.

It was, perhaps, one of the ironic misfortunes of King's career and of his leadership that he spent so little actual time in jail. The kind of movement he was attempting to lead and the vision he was proposing required time for reflection, meditation and the purification and renewal of one's own emotions and energies.(58) He needed some distance from the repeated calls for help, for speeches, for money, for advice. Jail was one of the few conditions that would have forced the release from daily pressures and could have provided the opportunity for extended thought and prayer. The comparison between the time King and Gandhi spent in jail is illuminating in this regard. Form the time of his first arrest in mid-January, 1956, until his death in Memphis some twelve years later, King logged a total of 14 arrests and 39 total days in southern jails.(59) Gandhi, by contrast, in a career extending over some 50 years, spent 249 days in South African jails and 2089 days in British jails in India.(60) The insights and implications flowing from a whole host of nonviolent demonstrations were too many and too diverse to be assimilated and developed in the time available. If the shock to white sensibilities caused by the civil rights movement was great and at times overwhelming, the shock to the feelings and energies of those actively engaged in the movement was no less momentous or exhausting. What is astonishing in retrospect is that the changes came as swiftly and harmoniously as they did.

King always regarded the nonviolent demonstrations as a means of education for both those who passively observed them and those who actively participated in them. That angry teenagers or hostile adults could march and demonstrate peacefully, if vociferously, was, he thought, a step toward a fuller commitment to social responsibility and to nonviolence itself in that it provided a constructive outlet for otherwise unruly and destructive passions and resentments.(61) He did not, perhaps, take fully into account the exhaustion and numbness that such intense activity could leave behind as well as the intoxicating feeling that accompanied active participation. William Kunstler has pointed out these phenomena and suggested some of the practical limitations of King's approach to social change. "King's formula," he wrote, "has been remarkably successful in focusing national attention on every aspect of Negro oppression. But too often it has left in its wake enervated and bitter communities with nothing else but a moment's glory to show for their monumental efforts."(62)

The politicalization(63) of nonviolence is almost certainly its downfall both as a spiritual movement and a credible practical alternative. Gandhi once rejected the likely realization of his revolution because it would have been the wrong kind of revolution, yet in the long run his revolution was taken away from him anyway.(64) King never had the extensive spiritual and moral authority and control over the civil rights movement that Gandhi had had in India, and his movement was taken away from him more swiftly and more completely. King always hoped and preached that reconciliation must be the outcome of militant nonviolence, but he had no way of insuring that the interior struggle he went through would be undertaken by all who joined in his movement.

Marie E. Byles, a dedicated disciple of Gandhi, has pointed out that it is not easy for people to love their enemies just because a leader like King or Gandhi tells them to do so. It is especially difficult to do so when the leader is also busy pointing out all the vileness and ill-treatment the enemy has heaped upon them in the past and is still perpetrating.(65) The increasing awareness on the part of many people that things in America were worse than had been thought, that, as the civil rights movement blended into the protest against Vietnam, racism was seen to be more deeply rooted than had been suspected and that violence and exploitation seemed endemic to the American social structure and way of life, all this turned King more and more into a social critic, possibly on the order and harshness of the prophet Amos,(66) and less and less a preacher of voluntary suffering and reconciling good will.(67) "Both Gandhi and King," observed Byles, "say that we must be prepared to suffer ourselves without inflicting suffering on the opponent, but self-suffering alone without the admission of evil in ourselves may very well only have the effect of increasing outwardly the latent sadism in the enemy."(68)

King's effort to use voluntary suffering as the clear dividing line between the violent and the nonviolent, between good and evil, justice and injustice, was bound to fail on several counts. He was able to portray this distinction clearly to the eyes of a viewing nation in Birmingham and Selma, but in Chicago and Memphis he had no such good fortune, and he was equally unsuccessful in his anti-Vietnam efforts. Indeed, his Chicago and Memphis demonstrations tended to hide the real suffering and oppression that ghetto life and gross economic inequality inflict upon people, which suggests, at least, that militant nonviolence is of dubious worth in solving problems of economic and cultural inequality. In addition, King's inability to portray a clear and obvious enemy in Chicago,(69) other than the blue-collar ethnics who responded with fear and violence to the invasion of their neighborhoods, highlights that voluntary suffering to be politically effective relies not so much on a perception of justice and injustice as on its ability to image heroes and villains.

As King's career unfolded, the personal burden of responsibility grew, but suffering as an essential element of militant nonviolence became increasingly irrelevant to his purposes. He spoke more about massive civil disobedience and of filling the nation's jails,(70) but such behavior seemed to be beside the point. Hard work and organization were called for rather than suffering. Bayard Rustin did not tire of pointing out to King that "you cannot demonstrate yourself into a new school system, full employment or the destruction of slums."(71)

The identification of self-suffering with receiving overt, external violence was one of the unhappier developments in King's movement and was, in part at least, responsible for the rejection of King's approach to social change. At its roots it signals a confusion between truth and sincerity. The willingness to suffer is, indeed, a sign of sincerity but not of truth. King's original perception of the reality of suffering in the life of every black American was a mandate to seize upon the reality of suffering as a call to mission and service. Such suffering could be destructive, or it could prove to be life-giving if accepted as a fact, absorbed without bitterness, and human energies were directed to overcoming the causes of suffering. Unfortunately in his rhetoric King was a bit romantic and sentimental about the impact of suffering in human life, a sentimentality that goes back to his understanding of the way in which the suffering of Jesus was redemptive. To understand the cross of Christ as redemptive in a purely psychological, inspirational sense - the moral influence theory of atonement discussed in an earlier chapter - is to render the cross altogether contingent and extrinsic to human salvation. It is also to ignore some basic facts of historical experience. Kenneth Clark has reminded us that "in Hitler's Germany the Jews suffered nonviolently without stirring Nazi repentance; the early Christians who were eaten by lions seem to have stimulated not guilt but greed in watching multitudes."(72) Even earlier Lerone Bennett had pointed out that in the Black Belt areas of the South there was no empirical confirmation of King's contention that soft answers turned away wrath in the years between 1955 and 1960.(73)

The failure and the inability of suffering to do all that King claimed for it led to the unhappy debate over the issue of violence or nonviolence as the method of social change. The argument became - and remains today - hopelessly tangled up in a web of unclear and variously used concepts like oppression, liberation, integration and reconciliation. Violence came to mean anything and everything that limited personal development,(74) and King himself was arguing that the only human choice was between nonviolence and non-existence.(75) The apocalyptic tenor of such discussions quickly lost sight of the actual realities of the situation and of the real problems and possible solutions available. The rhetoric used in these discussions tended to solve problems either by moral exhortation or by definition.(76) Whereas voluntary suffering had once served as a hallmark of one's moral seriousness, and as a touchstone of reality,(77) increasingly it became identified with every difficult, unpleasant routine task, and hence an unbearable burden. Debbie Louis, in her reflections on the student participation in the civil rights movement, has indicated various reasons for student disillusionment and their withdrawal from an active role. Her judgment was that "the students generally lacked the kind of commitment [hard work] would demand. Further, efforts in this direction would fail, in being less than immediately rewarding and obvious, to provide the relief from the sense of responsibility and helplessness that really motivated them."(78)

The original invitation of King to his Montgomery followers to engage in nonviolent action for social change and to accept the suffering entailed by such action is better understood as an invitation to accept unmerited responsibility. In abstract justice the duty of acting to change the unfair racial situation in the United States was, without any question, incumbent upon the white majority which had created and perpetuated the situation. But as a matter of fact and morality King realized that change would not spontaneously be forthcoming from white people and to leave it at that and simply lament the fact would be useless and wrong. He willingly accepted and urged his followers willingly to accept the unmerited responsibility for change. In assuming this responsibility there was suffering involved, at first inconvenience, sore feet, wearying marches, and threats of every kind. In his own personal life King was faced with obscene and threatening phone calls, harassment of the petty and not so petty kind, but above all the responsibility for sustaining the unity and direction of the movement. By the time he had reached Chicago King found himself up against quite different forms of injustice and violence. He was still able to reveal white fears, hostility and resistance. He could mobilize reasonably disciplined masses of people for rallies and marches. But the positive programs that were needed, the political alliances and practical experience necessary to enact due rights could not be created simply by the willing acceptance of suffering. In such a context the debate about violence or nonviolence was largely irrelevant. That violence could avail nothing beyond the temporary satisfaction of frustration and desires for revenge was sufficiently clear to anyone who cared to pay attention. By 1968 King had ceased to speak very much about reconciling love and redemptive suffering. He was speaking in harsh and apocalyptic tones of rights too long denied, of justice and impending doom. His dream seemed to have gone up in the smoke of urban riots, yet he held to the faith that the United States was not beyond redemption and he continued to carry the unmerited responsibility for helping his country change. The victory that he won for himself, and to which he gave witness shortly before his death, (79) was truly the victory of nonviolence and of unmerited responsibility willingly accepted. Unlike so many advocates of violence and hatred who failed to persevere, King endured to the end. He, like an earlier, wandering Christian

282

preacher, St. Paul, kept the faith and finished the race. The work of further articulation and implementation of his dream was left to those who had been touched by the example of his own courage and nobility. He left behind no blueprint or guaranteed technique for achieving the dream, only the hope of moving closer to the beloved community. To conclude this study of militant nonviolence, then, we turn to a consideration of the dream and the life of the beloved community.

NOTES: CHAPTER VIII

1. One of the earliest understandings of the hermetical and monastic way of life was that they were substitutes for the martyrdom that was no longer likely. See Louis Bouyer, Introduction to Spirituality, trans. Mary-Perkins Ryan (Collegeville, Minnesota: Liturgical Press, 1961), p. 134.

2. The words are Martin Luther King, Jr.'s. They are cited from Coretta Scott King, "Creative Suffering: The Ripple of Hope," National Catholic Reporter (April 2, 1969), p. 6.

3. Miller, Martin Luther King, Jr.: His Life...., p. 53, is the biographer most sensitive to this aspect of King's motivation.

4. BU Coll., VII (28); the letter was dated 2/17/61.

5. A good, if repulsive, example of this is Richard Gregg, The Power of Nonviolence, pp. 43-51. The chapter referred to is called "Moral Jui-Jitsu," and represents a strange notion of moral. King wrote a brief introduction for this book in 1959.

6. King, The Trumpet of Conscience, p. 5; "The nation and the world were sickened and through national legislation wiped out a thousand Southern laws, ripping gapping holes in the edifice of segregation."

7. In King's last published article, "A Testament of Hope," Playboy (January 1969), there is no mention of such an idea. More typical of the direction he was moving in were the following words: "[Negroes] are stirring the mass of smug, somnolent citizens, who are neither evil nor good, to an awareness of crisis. The confrontation involves not only their morality but their self-interest, and that combination promises to evoke positive action.", p. 236.

8. King, Stride Toward Freedom, p. 83.

9. BU Coll., XIV (67).

10. *Ibid.*, XIV (27).

11. *Ibid.*, XIV (33).

12. *Ibid.*, XIV (67).

13. *Ibid.*, XIV (71); there is a great deal more of this kind of interpretation in King's notes.

14. King, *The Trumpet of Conscience*, pp. 74-75; It is interesting that in all the illustrations, King says nothing of death, physical, psychological or spiritual, and badly underestimates in his rhetoric the power of evil. Rhetorically that is, perhaps, a wise move.

15. Bishop, pp. 10-15; in fairness Bishop also acknowledges King's courage at different times in his life.

16. BU Coll., VII (51); the telegram was dated 5/31/61.

17. Lewis, p. 300; August Meier, "On the Role of Martin Luther King," *New Politics*, pp. 52-59, was the first to make this observation.

18. Lewis, p. 315.

19. Bishop, pp. 264-267.

20. Washington, *The Politics of God*, p. 159.

21. *Ibid.*, p. 156.

22. *Ibid.*, p. 155; confirmation for Washington's view may be found in the story of Jesus' agony in the Garden of Gethsemane. Jesus doesn't want to suffer. It is God's Will that he do so.

23. Lewis, p. 339.

24. Washington, *Black Religion*, p. 27; this criticism is, of course, a complaint against the tactic, not the principle of self-suffering.

25. *Ibid.*, p. 26.

26. BU Coll., VII (13A); from a letter to a Mr. Lacy Harris dated 1/27/61.

27. Washington, The Politics of God., p. 156.

28. Ibid.

29. King, Stride Toward Freedom, p. 48.

30. Washington, The Politics of God., p. 162.

31. BU Coll., I (11A); statement made 9/5/58.

32. Ibid., VII (13); from a letter to Mr. Charles J. Hart, 10/10/61.

33. King, Where Do We Go From Here?, pp. 44-54, where he discusses the pros and cons of the Black Power slogan.

34. John M. Swomley, Jr., Liberation Ethics (New York: The Macmillan Company, 1972), p. 13.

35. BU Coll., I (38); notes for "Pilgrimage to Nonviolence," for the Christian Century (April 13, 1960).

36. For the notion of the moral truth of one's existence and its relation to social ethics see Frederick S. Carney, "Living the Truth in Love," Perkins Journal (Fall 1981), pp. 36-39.

37. BU Coll., IV (40); from a news release by King to the press at the start of a Youth Leadership Conference in Raleigh, N.C., April 15, 1960. Out of this conference there developed the Student Non-Violent Coordinating Committee (SNCC).

38. Miller, Martin Luther King, Jr.: His Life...., p. 49.

39. The words are Martin Luther King's. They are cited from Coretta Scott King, "A Ripple of Hope," p. 6.

40. Berrigan, They Call Us Dead Men, p. 188.

41. For violence being a reality that belongs to the realm of necessity and so removed from the moral realm see Jacques Ellul, Violence; pp. 127-130. To place violence in the realm of necessity, however, does not eliminate all the moral

286

problems surrounding its use. As James M. Gustafson, <u>Christ and the Moral Life</u> (New York, Evanston, London: Harper and Row Publishers, 1968), pp. 28-30, has pointed out in another context, one cannot get away from the problem of concrete moral reckoning no matter how one transforms the ethical enterprise.

42. By questionable I mean that it requires conversion in the positive religious sense of that word before it could ever become the basis for action. Hence, it would seem not to be a very realistic expectation in a pluralistic society. On conversion see Charles E. Curran, "Conversion: The Central Moral Message of Jesus," <u>A New Look at Christian Morality</u> (Notre Dame, Ind: Fides Publishers, Inc., 1970), pp. 25-71. On the relationship of suffering and political action and theology see Jon P. Gunnemann, <u>The Moral Meaning of Revolution</u> (New Haven and London: Yale University Press, 1979), esp. pp. 30-41.

43. Miller, <u>Martin Luther King, Jr., His Life....</u>, p. 286; this notion of unmerited responsibility is, I would suggest, a much more fruitful and adequate concept for Christian faith than the notion advanced by liberation theology of "solidarity with the oppressed."

44. Washington, <u>Black Religion</u>, p. 44.

45. Cleage, p. 97; this difference continues among black theologians. The debate is carried on in terms of liberation and reconcilation. See Wilmore and Cone, <u>Black Theology</u>, pp. 612-614.

46. King, <u>Where Do We Go From Here?</u>, pp. 71-72.

47. <u>Ibid</u>., p. 73.

48. I use "ideology" here in the classic, sociological sense explained by Karl Mannheim. I refer to both the particular and total conceptions he has delineated. Karl Mannheim, <u>Ideology and Utopia</u>, trans. Louis Wirth and Edward Shils (New York: Harcourt, Brace and World, Inc., 1936), pp. 55-59.

49. Lerone Bennett, <u>Confrontation: Black and White</u>, p. 232, claims King did not believe in self-defense. Being a close personal friend and colleague of King's, he might well be correct about King's personal position on the matter. Be that as it may, King was certainly not consistent in holding that position, he did stress the social character of militant nonviolence - it was after all a method for eliminating <u>social</u> evil - and he never wrote anything about the private defense of one's self, home or family. In addition see King, <u>Where Do We Go From Here?</u>, p. 31, where the use of violence in a private capacity is clearly distinguished from the use of violence to effect social change. The two are different questions and must not be confused with one another.

50. Cone, <u>Black Power and Black Theology</u>, p. 120.

51. <u>Ibid.</u>, p. 121. There are warnings against this sort of approach to the gospel from other black theologians. See, e.g., J. Deotis Roberts, <u>Liberation and Reconciliation: A Black Theology</u> (Philadelphia: The Westminster Press, n.d.), pp. 21, 161-162.

52. James Baldwin, <u>The Fire Next Time</u> (New York: Dial Press, 1963), pp. 22-23; King cites this passage in <u>Where Do We Go From Here?</u>, p. 70.

53. James W. Vander Zanden, "The Non-Violent Resistance Movement Against Segregation," <u>The American Journal of Sociology</u> (March 1963), pp. 544-558; the discussion which follows draws heavily from this article.

54. <u>Ibid.</u>, p. 547; of course Vander Zanden ignored a very significant point. The definition of militant protest as immoral and unacceptable was a white definition. The redefinition made possible by King enabled the southern blacks to define their own reality and to do so in a more truthful way. That is the first step toward human freedom.

55. Vander Zanden provided the following references to King in support of this contention; <u>Stride</u>

Toward Freedom, pp. 97, 143, 177; King, "Love, Law and Civil Disobedience," New South (December 1961), p. 6.

56. The attraction was toward greater militancy and violence, toward black unity and a rejection of integration; that it took the shape of Black Power rather than the Muslim option and was secular rather than religious is the difference in content mentioned here.

57. King, Where Do We Go From Here?, pp. 52-54.

58. King himself often acknowledged the need of such periods, though time in American jails would not have provided them, unless he had received extraordinary treatment, as Gandhi, and, it might be added, St. Paul, did.

59. The total of days is my own reckoning; the number of arrests is from Time (January 3, 1964), p. 13.

60. Ashe, p. 357.

61. King, The Trumpet of Conscience, p. 58.

62. William M. Kunstler, Deep in My Heart (New York: William Morris and Company, 1966), p. 355.

63. By "politicalization" I mean the reduction of nonviolence to a set of pragmatic techniques whose only ruling norm is their effectiveness in achieving a desired end.

64. Ashe, pp. 364-373.

65. Marie E. Byles, in Nonviolence After Gandhi, p. 83.

66. Roberts, p. 182.

67. For a critical assessment of this development see Vincent Harding, "The Religion of Black Power," The Religious Situation, pp. 3-37, especially pp. 32-36.

68. Byles, p. 85.

69. Lewis, pp. 348-349.

70. King, _The Trumpet of Conscience_, pp. 14-15.

71. Bayard Rustin, "The Negros, the Cops, and the Jews," _The Movement Reexamined_ (New York: A. Philip Randolph Foundation, 1967), p. 42.

72. Kenneth Clark, "The Civil Rights Movement: Momentum and Organization," _The Negro American_, ed. Talcott Parsons and Kenneth Clark (Boston: Beacon Press, 1967), p. 613.

73. Bennett, _Confrontation: Black and White_, p. 236.

74. Swomley, pp. 19-20, argues, with apparent seriousness, that justice, in the sense of the substantive ideal of justice, is a person's birthright as a human being. Upon whom could one possibly make such a claim and who could honor such a claim, except God?

75. King, _The Trumpet of Conscience_, p. 64; _Where Do We Go From Here?_, p. 223. Certainly the claim has a degree of truth to it, but it would, with equal certainty, need a great deal of careful specification.

76. For an example of solution by moral exhortation see King, _The Trumpet of Conscience_, pp. 37-50; for a solution by definition, see Swomley, pp. 41-53. Liberation theology seems to me to avoid both these pitfalls by its emphasis on the importance of the base communities, or, if one prefers, the local church.

77. The function of self-suffering in Gandhi, as interpreted by Bondurant, p. 25, is "that the only test of truth is action based on the refusal to do harm." Stated in those simple terms it is a human impossibility. Erikson, _Gandhi's Truth_, pp. 412-423, takes the idea more deeply and sees that the refusal to do harm to another is based upon the demand "to respect the truth in him." "Gandhi claimed that only the voluntary acceptance of self-suffering can reveal the truth latent in a conflict - and in the opponent." To this we should add also the truth, or lack thereof, in ourselves.

78. Debbie Louis, <u>And We Are Not Saved</u> (Garden City, New York: Doubleday & Company, Inc., 1970), p. 320.

79. Coretta Scott King, <u>My Life</u>, pp. 316, 348-349.

CHAPTER IX

THE DREAM OF A MAN

Martin Luther King, Jr. was a human being who lived and died in faith and hope. His faith was deep and persistent, taking the basic form of a belief in the goodness and power of God and in the potentiality for good in human beings who were created in God's image. His hope was a simple one, often disappointed, but alive to the end, that the United States of America would one day live the republican and democratic principles its founding documents and public rhetoric proclaimed. People have had hopes and dreamed dreams before King, and there was nothing novel or unique about King's dream. It was, as he told a quarter-million of his fellow-citizens on an August afternoon in his nation's capital city, a dream deeply rooted in the American dream that all human beings are created equal,(1) and it carried with it the hope that the American people would one day make this equality a lived reality for all citizens. It was a dream of brotherhood and sisterhood, of justice and equality, of peace and freedom. Always King's eyes looked forward to the realization of the beloved community.(2)

Behind the sweeping vistas and glittering abstractions there were conceptions of human relationships and social systems which made the beloved community a more determinate concept and added meaning to the dream that King had. There was a warm acceptance of certain structures and values dominant in American society and an uncompromising rejection of other structures and dominant values. This rejection suggests that King was inviting his fellow citizens to a new way of living together. A fundamental element in King's dream was the conviction that "all men, created alike in the image of God, are inseparably bound together."(3) This conviction King regarded as the very substance and charter of the Christian gospel as well as the substance and purpose of his nation. King's basic understanding of the United States as a people was reflected in the preamble to the constitution and by-laws of the Southern Christian Leadership Conference.

Our nation came into existence as a protest against tyranny and oppression. It was

created upon the fundamental assumption
that all men are created equal and endowed
with inalienable rights. The Government
exists to protect the life and liberty of
all without regard to race, color, or
religion.(4)

This core truth of human equality, common as he
thought to both the gospel and the nation, became his
charter for action. "We face," he once wrote, "the
hard challenge and wonderous[sic] opportunity of
letting the spirit of Christ work among us toward
fashioning a truly Christian nation."(5)

This identification between the basic purpose of
the gospel and the nation led to certain confusions
in King's thought, especially as it affected his
understanding of the relationship of the Church to
the society as a whole, of religion to politics, and
of what he held to constitute liberation, freedom,
equality, and militant nonviolence. It will be
useful to examine some of those elements here and
their place in King's dream as part of a final
assessment of militant nonviolence.

King's understanding of the nature and mission
of the Church was unsystematic and impressionistic.
The Church he took to be the sum of those organizations which have been formed to serve as organs of
Christ for the expression and promotion of his
religion,(6) but he suggested no norms or signs by
which one could identify such organizations or
distinguish true from false organs. At the same time
he held the Church to be both visible as organized
and invisible as a spiritual reality,(7) without
explaining the relationship between the visible and
invisible Church. By the invisible Church he understood that fellowship of sharing which took place
under the guidance of the Holy Spirit, and in this
sense the Church was identified with the Kingdom of
God on earth. He expressly rejected any conscious
founding of an organized Church by Jesus of Nazareth,
as well as any claim by the Church to possess absolute truth or to have infallible guidance.(8) In
another formulation the essence of the Church was no
more and no less than all the people who followed
Jesus, who were moved by his Spirit, his example, his
ideals.(9) The individual's relationship to the
Church should involve both a critical and a creative
relationship to the organized society of Christians

and an understanding of the historical development of the Church. There is also a need to appreciate the universal nature of the Church which transcends the barriers of race, nation and class.(10)

As an organized and visible body, the Church finds embodiment in the local community of Christians, the local or parish church, which is essentially a nucleus of fellowship. It is the task of the Church, understood in this way, to make people feel at home, to give them a sense of finding peace and joy in the fellowship we have with one another. This fellowship is far more important than any kind of creedal or doctrinal agreement. The actual experience of it is far more fundamental to the life of the Church than any sort of doctrinal conformity. The difference between the fellowship of the Church and that which can be experienced in any other organized group is that the Church's fellowship has the additional dimension of confronting the members with the fact of the living God and with the light and judgment his existence sheds on history and on present events.(11) In performing this last function the members of the Church are turned into the light-bearers for humankind.

Another function of the visible Church is found in King's suggestion that the Church is a religious institution for the perpetuation of a religious tradition. It has gathered together various insights of the spiritual giants throughout the ages and included them in a body of beliefs and convictions which it passes on through history. Without the institution of the Church these insights would have perished. While the Church itself does not live perfectly the ideal for which it stands, it does, despite its failings and weaknesses, enlarge our sympathies and reinforce our power by uniting us with those who have followed Jesus before us and will follow after us.(12)

In addition to the functions of providing fellowship and preserving insights, the Church has another task. It is to serve as the conscience of society with respect to the ethical principles of Christianity.(13) It should provide a challenge to the status quo by broadening people's horizons and be a guardian of the spiritual and moral life of the community. The Church is to stand firmly against injustice and exert its influence and power for justice.(14)   It is never easy to tell when King passed from descriptive to normative discourse in his comments on the Church, nor is it always clear what pertains to the visible Church and what to the invisible.   The fact that his American society was simply rife with Christian denominations, often at bitter odds with one another over the ethical principles of Christianity and their practical implication, does not seem to have affected his thinking on the Church.   He was not particularly bothered by the fact of denominational differences, so much as denominational claims to be right or to possess absolute truth.   "Such narrow sectarianism," he proclaimed, "destroys the unity of the Body of Christ.   God is neither Baptist, Methodist, Presbyterian, nor Episcopalian.   God transcends our denominations.   If you are to be true witnesses to Christ, you must come to know this, America."(15)

The present writer frankly confesses himself puzzled by such a doctrine of the Church, or more accurately by his inability to find it either coherent or intelligible.   And he is equally mystified in trying to determine the resources the Church has which would enable it to perform its various functions.   What does seem clear is that King expected, exhorted, and demanded that all the citizens of the United States live what Christian believers are charged to live in virtue of their faith.   He took the entire country for his parish because he thought he had discovered identical charters for action in the gospel and the Constitution.   For that reason his ideas and expectations were often unclear and his appeals unpersuasive.   We have referred earlier to his own bewilderment when this confusion was noted and resented.(16)

This same confusion touched deeply King's hope and dream for America.   In 1961 Look Magazine had asked King to write a few paragraphs on his expectations or hopes for the world in twenty-five years. After expressing the hope that war, racial segregation, poverty and militarism would be "ugly relics of a vain quasi-civilization," King ended by saying, "I will expect the Christian era to begin."(17)   This kind of millennial hope, expressed often in terms of human possibility, appeared again and again in King's rhetoric and reflected a confusion about the nature of the problems that human beings actually faced, to say nothing about a confusion over the meaning of

Christ's death and resurrection. The sentence quoted immediately above, expressing King's hope for the start of the Christian era, appeared again at the very end of his last published article.(18)

King's understanding of the Church, its role in society, and his millennial expectations are of more concern than simply as a matter of theological adequacy. His understanding had practical implications for his own work and for the realization of his dream. He correctly located the locus of God's Will and activity as the larger society; he did not restrict the grace of God to the Church. But he then concluded that the people called to live in accord with the principles and ideals of Jesus were his fellow citizens and not just his fellow believers. The confusion here is not merely over the relationship of Church and society, and the significance of action in either sphere for the other sphere.(19) The confusion seemed to be of no great practical import when militant nonviolence was regarded as simply a form of non-cooperation with evil, a conscious withdrawal from participation in a system of injustice, as was the case in the Montgomery bus boycott. Throughout the boycott King thought he was engaged in giving moral witness and making moral appeal to white consciences, as was certainly the case in part. But at the same time the boycott was an exercise of economic and political power which represented a distinct challenge to the city officials and the dominant white establishment. The organization of the black community for concerted action of any kind that went beyond their own internal affairs posed a major threat to segregationist control of southern communities. Every means, legal and extra-legal, manipulative and violent, had been historically employed to prevent such organization. The most significant social achievement in Montgomery was not the moral witness of nonviolent protest but the political fact of organized black action.

The theme of nonviolence struck by King at the outset of the boycott was not, to be sure, altogether gratuitous or irrelevant to his purpose, and not only because he was also concerned about the souls of his people.(20) But it was not the central feature in the achievement of desegregated communities. The importance of nonviolence was simply that it was a functional pre-requisite of organization and so for political action. One can, of course, organize

297

people for violent purposes, but not by means of violence.(21) Violence can prevent or destroy organized activity but it cannot create it. It was unfortunate that King's rhetoric led the civil rights movement into arguments over the uses and abuses of violence, for that was not the central question in the events that were transpiring. Militant nonviolence was simply a necessary discipline which King was able to establish so as to keep the energy born of genuine grievance, of frustration and, in some cases, of hostility from being wasted in unorganized, and so politically ineffective, action. C. Eric Lincoln was quite accurate in assessing King's genius to be the ability to channel religious fervor and conviction into political participation.(22) But the religious fervor could find a substitute. Where the religious conviction which sustained the nonviolent discipline was lacking, as it was frequently in the northern ghettoes, no effective political participation was forthcoming.

What happened to King's thinking as his movement developed was that he slowly came to realize that his conception of a democratic society did not blend smoothly with the American reality nor with the ideas of many of his fellow citizens. The continued struggle to reform society to match his own conception he carried on through moral exhortation and public marches designed as appeals to conscience. The criticisms and judgments of the younger black militants, however, tended increasingly toward systemic analysis of society's ills, with the major emphasis being placed on capitalism as the chief villain. Since King shared this antipathy for capitalism with them, he simply incorporated it into his own analysis and continued his moral exhortation.(23) But this new admixture of themes was confused and confusing as can be plainly seen in the last major demonstration which King planned, the Poor People's March on Washington.

The greatest moral outrage in King's mind, and one intimately linked with racism, was the conflicting extremes of wealth and poverty, that some people should enjoy luxuries while others lacked basic necessities.(24) The indubitable and documented fact(25) of poverty in the most affluent society in the world struck him as a sin and an injustice calling for immediate rectification. His trip to India brought him to a felt awareness of the world-wide dimensions of the problem, while the American involvement in Viet Nam served as the hinge to link all the social injustices which grieved his conscience. But his understanding of the Christian faith and his common sense made it obvious that racism, poverty, war and imperialism were not going to be overcome by violence. One could certainly in theory shoot the racists and the rich, the militarists and the imperialists, if one could identify them, but not without becoming one of them in the process. To his mind that would change nothing. Violence was simply neither a practical nor a moral imperative.

In the face of injustice King had originally thought that two things could be done. First, the injustice could be dramatized and made plain for all to see, thus offering an appeal to the consciences of people of good will. This expectation was a hope disillusioned in Chicago and ended in the Poor People's campaign. Second, he had thought that injustice could be opposed by refusing to co-operate in the system that inflicted it. The sit-in movement changed his perspective from withdrawal to making an open challenge to the system through civil disobedience. The success of the sit-in movement and of the campaigns in Birmingham and Selma which led to the welcome civil rights legislation of the mid-1960's proved, however, to be deceptive. For while it confirmed the basic soundness of the Constitution and the political processes of the nation, its effect on the economic, cultural and social institutions was only indirect and minimal. But it did effect one important change in the life of society, the evident need and opportunity for organizing the black community and its white allies.

By 1966 it could be fairly said that King and the various people and movements related to and inspired by him had achieved significant psychological and legal victories through nonviolent, political means. A people was in the process of self-liberation; humanly created, restrictive bonds had been loosened. There existed both a charter and a space for public action.(26) The perceived need was for power and so the cry arose. King's own hesitation in the face of the Black Power slogan and his analysis of the dangers and weaknesses of it were accurate enough,(27) but somewhat beside the point. For they betray a confusion about the various dimensions of human life, spiritual, political, economic and so on.

The faith - or the truth - that "all men are created equal" has different applications in different dimensions of human existence. For the Church of King's faith human equality is an equality before God and denotes the universal character of salvation. The gift offered by God in Christ is open equally to all human beings and the Christian fellowship embraces all who accept and respond to the gift of faith. It is emphatically not a claim that all are equally endowed with natural and supernatural gifts. For political society human equality can only mean equal status before the law and equal access to political participation, what is commonly called equality of opportunity. Such equality requires political institutions, which is to say it is a structured equality, a social fabrication.(28) It is and cannot be a natural or personal reality. Both the Church and political society, as institutions, are necessary to human freedom for as social fabrications they afford a space for human action and the possibility of freedom. Both institutions are deliberate attempts by human beings to carve out of the bonds of necessity some space in which necessity no longer reigns and free action is possible. Society, however, is not a total fabrication, for it remains always under the burden of certain necessities imposed by human beings' natural needs for food, shelter, clothing, social intercourse and so on. There is a necessity present in the economic, social and cultural dimensions of human life that is not present in the spiritual and political arenas, and which must qualify significantly the meaning of equality of opportunity in regard to these dimensions.(29)

The profound ethical significance of King's insistence on militant nonviolence would seem to lie in the primacy it puts upon the spiritual and political - free, moral, human - dimensions of human life. It appears to be an effort to remind human beings that they are responsible agents and that they will find their freedom and humanness only to the degree that they actively exercise that responsibility.(30) To allow elements inconsistent with the basic charter of free action to creep into the domains of freedom is to surrender freedom. Violence is one such element. It is an enemy of human freedom because it

300

belongs to the order of necessity and to resort to the use of violent means is precisely to forsake freedom for the necessary.(31) Even the traditional defense of the possibility of a just war spoke of violence as a last resort and as an obligation, as something that ought to be done, only when there were no other choices for action, and to do nothing was to abandon responsibility. When there are no other choices, freedom is gone. The just war theory, and its application to questions of revolution, is surely misunderstood if it is seen merely as providing a justification for war or violent revolution as a means to achieve political or moral purpose. Necessity can have no moral justification. The theory itself is designed to do two main things; to prevent a premature escape from the difficult realm of responsible freedom into necessity, and then to limit, as far as may be, the extent that necessity claims one's deeds in war or revolution.(32)

The major questions in militant nonviolence which we have discussed, the means-end relationship, the recourse to civil disobedience and the appeal to a higher moral law, the voluntary acceptance of suffering, all point to this same emphasis on the moral dimension of life as supreme and are appeals to the possibility of exercising freedom rather than submitting to necessity. I have argued above how it is possible for human beings to care, to exercise responsibility only in the present, only for the process. To have one's actions and choices dictated or determined by an end is to act under the burden of an imagined necessity. Ends, whether understood as proposed intentions or expected consequences, direct and guide free human energies and deeds. But when it is argued that the end justifies the means, what is usually meant is that the act in question was necessary and not freely chosen, that there was no other choice,(33) and that one was under the necessity to act. In such cases one is not talking about freely assumed responsibility but regretable necessity. The spirituality of militant nonviolence is an attempt to construct a barrier against the premature admission of such necessity into the domain of human freedom.(34)

The practice of civil disobedience with its appeal to a higher law, be it federal law over local law, constitutional law over statutory law, or the higher divine law over human law, is once again an appeal to freedom over necessity. For it attempts to place human beings in a structured situation in which there is more space to act, in which the range of human choice is enlarged, in which one can find a new basis and authority for action. King's conception of evil as that which is not able to organize itself permanently, and which led him to conclude that the universe is on the side of justice, is only one way of affirming that only those actions which enable a real future can be considered humanly free, and only such free deeds are in accord with the moral law. It is only the anarchist and the libertine who perceive all law, all structure, as a restraint on human freedom. But without a structured space for action, there would be no possibility of human freedom. There would be only necessity and the chaos of undirected spontaneity. To speak of and appeal to a moral law of the universe as the authorization of human action is to point to the appropriate structures which define the possible areas of human freedom.

Finally, King's insistence on the importance of voluntary suffering is also an effort to transform necessity into freedom. To allow another person or event or situation to dictate my response, be it a response in word, deed, thought or emotions, is to submit to necessity. Such submission is reflected in the frequently used justification, "I couldn't help myself." Suffering itself is of the order of necessity. It is not only something human beings do not freely pursue for its own sake; it is not something they can freely so choose, even if they would. What it means to suffer willingly, therefore, or more accurately to accept unmerited suffering as redemptive, is to find a domain of freedom within the domain of necessity which is suffering. To do this requires a spiritual and psychological struggle with oneself and one's God which involves an interior self-testing which might be called a this-worldly asceticism.(35) King was, perhaps, overly optimistic about the readiness of his fellow citizens to undergo such struggle and testing, though impressive numbers of black southern Christians certainly were. It may be that his critics like Washington and Cleage showed more realism in this regard. But one point fundamental to militant nonviolence deserves to be stressed here, and that is the intrinsic unity between the inner process of self-testing, of securing freedom in the midst of necessity and its external expression through action in the world. The test of black-white relationships, the triumph over hatred, bitterness and racism required more than a conversion of heart, or the cultivation and protestation of good will.(36) The change of heart, to be authentic, also entailed a change in the external world. It called for the establishment of new kinds of relationships, and so of new structures and systems. For King it meant concretely integration.

When King turned his energies away from the struggle against legal injustice and challenged the evils of poverty, war and social racism, he found himself contending with enemies of a different sort. To speak of a violent assault upon these enemies is meaningless. How does one wage war upon war in a violent way? Or even if one agreed with the debatable proposition that the problems of national and international poverty are caused exclusively by human greed and selfish exploitation of others, how do you violently attack such an enemy? The problem of social racism, as distinguished from legal racism, is no more easily addressed through violent means. Seen in that light King's continued advocacy of nonviolence is little more than common sense, though it is certainly not itself a method for eliminating these social evils. Fortunately or unfortunately King was no economist and he seemed to think that the problems of poverty on both a national and world scale could be solved by purely political means; hence the Poor People's March on Washington. The systemic analysis which came to see capitalism as the devil at the heart of the world's problems (37) raised an enormously difficult problem for King. How does one practice civil disobedience against an economic system or overthrow it nonviolently, especially a system to which one's victories over legal racism have afforded increased access and a larger share to one's natural constituency? How do you refuse to cooperate with the injustice of poverty, short of taking a vow of poverty oneself?(38) It was difficulties like these which opened to King the wider dimensions of the struggle in which he was engaged and altered somewhat the nature of his response.

What was at the heart of King's objection to capitalism was the strong spirit of individualism and the competitive disregard of others it seemed to entail.(39) This perception owes something to the Marxian analysis of the inherent logic of the capitalist system, but for King that analysis was neither necessary nor especially compelling. Far more determinative of his view were the evident inequalities in human life. People were hungry, without work, without shelter, without the means to provide for their families, while others frolicked in luxuries beyond imagination. Something was wrong with a system that fostered and accepted such inequality. Furthermore, the centrality of a sink-or-swim competition in the free enterprise or capitalist ideology stood out as the element most in opposition to what King envisioned as the beloved community. For this was a community in which people lived together as equals, where one did not profit at the expense of another, where mutual cooperation rather than competition was the rule, where mutual enhancement of life replaced individual striving for betterment. Consequently the real sin of American society was seen to be individualism, the excessive absorption in and concern for one's own welfare in complete disregard of how others fared. This central sin was reflected in many other areas of life and wore many masks - poverty, racism, social apathy, militarism, and so on - but, once unmasked, its face was recognizable as that most ignoble of human sins, greed.(40)

Neither Martin Luther King nor anyone else had devised a method to eliminate greed and the tenacity of self-interest from human life. In planning for the Poor People's March King was beyond believing that the sight of the poor would touch the nation's conscience sufficiently to move it to some unspecified course of action. He did hope that the persistent presence of the poor, with their spoken and unspoken demands, joined to the inconvenience and expense their presence would cause, might move Congress to see it was in everyone's self-interest to act. He was engaged quite plainly in traditional politics, and it was clear that militant nonviolence was not some new and purer way to effect social change.(41) A bullet fired in Memphis one April day made it clear that militant nonviolence had not brought about a new society.

It seems to me that it would be impertinent, as well as impossible, for a white American to assess what King meant to and accomplished in the black community. The value of his efforts and the uses of militant nonviolence for the continued expansion of black freedom are not for me to judge. But the dream of Martin Luther King and the challenge that his life was, was something he shared with all Americans, and, indeed, with all the world. In addition, he tried to live and proclaim the Christian gospel, and that is something any Christian theologian must take serious note of and evaluate. To the task of an overall evaluation of King's proclamation, then, the final pages of this study will be devoted.

To begin with some negative criticisms, it seems clear that King was ill-served in some ways by his liberal theology, and that his failure to come to terms with Niebuhr at greater depth cost him the one realistic(42) chance he had to amend some of these theological weaknesses. These weaknesses appear particularly in three areas: the divorce between power and goodness (love) in the nature of God; a view of original sin that considers it a variable factor in human life; and his nebulous conception of the nature and mission of the Church.(43) Aside from the technical importance of these doctrines to any adequate Christian theology, they were not without significant impact on King's practice and on his movement. While I fully agree that good doctrine (orthodoxy) will not necessarily make for good practice (orthopraxis), and the latter is far more central to Christian life, bad doctrine acted upon will make, sooner or later, for bad practice.

For many years King spoke about love as the most powerful force in the universe. Yet he understood God's own love for his human creatures to involve a self-imposed limitation upon God's power in relation to his creatures. His doctrine of nonviolence rested squarely upon the human person's obligation to impose a similar self-limitation upon one's power in relation to fellow human beings. Love and power seemed somehow to be at odds with one another, even while love was being proclaimed as powerful. Love, to be quite sure, is powerful, but it is not power. Love is a characteristic of personal strength, it is a virtue and is altogether a personal reality. Only individual persons love. Love can be considered powerful precisely because it has the capacity to unite people and so to make common action for a shared end possible. But it is not the only thing in human life that is powerful in this way. The claim of the Christian gospel is that there is no power in heaven or on earth or beneath the earth that can separate human beings from the love of God in Christ, which is but another way of saying that God's love for his creatures is eternal and unchanging. But such love is not a human possession nor is it the cement of political society. It is not even especially important that it be so. To this degree I find that King's rhetoric clouded his own thinking and that of many of his followers. It is, of course, a moot point now whether clarity in this matter would have spared him some of the disagreements he had and the anguish he felt over the rise of the black power slogan, but it could have clarified his essentially political task much sooner.

More specifically, however, clarity on the difference between love and power might have spared us all from the interminable and fruitless arguments over nonviolence as the way of love and violence as the way of power. Not only was such language wholly strange and unfamiliar to American political discourse, it was also without relevance to the reality of American political life. As DeOtis Roberts has suggested, the practical significance of Gandhi to American society was small; his theoretical relevance was nonexistent.(44) It may or it may not be too late for the American People to recapture and live the hope of their Founding Fathers to create a free society rather than an affluent one, a society in which liberty is prized more than luxuries and free human beings are clearly distinguished from and honored more than those who are merely rich. But it is certain that vast numbers of American people, black and white, need power to be free, and not simply love. The major significance of what King launched at Montgomery and left behind him after his death at Memphis was precisely the binding together of people in common action for common goals. They shared the experience of power in relation to the larger society. Love is not irrelevant to this enterprise, but it is not at the heart of it. Love is central in determining the common goals, but power is essential to realizing them. Powerless people have trouble loving wisely and well because what their love can realize is so unduly restricted. Powerful people can understand their responsibility because they at least have a real choice in the matter. In such a context a debate over power or love in terms of the choice between violence and nonviolence is misplaced.

Secondly, King's failure to grasp the profound and all-pervasive nature of original sin may have been one of those ironic blessings in disguise. Had he known at the outset the virulence and tenacity of his enemy, racism, it might have discouraged him at the start or made him more cautious and less militant.(45) Aside from certain theological inconsistencies that a sounder doctrine of sin would have spared him, on a practical level it may have prevented the tone of self-righteous indignation and unabashed condemnation of American society as racist which often prevented King's message from being heard, or saw it welcomed with the most noxious kind of breast-beating and a sick acceptance of guilt. It is not my intent here to deny the very real presence of racism - and sexism - in American society. But far too many Americans have no history in their country before the twentieth century; even more have no history there before the civil war. To such people the burden of a national guilt(46) for a history that is not their own is simply incomprehensible and unfair. The unalloyed charge of racism often misses by a wide margin the real fears, insecurities and hesitations of such people. One is not dealing with pure, unalloyed evil. So also the utopian dreams of God's Kingdom realized on earth, and the apocalyptic warnings of doom that usually accompany such dreams, may make for fine-sounding rhetoric, but have never made for a free society. Disappointed expectations and frustrated hopes have never made for reconciliation. King himself was aware of over-promising or of raising hopes to an unwarranted degree.(47) The excessive or unrealistic hope that is deflated can leave people so discouraged, so guilt-ridden and feeling so hopelessly inadequate that they despair altogether of any public action.(48)

Thirdly, there is the matter of King's nebulous and inadequate doctrine of the Church and the confusion it leads to in regard to acting in society.(49) For one thing King's view of the Church and its mission continues to foster the false belief of many people that the United States is a Christian country founded upon and committed to Christian ideals and principles which are regarded as the charter and norm of a public morality. Such a belief blurs if it does not altogether obscure the actual basis of American unity and action. Racial segregation is undoubtedly immoral and contrary to the

Christian faith. More to the public point, however, is that it is unconstitutional and violates the inalienable rights the government is designed to protect and insure. To place every public issue and discussion immediately on the level of morality and Christian principle is both dangerous and dishonest. It is dishonest, for Christian faith and Christian principles are not the basis of our common life as a nation nor does the Church exist to achieve the same purpose as the nation. It is dangerous because it prevents the recognition of honest political dis-agreements and does not allow a political issue to be discussed on its own merits. The Vietnam war and the debate over nuclear weapons both afford excellent illustrations of this point. The pressure to decide on the morality or immorality of the war and the building of nuclear weapons on the basis of some Christian principle or value, forces people to take sides on an issue, most often in response to rhetoric or some slogan, without ever inquiring into whether, whatever the abstract values involved, the proposed course of action might not be a terribly stupid and useless political exercise, one that in no compre-hensible way promotes or protects the common good.

When combined with an inadequate understanding of sin, this confusion between the task of the Church and political society has two additional results, both of which are noticeable in King's career. The first result is that the very real problems which evil and human sin create for human decision and choice are either ignored or defined out of exis-tence. Again it was an effort to achieve some measure of realism in this regard that prompted so much of Reinhold Niebuhr's writings. King's ambiva-lence and lack of clarity about the problems that human beings' evil choices pose is evident in his unhesitating acceptance of law enforcement officials to act as a restraint upon illegal and violent behavior. If it is true that law can and should keep a person from lynching me, than all talk about nonviolence as a method to eliminate social evil is either equivocal or utopian. In King's case it is probably utopian in as much as he allows that force or violence, or the threat of it, can restrain social evil, while it takes militant nonviolence actually to eliminate it. But in that case it is not at all clear how militant nonviolence effects <u>social</u> change. It would seem more immediately to appeal for a personal change of mind and heart, and to effect such change only in the person who responds to the appeal. It is a method for changing individual minds and hearts, not social structures and systems. Its focus is on what King called the unenforceable, while political society properly concerns itself only with what is, in principle at least, enforceable. The practice of militant nonviolence, then, is curiously irrelevant to the ethical and political question of whether, under what conditions, and to what extent the use of force or violence can be legitimate.

A second result that follows upon the combination of an inadequate doctrine of sin and a confused doctrine of the Church is, ironically, a disillusionment about human beings and a conviction that they are worse than they really are. Given his beliefs and convictions, King logically had to assume that all his fellow citizens were or should be committed to the same faith and values that he held, and that the work of the Church and the State were essentially identical. He saw one distinctively Christian role for the Church in the social process to be the critic and guide of the process, though whence the Church drew the wisdom to play this role is something of a mystery. Unfortunately such a picture of the Church's role does not match the facts of life in a pluralistic society committed to religious freedom, and is a disservice to both religion and politics. There may well be a true sense to King's belief that religion is life or it is empty, but that does not deny a certain autonomy to the various dimensions of our existence. Christian beliefs, values and principles, apart from a living Christian faith, remain abstractions of some possibly useful guidance to action. Believing that people are deeply committed to such principles and values, one can only be disappointed and embittered when they do not act vigorously to realize them. So many black power advocates quickly came to reject the reality of the American dilemma because they saw there was no commitment to the American creed as King preached it and they understood it. This disillusionment inevitably grew to see nothing of worth, nothing of merit in the actual basis of common life,(50) and to conclude that things were much worse than they actually were. Out of such experience grow the apocalyptic warnings and totalitarian solutions which exhaust human energies but do not advance human freedom.

On the positive side, the importance of Martin Luther King, Jr., in addition to the personal worth and power of his example as a noble human being, seems to me to lie in the fact that he restored and renewed in his own nation, and perhaps in other parts of the world, the awareness that all social relationships are essentially ethical in character, and we ignore the ethical quality of them at our own peril. For gross inequities in a society cannot long sustain the social fabric(51) and are an imminent peril to us all. He also demonstrated that the freedoms of a people are only to be preserved, appreciated and enjoyed in and through action.(52) His insistence upon militant nonviolence, especially as that stressed the refusal to cooperate in one's own abasement or enslavement, is a clear reminder that the ethical shape of a society is altogether dependent upon the ethical character and behavior of the individuals in that society. It is a function of their willingness to assume personal responsibility for the shape of society and cannot be left to some system. Systems, structures and institutions are essential to human existence, but they need not be determinative of our existence. They can and at times should be changed, and that is possible without the use of violence.

These two lessons, which originated far more in King's faith and experience than in any theory of nonviolence, were given to American society at a time when it was losing any understanding of what a free society meant, any sense of public life and public action, any sense of a living national community with a transcendent purpose beyond its own survival.(53) The truly innovative and noble experiment and risk which was American democracy was slowly being surrendered to the desire to be rich and comfortable, and the American dream was being abased when American affluence was held up as the sign of national greatness.(54) The fact that not everyone was as large-minded and as open-hearted as King so that they could hear the message to build their lives and freedom on the basis of their universal humanity does not mean that King's dream had been wholly in vain. The resurrection of ethnic pride, for one example, not only among Afro-Americans, but among other ethic groups in the nation, is a positive response to King's dream, even while it bears with it its own problems and dangers. For the absence of such pride and joy in one's ethnic heritage can only lead to apathy, drift and chaos, or to lawless and pointless violence. The meaning of the nonviolent claim to any people is that you can love and embrace and foster your heritage without denying its tragedy and pain (voluntary suffering) and without putting down anyone else's historical experience. We do not build ourselves up by putting our fellow human beings down. Nor do we build up our fellow human beings by letting them put us down. As best I can tell there is the essence of militant nonviolence.

The beloved community to which King looked forward remains only a community in the making, and it has real existence among us only in the continuous struggle to balance the various claims for liberty, justice and equality. But if King did nothing else and if nonviolence means nothing else, at least he generated among those who heeded his presence new energies for the struggle and left them with the knowledge that human beings are charged by their Maker to be the co-creators of their own freedom, the co-claimants to their own equality, the coworkers in establishing justice. To do this work at the price of someone else's freedom, equality or just treatment was to lose what made being human worthwhile. At the time of his death Martin Luther King, Jr. had been graced with this knowledge.

That King's assassination signified to many black Americans that it was their survival as a people that was at stake(55) in the United States rather than any hope of equal justice or a beloved community points, I suggest, not to the destruction of King's dream nor to the death of his hope. It does mark an end to excessive hopes and rhetoric in which the dream was originally couched, but the dream is no less real and important for the absence of its most eloquent spokesman. The lingering tragedy of King's assassination is that so many Americans have been so slow to acknowledge the symbolic importance of his time among them,(56) and have retreated into private life and private concerns or to wistful images of the past. Unlike the founding fathers of the republic, they have appeared to lack the will and courage to pledge their lives, their fortunes and their sacred honor to one another for the sake of establishing a free society.

When King proclaimed that his own dream was deeply rooted in the American dream, historically and on balance he was not mistaken. Nor was he mistaken in pointing out that the unrestrained pursuit of wealth and the obvious legal inequities in society were the biggest threat to the realization of the dream. To his everlasting credit he confronted the nation with a choice that made it plain that a people's freedom was dependent, not upon historical necessity nor the blind turnings of chance or luck or good systems, but upon their own willingness and ability to struggle with the truth and do the good. Or, as he preferred to preach it, it depended upon their obedience to God. Whether or not his hope that the people of the United States were not too tired, or too frightened or too callous to respond affirmatively to the challenge should prove vain, the depth and meaning of his own Christian faith can be seen in the life of dedication and service he gave to the dream. He did not give up; he lived it, even if no one else was willing to try. He did not wait or complain or point at others. He assumed the unmerited responsibility to do something about injustice even while caring about justice for all. In more historic terms he pledged first his own life, fortune and sacred honor(57) to his fellow citizens both black and white alike. He did not find a new theory in nonviolence, but renewed an old truth, that the practical meaning of Christian faith is that freedom lies in action, love in giving and living in laying down one's life for others, in the actual place and time in which the person finds oneself. I cannot find, and I now think it is a mistake to try to find, that King left behind him, as he may have thought, a new theory and method of social change.(58) His legacy is no less important as the renewal of an old lesson embodied and refreshed in his own life. Freedom is both God's gracious gift and a painfully achieved human accomplishment, it is worth dying for but violence is of precious little use in its attainment or preservation. One of King's printed sermons bears the title, "Our God Is Able."(59) The salient point about King and his doctrine of militant nonviolence is that his faith was not misplaced. He learned to live free even while he helped enhance the freedom of the rest of us. His God was able indeed.

312

1. <u>BU Coll.</u>, I (11A); August 28, 1963. This was not the first time that King used the dream image in a speech.

2. King, <u>Where Do We Go From Here?</u>, pp. 70-77.

3. <u>BU Coll.</u>, V (177); from a manuscript entitled "A Non-Segregated Society."

4. <u>Ibid.</u>, I (26).

5. <u>Ibid.</u>, V (177).

6. <u>Ibid.</u>, XIV (75).

7. <u>Ibid.</u>, XIV (67).

8. <u>Ibid.</u>; in a manuscript copy of his famous sermon, "Paul's Letter to American Christians," King has a long diatribe against the Roman Catholic doctrine of papal infallibility in which it is clear that he has badly misunderstood the meaning and the reach of that doctrine. His criticism of the doctrine does not appear in the published version of the sermon. Compare <u>BU Coll.</u>, I (11) and King, <u>Strength To Love</u>, p. 159. King may be forgiven his misunderstanding in as much as Catholics themselves debate the meaning and scope of the doctrine. Hans Kung, <u>Infallible? An Inquiry</u>, trans. Edward Quinn (Garden City, NY: Doubleday and Company, Inc., 1971); John J. Kirvan (ed.), <u>The Infallibility Debate</u> (New York: Paulist Press, 1971).

9. <u>BU Coll.</u>, XIV (47); I do not know if King meant to use these three words, spirit, ideals, example, interchangeably or whether they represent three distinct elements. In the latter case, I do not know if people make up the Church who are moved by any one of the three elements, or whether it is necessary to be moved by all three. My guess is that he never even considered the question.

10. <u>Ibid.</u>, XIV (29); again I do not know whether the relationship to the organized society of Christians refers to any organized society of

Christians or if King thought there was something that could be called "the organized
society of Christians." Nor can I find any
norms for the creativity and criticism the
individual is to exercise.

11. *Ibid.*, XIV (75).

12. *Ibid.*

13. King, *Strength To Love*, p. 157.

14. *Ibid.*, p. 161.

15. *Ibid.*, p. 159.

16. King did learn to make some adjustment to
non-Christian sensibilities. In a letter to
Harold Fey, the editor of the *Christian Century*,
dated June 4, 1961, King included a form letter
appealing for funds in which he spoke of "a
challenge to the Christian conscience of America." At the bottom of the letter to Fey he
added a note to omit "Christian" when the letter
was mailed to Jewish groups. BU Coll., VII
(10).

17. BU Coll., VII (26); King sent the letter to *Look*
on 8/4/61. It appeared in *Look* (January 1962),
the 25th anniversary edition.

18. King, "A Testament of Hope," *Playboy*, p. 236.

19. Mac Iver, pp. 4-5; the relationships involved
here are quite complex and more wide-ranging
than the text needs to cover. For an illuminating explanation of the complexities involved see
E. A. Goerner, *Peter and Caesar* (New York:
Herder and Herder, 1965), pp. 15-25.

20. King, *Where Do We Go From Here?*, p. 74; "I am
concerned that Negroes achieve full status as
citizens and human beings in the United States.
But I am also concerned about our moral upright-
ness and the health of our souls. Therefore I
must oppose any attempt to gain our freedom by
the methods of malice, hate and violence that
have characterized our oppressors."

21. Arendt, *On Violence*, pp. 48-49.

22. Lincoln, <u>Martin Luther King, Jr.: A Profile</u>, p. XIII.

23. For example, King, <u>Where Do We Go From Here?</u>, p. 191; <u>The Trumpet of Conscience</u>, p. 14.

24. King, <u>Strength To Love</u>, p. 158.

25. Michael Harrington, <u>The Other America: Poverty in The United States</u> (Baltimore, MD: Penguin Books, 1964).

26. For a discussion of the notion of a space for action as an essential condition of human freedom see Arendt, <u>On Revolution</u>, pp. 117-123. The other two essential conditions are authority and power. The three together constitute the necessary and sufficient conditions of human freedom.

27. King, <u>Where Do We Go From Here?</u>, pp. 51-77.

28. Arendt, <u>On Revolution</u>, pp. 173-175; also helpful in understanding the notion of social fabrication is Peter Berger and Thomas Luckmann, <u>The Social Construction of Reality</u> (Garden City, N.Y.: Doubleday and Company, 1966).

29. Perhaps an example would be helpful here. The human rights to freedom of conscience and to political participation are absolute; the rights to a job, to an education, to live where one wants are always and inescapably relative. Or again no human being has the right to deprive me of God's gift of salvation or of my right to vote, though I can and may deprive myself of them, but not with right. The same cannot be said, however, for the other rights mentioned. See Hollenbach, <u>Claims in Conflict</u>, pp. 95-100.

30. The argument put forward here seems fully compatible with Gandhi's views as well. Dhirendra Mohan Datta, <u>The Philosophy of Mahatma Gandhi</u> (Madison: The University of Wisconsin Press, 1953), p. 140; "Democracy can grow only by the voluntary efforts of the individual and it cannot be enforced from outside. Gandhi says: I hold that democracy cannot be evolved by forcible methods. The spirit of democracy cannot be imposed from without. It has to come

from within! The good individual is, therefore, the essential requisite of a good democracy."

31. For freedom as liberation from necessity, and violence as a necessity, see Ellul, On Violence, pp. 91-92, 127-128. Unlike Ellul, however, I don't think this exempts violence from any further moral reckoning.

32. John Courtney Murray, "The Uses of a Doctrine on the Uses of Force," We Hold These Truths, p. 257.

33. Many of the examples used by Fletcher, Situation Ethics, to defend this proposition are exactly cases in which there seems to be no other possible course of action as he presents them. See especially the cases on pp. 163-168.

34. The notion of regretable necessity seems to me to be the strength of Ellul's argument about the use of violence. See note 31. But to say that violence is of the order of necessity is not to resolve all the ethical problems attendant on its use, which is why there continues to be a place for just war considerations.

35. Alfred T. Hennelly, "Pope John Paul's Spirituality of Work," America 146, 2 (January 16, 1982), pp. 31-33 has some initial suggestions, derived from the encyclical letter Laborem Exercens, about how one's daily work could be the occasion of this kind of spiritual struggle and growth. The encyclical itself can be found in Origins 11 (September 24, 1981), pp. 225-244.

36. I refer the reader back to Lomax's suggestion at the beginning of Chapter 4. I agree with him that King was taking on the hypocrisy of one version of southern Christianity and we are again at the heart of the matter. Inner experience which does not find expression in action is worse than empty. It is deceitful and false. But for King it should be noted that external action without the inner experience is also deceitful and false. This is germane to the debate in black theology over the relationship of liberation and reconciliation.

37. A very helpful illustration and evaluation of this systemic analysis can be found in Arthur F. McGovern, <u>Marxism: An American Christian Perspective</u> (Maryknoll, N.Y.: Orbis Books, 1980), pp. 135-171.

38. That was Gandhi's direction: "I shall bring about economic equality through non-violence by converting the people to my point of view by harnessing the forces of love as against hatred.... For that I have to reduce myself to the level of the poorest of the poor." <u>Gandhi on Non-Violence</u>, pp. 58-59. In his case there was honesty in his "solidarity" with the poor and the oppressed, but such solidarity does not solve the basic economic problems of production and distribution.

39. <u>BU Coll.</u>, XIV (55) where King noted that the modern Protestant Church had become too individualistic under the shadow of capitalism. A not untypical example of the antipathy to rugged individualism is David Ilorens, "Ameer (Leroi Jones) Baraka," <u>The Black Revolution: An Ebony Special Issue</u> (Chicago: Johnson Publishing Company, Inc., 1970), p. 75. "We recognize personality, but not individuality," This point is essential to any understanding of the value orientation of black nationalism.

40. King, <u>Strength To Love</u>, p. 158; <u>Where Do We Go From Here?</u>, p. 76. "Violence has been the inseparable twin of materialism, the hallmark of its grandeur and misery. This is one thing about modern civilization that I do not care to imitate." For an excellent analysis of greed in the contemporary setting see Fairlie, pp. 133-152.

41. King, "A Testament of Hope," <u>Playboy</u>, p. 236.

42. By realistic I mean to suggest that Niebuhr seems to have been the one author King paid serious attention to who might have provided the necessary corrective. I do not mean to commend Niebuhr's theology as ideal or itself without problems.

43. This last criticism might well be expected from a Roman Catholic theologian vis-a-vis Baptist

ecclesiology. But the basis of my criticism is essentially ethical and practical, not doctrinal.

44. Roberts, pp. 196-197, where he makes this point in a more practical and more sympathetic way.

45. E. J. Hobsbawn, _Primitive Rebels_ (New York: Norton, 1959), pp. 60-61 makes the case that without the hope and moral passion that evil can be overcome which are inspired by millennial beliefs, no revolution would be achieved. He considers such beliefs "probably a necessary social device for generating the super human efforts without which no major revolution is achieved." Niebuhr, _Moral Man and Immoral Society_, p. 277 makes the same point. Gunnemann, pp. 90-93 discussed the claim from a Christian theological perspective.

46. I mean guilt, which is not the same thing as acknowledging some responsibility for changing things. See Robert Morris (ed.), _Guilt and Shame_ (Belmont, California: Wadsworth Publishing Company, Inc., 1971); Bernard Haring, _The Law of Christ_, I, trans. Edwin G. Kaiser (Westminster, Maryland: The Newman Press, 1966), pp. 35-53.

47. King, _Where Do We Go From Here?_, p. 52.

48. This is particularly where Niebuhr might have proved of help on a theoretical level. See McCann, pp. 19-27, 101-104, where McCann also discusses the inadequacies of Niebuhr's theoretical perspective, and p. 128 where he makes generally the same claim and criticisms practically about Niebuhr that I am making about King, even while their theoretical perspectives were different.

49. There is a very interesting illustration of this confusion in a letter to King from Grady Wilson, written on behalf of Billy Graham, in reply to a protest King had made about having a governor, avowedly in favor of racial segregation, appear on a platform with and introduce Graham at one of his crusades. The letter is dated 7/28/58 and I quote a bit of it here. "Billy Graham has never engaged in politics on one side or the

other.... We were surprised to receive your telegram and learn of your feeling toward the Governor of...Texas. Even though we do not see eye to eye with him on every issue, we still love him in Christ, and frankly, I think that should be your position not only as a Christian but as a minister of the Gospel.... Perhaps you should know that we received scores of letters and telegrams concerning your coming to our meeting in New York, and yet Mr. Graham was happy to have you come as a fellow minister in Christ." BU Coll., IV (1a); if I accuse King of confusion, he was certainly a lot clearer about the significance of public action in relation to Christian faith than the author of the letter.

50. Vincent Harding, Black History and The Search for the New Land, pp. 16-19; McKissick, p. 24; "Morality is a nonexistent force in America." By way of contrast and corrective, John Conyers, "Politics and The Black Revolution," p. 226 observed: "We are not in the midst of a revolution - in politics or in anything else. Black Americans by the millions are angry because they are aware of the republic's shortcomings. But the majority of blacks have few fundamental objections to the Constitution and to the form of government we have. (It is interesting to note that, when the chips are down, many who style themselves 'revolutionaries' turn unfailingly to the Constitution in defense of their right to participate in revolution.)." Conyers' view would be much closer to King's actual views than to King's rhetoric.

51. That is why totalitarianism must resort to the use of force and the denial of all human rights not dependent upon the pleasure of the State. It is easier to sustain the social fabric where there is no justice, only privilege, than where some, but not all, are accorded some measure of justice.

52. Bennett, The Challenge of Blackness, p. 5, "...knowledge is action, not contemplation. There can be no knowing without doing." This is not to depreciate the contemplative dimension of the intellectual, artistic or spiritual life. To engage in these ways of life seriously is an intensely active existence which only anti-

intellectual, anti-artistic or anti-mystical prejudice would deny.

53. As instances of this development, Walter Lippmann, The Public Philosophy (A Mentor Book: The New American Library, 1955); Robert A. Nisbet, Community and Power (New York: Oxford University Press, 1962); John Courtney Murray, We Hold These Truths; Robert N. Bellah, The Broken Covenant (New York: The Seabury Press, 1975).

54. Arendt, On Revolution, pp. 218-219.

55. The most distinctive example of the extent and depth of this disillusionment is Samuel F. Yette, The Choice: The Issue of Black Survival in America (New York: Berkeley Publishing Co., Inc., 1971). This work testifies to the depth of both hope and disappointment.

56. Did anyone have any good reason at all to deny his birthday - or death-day - the status of a national holiday?

57. Since I have used the term "sacred honor" in relation to King's life, it is necessary, perhaps, to say something about the assault on his honor by the dishonorable - and illegal - activities of the FBI and the resulting accusations about King's sexual immorality. See the fine work by David J. Garrow, The FBI and Martin Luther King, Jr. (New York: N. W. Norton, 1981). While the accusations seem to have a factual basis, Oates, pp. 314-318, 331-334, they only prove that King, too, knew the power of sin in his own life to tempt and defeat him. They say nothing against the heroic life he lived nor do they give lie to the truth of the moral choice he placed before his fellow citizens. We may reasonably ask our God to be without flaw, but not our fellow pilgrims who become our heroes and saints.

58. I mention this both because I set out on this study with the expectation of finding a new theory of social change in King's writings and work and because I sense - that is not scholarly evidence - a movement to turn King into some kind of innovative and theoretical genius. He was not, and if it is any consolation to his

admirers, neither was Jesus or St. Paul. Their genius was eminently moral and practical, with strong, theoretical overtones.

59. King, <u>Strength To Love</u>, pp. 124-132.

Abernathy, Ralph, 40, 51
Acton, Lord John, 8
Agape, 93-96, 130, 194, 195-200, 251
Aggression, 9-11
Alexander, M. K., 49
Ambrose, 210
Amos, 279
Analogy, 76
Anarchy, 8, 157, 238, 239, 302
Arby, Robert, 10
Arendt, Hannah, 6, 7, 24, 60, 112, 147, 185
Arianism, 83
Aristotle, 101, 216
Atlanta, 267
Atonement, 85
Augustine, 85, 86, 210
Authority, 6, 7, 45, 78, 97-99, 214, 251

Baker, Ella, 43
Baldwin, James, 47, 52, 60, 275
Baptist, 40, 69, 71, 78, 147, 150, 296, 317-318
Barbour, J. Pius, 116, 117, 118, 158
Barclay, Robert, 211
Barth, Karl, 77, 98
Bennett, Lerone, 55, 281, 288
Berrigan, Daniel, 272
Bible, 73, 92, 96-100
Birmingham, 39, 167, 237, 244, 247, 252, 253, 254,
          280, 299
Bishop, James, 48, 55
Black Experience, 134, 161-166
Black Muslims, 164, 277, 289
Black Power, 44, 45, 52, 251, 274, 275, 299
Black Religion, 165, 275
Bonhoeffer, Dietrich, 190
Boycott, 1, 40, 47, 142, 187, 220, 297
Brightman, Edgar, 70, 71
Brown, H. Rap, 8
Brown, Robert McAfee, 14, 15, 28
Browne, Borden P., 70
Byles, Marie, 279

Calvin, John, 74, 90, 128
Camera, Helder, 14
Capitalism, 120, 146, 147, 170-171, 298, 303
Carmichael, Stokely, 45
Celsus, 210

Chalmers, Allen, 159, 176
Chavez, Cesar, 1, 2, 22
Chicago, 43, 167, 266, 268, 275, 280, 282, 299
Christology, 82-84
Church, 72, 92, 97, 142, 147, 241, 300
Civil Disobedience, 1, 2, 46-47, 236, 241-245, 248, 301-302
Civil Rights, 42, 44, 47, 149, 240, 281
Clark, Kenneth, 281
Cleage, Albert, Jr., 51, 55, 273, 274, 302
Clement of Alexandria, 98
Cobbs, Price, 9
Coercion, 7, 120, 253-254, 268
Communism, 125, 136, 146, 147, 157, 275
Cone, James, 27, 28, 52, 161, 274-275
Constitution, U.S., 145, 170, 225, 240, 241, 252, 299
CORE, 160

Dante, 87
Darwin, Charles, 87
Day, Dorothy, 1, 2, 22, 199
Death, 18-19, 152-153
Democratic Party, 44, 240
Democracy, 2, 145, 152, 220, 244
Development, 71, 96-97, 121-123, 132, 184-186
Dewey, John, 36
Dewhurst, J. F., 237
DeWulf, Harold, 70, 71
Dolci, Danilo, 1, 22
Doubt, 72-73, 87, 142

Ecclesiology, 147-148, 294-297, 307-309, 313-314
Edwards, George, 13
Eisenhower Commission, 9
Eisenhower, Dwight, 238
Ellul, Jacques, 12, 15, 27
Eros, 93, 195
Eschatology, 87-90

Face the Nation, 244
Faith, 69, 74, 90-92, 100, 112, 128-129, 154-155, 241, 293
Family, 72, 267
Fanon, Frantz, 9
Farmer, James, 223
Fellowship of Reconciliation, 48, 160
Force, 6, 7, 8, 120
Francis of Assissi, 181
Frazier, E. Stanley, 141-142

323

Freedom, 3, 7, 78, 81, 93, 94, 123-126, 132, 133,
          153, 188, 223-224, 254
Freedom Rides, 266
Freud, Sigmund, 152
Friedman, Maurice, 53-55
Friendship, 39, 194, 205
Fromm, Erich, 10, 11
Fundamentalism, 72, 73, 97

Gandhi, Mohandas, 1, 2, 3, 4, 5, 6, 8, 16, 17, 18,
                  19, 42, 48, 49, 64, 65, 85, 117,
                  119, 120, 134, 135, 149, 150,
                  155-156, 158-160, 176, 184, 186,
                  193, 196, 202, 211, 214, 220, 225,
                  226, 227, 232, 233, 237, 257, 273,
                  278, 279, 290, 306, 315, 317
Goodness, 75, 79, 82, 87, 101, 130, 131, 139, 249,
          265
Grace, 112, 139, 144, 186, 196-197, 273
Graham, Billy, 47, 318
Gregg, Richard, 3, 23, 284
Grier, William, 9

Halberstam, David, 48
Hamilton, Charles, 45, 255
Harding, Vincent, 67, 161
Harnack, Adolph, 74
Hate, 73, 125, 132, 195, 271
Hegel, G. W. F., 40, 80, 82, 98, 107, 119, 140
History, 8-9, 11, 161
Hitler, Adolf, 15, 190, 197
Hobbes, Thomas, 10, 26
Hofstadter, Richard, 8
Homer, 244
Hope, 92-93, 95, 162, 165, 199-200, 293
Houtart, Francois, 2, 23
Hoyt, Robert, 50, 55

Ideology, 1, 4, 39, 165, 182, 274-275, 287
India, 48, 65, 150, 156, 225, 240, 278, 298
Individualism, 7, 120, 122, 165, 303-304, 317

Jail, 266, 270, 278, 289
James, William, 92
Jefferson, Thomas, 8
Jesus, 2, 31, 40, 42, 72, 75, 82-84, 87, 88, 90, 92,
        94, 96, 98, 99, 101, 109, 121, 133, 142, 154,
        158, 181, 196, 222, 243, 264-265, 268, 270,
        271, 274, 281, 285, 294, 295, 297, 321
Job, 42, 50, 53-54, 55

Johnson, Lyndon, 190
Jones, Leroi, 120, 122
Joseph, 50-51, 55
Judaism, 145, 170, 314
Judgment, 88-89
Justice, 3, 7, 82, 88, 93, 95, 124, 204, 236

Kant, Immanuel, 82, 88
Kelsey, George, 71
Kilpatrick, James, 245
King, Coretta, 55, 65, 154, 254
King, Martin Luther, Jr., 1, 2, 3, 5, 6, 8, 16, 17,
                        18, 20, 32, 33, 36, 37-56,
                        69-101, 115-134, 141-167,
                        183-188, 193-195, 198, 200,
                        208-209, 211-213, 217-227,
                        237-255, 264-267, 269-283,
                        288, 289, 293-300, 302-312,
                        313-314, 316, 318, 320
    and the Beloved Comunity, 39, 95, 122, 187, 293,
                        304, 311
    Black Power, 43, 45, 52, 250-251, 274-275, 299,
        306
    Communism, 58, 119, 120, 125, 136, 146, 157, 275
    Father, 69, 71, 72, 73, 74, 102
    Heresy, 83, 86, 139, 142, 168
    Holy Spirit, 93, 98, 121, 129, 294
    Kingdom of God, 89, 90, 145, 147, 294, 307
    Liberal Christianity, 19, 24, 70, 73, 74, 82-83,
                        87, 97, 115, 149, 305
    Moral Absolutes, 36-37, 100, 118, 124-125, 242,
        246
    Mysticism, 91-92
    Protestant Reformation, 78, 85, 86, 97, 127, 128
    Utilitarianism, 4, 100, 215
Knudson, Albert, 70
Kunstler, William, 278

Law, 8, 185, 188, 218, 235-255, 308
Lenin, 119
Lewis, David, 43-44, 45
Liberalism, 137
Lincoln, Abraham, 37, 87
Lincoln, C. Eric, 42, 298
Lithuli, Albert, 1, 22
Little Rock, 238
Livingstone, David, 87
Locke, John, 119
Loe, Eugene, 270
Lokos, Lionel, 46, 55, 248, 252, 253, 254

Lomax, Louis, 42, 141, 142, 168, 316
Lorenz, Konrad, 10
Louis, Debbie, 281
Luther, Martin, 74, 78, 90, 128

Macquarrie, John, 5, 24
Malcolm X, 51, 145
Mao Tse Tung, 157
Marcuse, Herbert, 152-153
Maritain, Jacques, 214
Marshall, Thurgood, 240, 257
Marx, Karl, 119, 144, 157, 181, 256
Materialism, 119, 317
May, Rollo, 9, 112, 184, 196
Mayerhoff, Milton, 215
Mays, Benjamin, 71
McCall, Walter, 117, 135
Means-ends, 4-6, 16, 45-46, 94, 207-227, 301
Meier, August, 47, 55, 154
Merton, Thomas, 5, 24
MIA, 40, 141, 159, 213, 217, 218, 243
Miller, William, 23, 43, 55, 271, 273
Mission, 73, 133, 164, 200, 269
Montague, L. Ashley, 10
Montgomery, 41, 47, 49, 116, 117, 141, 155, 166, 208,
          212-214, 217, 243, 269, 270
Morris, Colin, 12, 13
Morris, Desmond, 10
Moses, 42, 50-53, 55
Muste, A. J., 237
Myrdal, Gunnar, 33-37, 42
Myth, 32, 55, 59

National Bar Association, 238
Niebuhr, H. Richard, 181
Niebuhr, Reinhold, 98, 119, 120, 134, 148-155, 158,
              196, 305, 308, 317
Nietzsche, Friedrich, 119, 182, 183

Order, 8, 188, 235
Origin, 210
Orpheus, 130

Pacifism, 7, 12, 17, 150, 207-212, 263
Paul, Saint, 39, 42, 142, 189, 265, 283, 321
Peace, 5, 93, 95, 230
Pelagianism, 85, 86, 139, 142
Personalism, 70, 71, 74, 148
Philia, 93, 194
Philosophy, 2, 8-9, 39-40, 60, 77, 94, 99, 100

Plato, 247
Politics, 1, 5, 7, 9, 43, 45, 47, 226, 297
Poverty, 42, 280, 298-299, 303, 317
Power, 7-9, 11, 12, 44, 86, 91, 101, 120, 133, 140,
        183-185, 249-254, 305-306
Pragmatism, 4, 12, 135, 158
Prayer, 86-87, 91, 195, 205
Psychology, 9-10, 11, 20, 226, 276
Punishment, 198-199, 206, 239

Racism, 10, 34-37, 130, 142, 162, 231, 270, 271, 274,
        279, 298, 303, 307
Rahner, Karl, 12, 27, 166
Rand, Ayn, 186
Rauschenbusch, Walter, 119, 120, 134, 143-148
Reason, 77, 91, 99, 122, 137
Responsibility, 18, 36, 50, 151-152, 182, 200,
                209-212, 215-216, 254, 263, 269-273,
                282-283, 287, 300, 310-312
Revelation, 77, 91, 96-100
Revolution, 12, 190, 207, 242, 248, 279
Richardson, Herbert, 38-40, 55, 60
Roberts, De Otis, 306
Rousseau, Andre, 2, 23
Rowan, Carl, 47
Rustin, Bayard, 67, 149, 160, 177, 280

Sadism, 10, 192, 279
Salvation, 84-87, 91, 97, 101, 128
SCLC, 43, 267, 293
Segregation, 37, 133, 187, 240, 259
Segundo, Juan Luis, 13, 17
Selma, 40, 167, 237, 244, 252, 253, 254, 280, 299
Shakespeare, William, 87
Sharp, Gene, 3-4, 22, 23, 187, 193
Sherwood, Charles, 43
Sibley, Marquis, 49, 237
Sin, 70, 86, 120, 124, 126-128, 143, 144, 307, 319
Situation Ethics, 4, 24, 206, 215, 316
Sit-ins, 1, 187, 220, 245
SNCC, 8, 63, 285
Smith, Kenneth, 17, 29, 104, 148
Social Gospel, 118
Socialism, 8, 147
Society of Friends, 48, 159, 160, 237
Socrates, 31, 40, 42, 46, 117, 247
Sorel, Georges, 6, 9, 23
Spirituality, 118, 135-136, 155, 193, 200, 214, 301,
                316
Stephen, 265

Strength, 6, 256, 305
Suffering, 164, 191-193, 263-283, 290, 302
Symbol, 41-43, 76

Thoreau, Henry, 1, 22, 40, 118, 120, 184, 242, 249
Tillich, Paul, 69, 70, 76-82, 93, 194
Tolstoi, Leo, 1, 22
Truth, 2, 3, 4, 16, 18, 19, 32, 33, 57, 85, 96, 124,
     156, 168, 270-271, 280-281, 285, 290
Tyrranicide, 12, 190

Ulysses, 130
Utilitarianism, 4, 100, 163, 215

Vander Zanden, James, 276, 277, 288
Vietnam War, 42, 44, 190, 267, 275, 299, 308

Walker, Charles, 254
Walton, Hanes, Jr., 17, 46, 55, 241
War, 1, 12, 184, 207
Washington, Joseph, Jr., 40-41, 55, 63, 71, 99,
                         267-271, 273, 302
Wassermann, Lois, 148
Weiman, Henry, 69, 70, 76-82
West, Charles, 14
Williams, John, 44, 55
Williams, Robert, 266
Wolff, Robert, 7
Wycliff, John, 265

Yungblut, June, 159

Zepp, Ira, 17, 29, 104, 148